The Highl
and its

'S i phìob as fheàrr gu cèol
Cèolmhor, eutrom, eibhinn, alainn

Inscription on the 'Strathy' pipes.

The Highland Bagpipe and its Music

RODERICK D. CANNON, FSA(Scot.)

JOHN DONALD PUBLISHERS LTD
EDINBURGH

ISBN 0 85976 416 8 (Paperback)

Phototypeset by Quorn Selective Repro, Loughborough.
Printed in Great Britain by Bell & Bain Ltd., Glasgow

Preface

This book is a history of the Scottish Highland bagpipe, and a survey of its music, past and present. I hope it will be read and enjoyed by fellow-pipers, and also by music lovers in the wider world who, having been stirred by the music of 'the pipes', are intrigued to know more of its true character.

The Highland bagpipe has a special, perhaps unique, position in the modern world. It is unquestionably a 'folk' instrument, centuries old and not much different from its medieval ancestor. Its music too has 'folk' origins, if by that we mean that it was originally composed and played by ear, and has strong local flavour. But pipers have maintained a tradition of technical training no less rigorous than classical musicians, and have achieved standards of musicianship to match their superb techniques. And pipe music has a classical tradition of its own — the Highland pibroch, once the exclusive property of a small minority of players, but now attracting much wider interest, both within the piping world and without.

The history of the bagpipe depends to some extent on tradition, and tradition has too often been compounded by ill-informed speculation or sheer romantic invention. I have tried to avoid these dangers by referring back to original sources wherever possible, and by leaning heavily on other people's careful research. Certainly, there are gaps in our knowledge, and I have emphasised some of them in the hope that this will stimulate further work.

In choosing the music, I have aimed for the best and at the same time the most typical examples of the various traditions, and I have presented them in a simplified way which I hope will be intelligible both to pipers and to non-pipers. Most of the tunes are well known and the full settings can be found in many old and new books of pipe music.

Many friends have helped with information and advice. I am grateful to the owners of photographs, and the copyright holders of tunes, who have allowed me to reproduce their work; also to the staffs of the British Library, the Cambridge University Library, the Imperial War Museum, the Ministry of Defence and especially the National Library of Scotland for their help in tracing obscure references. For copies of books and articles I am very much indebted to Roger Hurd of the Premier Drum Company, to Bill Boag of the Scottish United Services Museum, to Barrie Orme and to Norman Pirie. Hugh Cheape, Peter Cooke and Ruairidh H. MacLeod kindly donated pre-publication copies of articles of their own, and also read portions of this book. So also did Anthony Baines, Archie Kenneth, John MacLellan, Seumas MacNeill and Robert Wallace. The errors that remain are all mine. The high standard of production of this book is due to its editor, John Tuckwell; to Jeanne Johnson, who typed the whole of a dauntingly illegible manuscript; and to Mark Hayward, who wrote the music. Finally I thank Richard Powell, who contributed practical help, information and, above all, moral support at every stage.

Music Notation

Musical notes named in the text by capital letters, thus A, B, C . . . , refer to the notes of any octave; but letters in italics, thus *A*, *a*, *a'*, *a''* . . . , refer to actual pitches according to usual convention as shown thus:

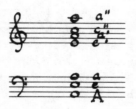

Music examples are written at the conventional Highland bagpipe pitch which is one semitone below the actual pitch.

Most of the music examples have been simplified by omitting the grace notes. In most printed pipe music, however, some notes which have time value are also printed as grace notes, so in order to preserve the overall musical effect as faithfully as possible I have found it necessary to write some of these notes as full melody notes, or to take other slight liberties. Pipers will have no difficulty in seeing what I have done. For examples of the same passage with and without the grace notes the reader may care to examine Exx. 4.1 and 4.23, 4.19 and 4.21, or 9.1 and 9.5.

Composers' names are given where known to me, and when a music example is taken wholly or mainly from one source, that too is indicated. In such cases, the expression 'arr. W. Gunn' means that the music is quoted strictly as arranged by the editor in question, but 'from W. Gunn' means that I have modified the original to some extent — usually by adding a key signature and removing the grace notes. Where no source is given, this means that the tune is well known and can be found in a number of standard collections.

Roderick D. Cannon
Norwich, 1987

Contents

CHAPTER 1

Origins

The sound of the bagpipe is so firmly associated with Scotland that many people quite naturally assume that the instrument was invented there — or if not, that it came to Scotland as a legacy of the Celtic as opposed to the Anglo-Saxon peoples. Both these ideas are almost certainly wrong: or to put it more cautiously, modern research does not support them. Indeed, two or three centuries ago, it would not have occurred to anyone to look to Scotland as the focal point, since bagpipes could be found in practically every country of Europe. Even today local varieties can be heard in places ranging from the Atlantic Coast to the Urals, and from Northern Sweden to Tunisia — mostly in remote country districts where old customs in general have tended to be preserved. The inference is that bagpipes were once more widely played than they are today, and historical research confirms this. From the works of artists like Dürer, Breughel and Teniers, we know of bagpipes in Germany and the Low Countries which seem to have gone out of fashion in the eighteenth century (H. Boone, 1983). In England the disappearance of the bagpipe can be charted quite accurately (R.D. Cannon, 1971). It receded northwards century by century, from the time of Chaucer when it was played as far south as Kent, to the nineteenth century when it remained only in Northumberland. At the height of its popularity, which was probably in the thirteenth century, the bagpipe was distributed over most of Europe.

This statement, however, conceals the fact that 'the bagpipe' is not one instrument, but the name for a variety of different instruments. Among the simplest is the one illustrated in Figure 1. This has two sounding pipes, both fitted with reeds. The *chanter* is the melody pipe, with finger holes. The *drone* is an accompanying pipe which gives a continuous fixed note. The drone is tuned by adjusting its length, but cannot be altered while playing. The two pipes are fed with air from the bag, into which the player blows through the mouthpiece, keeping the pressure constant by alternately blowing and pressing with the arm while taking the next breath.

Most bagpipes are in fact more elaborate than the simple one-chanter-and-one-drone variety. Some have two, three or even four drones. In some the drones point upwards, over the player's shoulder, but in others they are

1

Figure 1. A mediaeval bagpipe. The woodcut shows clearly the conical chanter and the single long drone; also the seam of the bag, and a decorative fringe attached to the drone. From *The Kalendyr of Shyppars* (i.e. The Shepherds' Calendar), printed at Paris, 1503.

fitted parallel to the chanter, pointing downwards. Some drones can be pre-set to different notes before playing. Some chanters are double pipes, with some holes in one pipe and some in the other. Many are restricted to eight or nine notes, but others have the scale extended with keys, or by overblowing to a higher register.

A classification of bagpipes

Although so many different kinds of bagpipes are known, not much is known in detail about the history of any one of them. The present-day historian who wishes to trace the development of the different forms of bagpipe is in something of the same position as the zoologist reconstructing the origin of species by classifying the various sorts of animals he can find in the world today: and musicologists have made some progress in doing this, notably Anthony Baines in his classic survey of bagpipes, published in 1960. Perhaps the most important finding is that bagpipes can be divided into two broad categories according to the design of the chanter. Two examples are shown in Plate 1. Chanters of one type are conical, the outer surface sometimes actually flared like a trumpet and the inner bore accurately shaped as a long narrow cone opening out from top to bottom. The other type are cylindrical inside and out. Conical pipes are always made of wood, turned on a lathe, and they are usually fitted with a double reed, like an oboe reed. Cylindrical pipes may be of wood, but they may be constructed more simply from ready-made tubes such as cane or bone, and some have a horn or horn-like extension attached at the bottom end. They generally have a rather primitive-looking reed made from a single piece of cane with a vibrating tongue cut in it. The musical characters of the two types are quite different: conical chanters produce a shrill and 'nasal' sound, best known today in the Scottish bagpipe, while cylindrical chanters of similar size are lower and softer in pitch, as on the Northumbrian pipes. Also conical chanters tend to be louder on the lower notes (presumably because the widening bore of the pipe has an amplifying effect like a loudspeaker), while cylindrical pipes tend to be louder at the top of the scale. From the point of view of understanding the origin of the bagpipe, the most important point is that this difference in design cuts across other non-bagpipe wind instruments as well. Corresponding to the conical pipe chanter is the shawm, known in Europe since the Middle Ages, and distributed widely in Asia as well. Corresponding to the cylindrical chanter is the 'hornpipe', rare but very widely spread, from Wales to India and from Russia to Sicily. In some countries, the same kinds of pipe co-exist with and without the bag. It seems therefore that in general the two kinds of pipe came first and the bag was added later as a more convenient method of blowing.

To the modern musician this may be a surprise, since anyone coming to the bagpipe from the flute, oboe or clarinet may think that blowing *via* a bag is a decidedly inconvenient method. What is not generally appreciated is that primitive or 'folk' reed instruments without bags are in practice played in much the same way as a bagpipe. The player does not squeeze the reed between his lips, but takes it wholly into his mouth and does not touch it with his tongue. When blowing he swells his cheeks, and when he needs to take a breath, he does so quickly, through the nose, at the same time contracting his cheeks so that the air supply is not stopped (Plate 2). 'Circular breathing' is the name sometimes given to this technique. Western musicians long ago abandoned it though glassblowers kept it up, for blowing large vessels, and so did chemists, when using a mouth blowpipe to produce a hot flame. Some Scottish pipers can blow the practice chanter continuously in this way. To them it is a trick, but to a Basque, Sicilian or Indian piper it is an essential skill. The Indian snake charmer indeed can fairly be described as a human bagpipe. Not only does he blow continuously, but his pipe has a drone, and sounds exactly like a bagpipe.

It is useless to ask when or where the two basic types of pipe were invented. Cylindrical pipes have been found in Egyptian tombs, and conical pipes were played in the Near East in Hellenistic times. There is no reason to doubt that people in other regions had such instruments, of which there is now no trace. On the addition of the bag, the authorities are a little more positive. There is slight but definite evidence that it was known in Ancient Rome, but that it did not come into general use in Western Europe until much later. A story that the emperor Nero played on a pipe 'with the armpit, a bag being thrown under it' indicates clearly enough some form of bagpipe (A. Baines, 1960, 63). But as Baines has pointed out, it is equally clear, from the lack of references to bagpipes in ancient literature as contrasted with later times, that the bagpipe was little known to educated people of the day, and was rated as unimportant by serious musicians. The Greek pipers used the continuous blowing technique, and they even used a special cheek-strap to relieve the strain on the facial muscles and so avoid what was called 'the disfigurement of Athene'. Next after Nero comes a description of a bagpipe, in a Latin document of unknown origin which was once thought to have been written by St. Jerome. It is important because it was copied in various monasteries in Western Europe, and illustrated with drawings that are so unrealistic that they show that the artists had never seen the instrument itself. Evidently the bagpipe, if known in Europe at all in the tenth century, was still rare. By 1200 AD the situation was quite different. Pictures in manuscripts, carvings in churches, and increasingly, references in literature, show bagpipes in places as far apart as England, Spain, Italy and Sweden. The earliest pictures seem to show more varieties of bagpipe than the later ones — pipes with many drones, and some with double chanters, but the commonest by far is the simple one already mentioned: a conical chanter, a single long drone, short blowpipe, and a bag shaped rather like a wineskin. It is the same instrument, as far as one can judge, which has survived more or less unchanged in the Spanish bagpipe of today. It seems therefore that the bag is the invention of some ingenious craftsman, designed to do more conveniently what pipers were doing already, that is, to blow continuously, and that once invented, the idea spread quickly and was applied to various different kinds of pipes.

The bass drone

The drone seems to have come into use at the same time as, or very soon after, the bag. At any rate it was widely used by the thirteenth century (Baines, 1977, 216). It is always constructed in the same way, as a series of wooden joints with slides for tuning, and with either a trumpet-shaped or a bottle-shaped 'bell' at the outer end. The bell has an important mellowing effect on the sound. The reed is a single-beating reed of the type already mentioned as normally associated with cylindrical pipes.

Scholars are still not sure when and how the drone came into being, but one thing that is clear is that it has a definite musical purpose. Any bagpiper knows this for himself even if he cannot explain it — the music simply would not be the same without it — and it is borne out by the fact that in nearly all European bagpipes, the relationship of drone to chanter is essentially the same. The chanter normally gives a scale of nine notes, and of these the key note is the one which is played with all finger holes covered except the lowest, which lies under the little finger of the lower hand. (This seems to be the basic finger position of most simple wind instruments, except that some, like the modern tin-whistle, have no hole under the little finger.) The highest note, played by raising the thumb of the upper hand, is one octave above the key note, and between these two the scale is a major scale — approximately so in some bagpipes, accurately in others. The drone, in relation to this scale, is a 'bass' drone, tuned two octaves below the six-finger key note. The actual pitch of the key note may vary from as low as D below the treble clef (Ireland) to B flat in the treble (Scotland), C or D (Spain) or even to B flat above the treble clef (Brittany), but in all these cases, and many others, the drone, or the largest drone if there are several, is two octaves below.[1]

No doubt the bass drone tuning arrangement was arrived at by experience: pipers must have discovered it added strength and colour to the music. But it can also be explained technically. The drone, because of its length and narrow bore, produces a particularly strong set of overtones (see below, p. 6). In other words, if for the sake of argument we assume that the fundamental note of the drone is A (that is, the A below 'middle C'; see above, p. vi), then in practice the drone sounds like a mixture of all the notes in the following series: $A, a, e', a', c''^{\#}, e''$, and so on. The next note in the series (the seventh) is actually not a true scale note, but lies between g'' and g'' sharp, after which comes a''. Since the chanter runs from g' to a'', this means that at least four of its notes, $a', c''^{\#}, e''$ and a'', are exactly in unison with harmonics of the drone. But more important is the effect of the drone's third harmonic, *e′*, which makes chords with *b′* and *c‴#* of the chanter. This effect can be heard quite clearly on the Highland pipes, if one makes the experiment of tuning the drones separately. Sound the chanter first with the tenor drones only: then the obvious correspondences are between the drones and the low A, E and high A of the chanter, but the D and the F sharp are also well supported, and a tune in D major goes well with the drones at this stage. Then, when the bass drone is brought in, the difference is clear. The sound is very much richer, and the note B is quite clearly supported. The G's too, while they cannot be said to be in harmony with the drones, are certainly not in disharmony. On a well-tuned bagpipe, nearly every note of the scale is effectively underpinned by the drone, and a tune which could quickly tire the ear when played on a solo pipe becomes rich and lively on the bagpipe.

Scottish pipers (nowadays at any rate) are very much aware of chanter-drone relationships, and when tuning up they test each note of the scale critically for the appropriate sound effect. The following diagram shows the scale and its relationship to the first few harmonics:

All the pairs of notes connected by arrows are in simple chord relationships to each other: octaves, fifths, fourths, and in the case of F#, major sixth. One other connection is not shown: as already mentioned, the seventh harmonic of the drone is actually somewhere between *g″* and *g‴#*. It happens that on many chanters the note 'high G' is a little sharp, and it might be thought that the presence of the seventh harmonic is the reason. However, this seems rather doubtful as measurements (by C.M. Harris and others in 1963) have shown that the seventh harmonic is actually very faint. The two G's of the chanter are important notes, and good pipers do listen to them carefully when tuning, but I doubt if they are really searching for a consonance.

The bagpipe in Scotland and Ireland

The earliest evidence of bagpipes in the British Isles relates to England: an Anglo-Saxon riddle of the eleventh century, for which 'a bagpipe' seems to be the answer (R. Sutherland, 1967), and a rather crude carving on a gravestone in Northumberland, thought to date from c.1200 (G.V.B. Charlton, 1927). Definite historical records begin with payments to bagpipers who played at the King's court. The word 'bagpipe' itself first occurs in such records in 1334, and in literature, in Chaucer's *Canterbury Tales*, c.1386. The oldest existing fragments of a bagpipe are also English. They were recovered by archaeologists from Weoley Castle in Warwickshire, and have been dated to the late thirteenth, or the fourteenth century (Baines, 1973). Bagpipes appear in Scottish literature somewhat later than this, for example in a play written by King James IV (1424–1437) and in a record of payments to court musicians in the early 1500s, including 'the Inglis (i.e. English) pyper with the drone'.[2] (The word 'drone' was occasionally used for the whole bagpipe at this time.) Evidence from the Gaelic regions is later still: for the Scottish Highlands, a reference in 1549, and for Ireland several mentions in history and literature of the late Tudor period. We shall return to these below.

In other words, we hear nothing of Highland or Irish bagpipes until the time when the bagpipe was already vanishing from Southern England and the more central parts of Europe. Must we conclude that the Scots and Irish acquired the bagpipe much later than the rest of the world? As a matter of fact, this may well have been the case, but the historical records themselves are not the best reason for thinking so. Records of any sort are scarce for the period we are interested in, and the oldest Gaelic literature is not of the sort which would give the kind of information we want. It consists mainly of collections of poems written down from oral tradition and dating back to much earlier times: tales of Fingal and Cuchullain, lives of saints, and battle poems in severely conventional styles. So bagpipes could have existed for some time before they came to be noticed by the bards. It has also been suggested (S. Donnelly, 1981) that Gaelic poets might have continued for some time to apply old names to new instruments, so that where they write *cuisle*, which strictly means 'flute', they could perhaps be referring to the bagpipe. What is clear is that by the time of the earliest historical references, bagpipes had already been adopted by the Irish and Scottish Gaels for purposes quite different from anywhere else; and for this to happen must have taken some time. In most places, the piper traditionally fulfils one (or both) of two roles: he is the village or town piper, a local 'character', in evidence mainly at fairs and weddings, almost a beggar, drunk and disorderly by reputation if not in fact; or he is a shepherd, swineherd or goatherd who spends most of his time in the open air and uses his bagpipe not only for amusement but to call in his animals and lead them from place to place. In Gaelic Scotland and Ireland, however, we hear of the bagpipe being used as the incitement to battle, and for lamenting the dead. No doubt there were village and pastoral pipers in the Gaelic lands as elsewhere, but the contrast between bagpiping in Scotland and Ireland, and in the rest of the world, is clear. At the battle of Pinkie near Edinburgh, in 1549, an army of Highlanders was involved, 'and while the French prepared for combat, the wild Scots incited themselves to arms by the sound of their bagpipes' (Beague, 1556). In 1581 the historian George Buchanan thought it worth mentioning that 'instead of the trumpet they use the bagpipe' (Collinson, 1975). Exactly similar things are reported of Ireland: Irish soldiers marching in London in 1544 'with bagpipes before them', and in 1566, playing bagpipes in battle instead of trumpets. The use of bagpipes in cattle raids is mentioned in 1561, and most strikingly of all, 'with it also they accompany their dead to the grave, making such sorrowful sounds as to invite, nay compel the bystanders to weep'.

We see, then, that the bagpipe was known to the Gaels by the mid-sixteenth century, and that by then it had been in use long enough to have become an integral part of their way of life. To fix a date any earlier than that with certainty is impossible, although there are a few clues of a negative sort. A long narrative poem by Barbour describing a Scots raid into England in 1327 mentions trumpets and horns in battle, but no bagpipes (Collinson, 1975, Ch. 3). At the siege of Rouen in 1418, large numbers of Irish soldiers were employed, but none of the English or Irish accounts of the event mentions bagpipes.[3] This is not much to go on, but it is at least consistent with a simple overall view. This is, that the bagpipe was invented or re-invented around 1100, somewhere in Europe; the idea spread rapidly, as did the use of the bass drone, which also reached the remotest parts of the Continent; it reached England before 1200, but was not accepted by the more conservative Gaelic peoples until later. Perhaps 1400 is the latest reasonable date. Contrary to general belief, there is nothing to indicate whether the bagpipe reached Scotland from Ireland, or *vice versa*.

There is, of course, no proof of this course of events, and presumably there never will be. Anyone who is determined to believe that the bagpipe was invented in the far North or West, and spread outwards from there, is at liberty to do so: but the idea flies in the face of the probabilities and is no longer considered seriously by the authorities on the subject.

NOTES

1. With some East European bagpipes (such as the *gaida* of Bulgaria), the three-finger note is regarded as the keynote. This corresponds to the note *d″* of the Highland pipe, and in such cases the drone is, again, two octaves below, sounding *d*.

2. Quoted by F. Collinson (1975), Ch. 2. Collinson also argues that references to 'pipers' in old records often denote 'bagpipers', but this is by no means always so. See H. G. Farmer (n.d.), p. 75.

3. Irish references in this chapter are taken from the careful recent work by S. Donnelly (1981). Earlier writings on the subject tend to be unreliable, especially those of W. H. Grattan Flood.

CHAPTER 2

The Highland Bagpipe

Description[1]

Figure 2 shows an exploded view of the modern Highland bagpipe, with the names of its more important parts. The bag is made of sheepskin or sealskin, tanned to a very soft leather. Its essential characteristic is that it must keep the air in, while letting moisture out, since the reeds must be kept reasonably dry or they will not stay in tune. The pipes are now played in every part of the world, and in hot or dry climates, so different sorts of bag are needed. 'Hide bags', i.e. cowhide, tanned to a tougher leather, are perhaps the favourite, though some players prefer a double thickness of the ordinary skin. Kangaroo skin, being soft and oily, is also effective. No one has yet found a plastic substitute. The bag is cut from a single flat sheet, folded and tightly sewn along a single seam which forms the bottom of the bag when the pipe is being played. Into the bag are tied the five *stocks*, short heavy wooden tubes with a deep groove at the inner end and metal or ivory (or plastic) *ferrules* at the outer end. The exposed ends of all parts of the bagpipe have mounts of this sort, not just for decoration, but to prevent the wood from splitting. The three drones, the blowpipe and the chanter are pushed firmly into the stocks, the joints being made tight with a lapping of thread, usually Indian hemp which stands up well to moisture. The sliding parts of the drones — *tuning slides* — are also lapped with hemp. At one time all woodwind instruments had lapped joints, but these were superseded by joints faced with cork. Bagpipe makers have not adopted this innovation, possibly because the joints of the bagpipe get much harder wear. Cork is however suitable for the tuning slides, and I have seen it used, but not often.

The outermost ends of the drones conceal a small round cavity, the *bell*, closed by a flat disc of ivory with a hole in the centre. As mentioned previously, this has the effect of smoothing the sound, by suppressing the highest harmonics. The bell is smaller nowadays than on the oldest pipes, possibly to economise on wood, but also possibly because pipe makers have found other ways of improving the tone. The dimensions of the inner bore are very important, as also is the quality of the wood. The casual listener

10

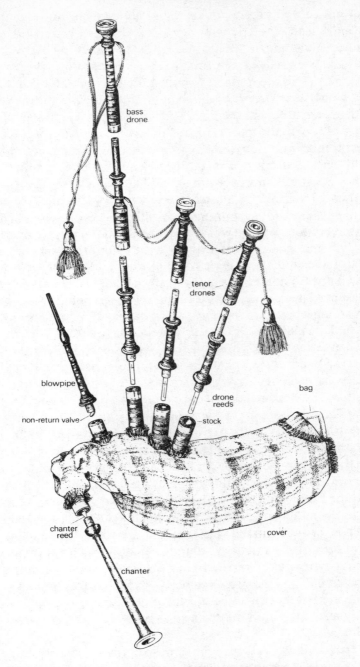

Figure 2. Exploded diagram of the Scottish Highland bagpipe.

may not notice, but pipers are keenly aware of the sound quality of the drones, and a really good rich-sounding set is a highly prized possession. A wide bore helps, and it should be highly polished inside. Metal-lined drones have been made from time to time, and are usually particularly good. One 'trick of the trade' is to adjust the reed so that when tuned the drone is pulled out to its maximum length: this increases the proportion of wider-diameter tubing in the pipe, and adds to the smoothing effect. The *chanter* is of course the most critical part of the whole assembly. It is also the most fragile, and this is one reason why old chanters are much rarer than old sets of drones. But another reason is that chanters are not generally thought to improve with age. Whether they actually deteriorate, or whether it is simply that tastes have changed with time (see below, p. 29), no one seems to know, but the fact is that the best players change their chanters every few years. Twenty years would be a long playing life for a chanter, whereas good sets of drones can be a hundred years old or more. Although the chanter is a single piece of wood, different parts of it have different names. The swelling at the top (see Plate 1) is the *knob* or *bole*; the narrowest part, just below, is the *neck*; the two holes bored crossways below the lowest fingerholes are the *sound holes*; the length of pipe below these is the *bell*, and the ivory disc is the *sole*. The sole has a slight effect on the tone and pitch of the lowest notes, as one finds if one has the misfortune to break it, but in the last few years chanters without soles have come into fashion. In place of the sole they have a substantial flange integral with the rest of the chanter. The wooden body of the chanter as a whole is sometimes called the *shell*. The topmost part of the bore is the *reed seat*. From here the bore tapers down slightly to its narrowest point, the *throat*, about halfway between the reed seat and the highest finger hole — the *back hole*, actually covered by the thumb of the upper hand; and from there it widens steadily, in an accurately cut cone, to the mouth at the lower end. The reamer used to finish the bore is sometimes made from an old rifle bayonet, carefully ground to the required profile. The *blowpipe* is made of two sections. The pipe itself is turned from the same wood, and mounted in the same way, as the rest of the pipes, but it has a separate *mouthpiece*, always of vulcanite or some other synthetic material, which is screwed on — or lapped if the blowpipe is old and has lost its screw thread. Most pipers hold the mouthpiece between their teeth, and indeed tend to grip it — while invariably teaching pupils not to do so — so the mouthpieces tend to wear out in time.

The reeds are always made of the same material — Spanish cane, *arundo donax*, the same as for oboe and clarinet reeds. Drone reeds are made to a very simple design, which has already been briefly mentioned. A length of cane is cut, retaining one of the nodes. A slit is cut near the node, and the wood is split downwards to form the vibrating *tongue*. The length of the tongue is controlled by a tightly tied binding of waxed thread, the *bridle* or 'tuning string'. Moving the bridle so as to lengthen the tongue makes the sound both louder and flatter; and *vice versa*. If the reed refuses to sound, it may be opened by inserting a hair crossways just above the bridle. This is often necessary with a new reed, but it produces a rough tone, and good players try to dispense with the hair as soon as possible. A reed can also be flattened by weighting the tip of the tongue with a blob of wax, or sharpened by cutting away some wood. Pipers in other countries do this regularly, but Scottish pipers do not.

The chanter reed will look familiar to those who know the oboe. It is a double reed, of two cane blades tied onto a short piece of tubing, the *staple*, usually made by rolling a piece of sheet copper. Compared with the oboe reed, the pipe chanter reed is shorter, broader and much stiffer to blow. There is also a difference in construction. The oboe reed is made from one strip of cane which is creased and folded into two, shaped, tied on and finally shaved until it parts into the two blades: but the pipe reed is made from two separate halves, cut to shape before tying. A detailed description of the method of chanter reed making was published recently (Anon., 1984a). Pipers do not generally make their own reeds, but a few have made a speciality of it, and a good reed maker can do a substantial business — or at least usefully augment his pension. Reeds can be made to order to suit the strong, medium or soft-blowing piper, and to suit the different makes of chanter, but even so they are chancy and temperamental things. The piper who has to buy them by post without trying them out cannot avoid buying a large selection and hoping to find just a few good ones. Ideally, he will establish contact with a maker who will get to know exactly what he wants, or else he will buy strong reeds and shave them down to suit himself. But even the best reed will require a lot of playing before it is properly 'broken in'. A test of a good reed is the quality of the 'crow' it gives when blown without the chanter. Also, when the reed is new it will tend to give a scratchy sound on the highest note, A. This too is called a 'crow', and is actually welcomed by the piper as a sign that the reed will eventually settle to a good tone.

When the pipe is blown up, the drones respond first. If they are good they will give a 'double tone' — that is, as the pressure is increased, the pitch suddenly drops by about a semitone, and the sound becomes smoother. The physical causes of this effect are not understood, although they have been studied and discussed a good deal (C.H. Harris and co-workers, 1963; see also a lengthy correspondence in the *Piping Times*,

February 1970–May 1971). At any rate it is well known that without the double tone, the drones will be rough and unsteady in pitch. As the air comes to full pressure (about one pound per square inch is typical — A. Carruthers, 1977) the chanter will 'speak'. At this stage the piper is holding the chanter with one hand, fingering a suitable note, usually E or the top note, 'high A', while he adjusts the drones. If necessary, he stops two of the drones while tuning the third. This is easily done by momentarily blocking the end of the drone with the finger. The reed closes under the air pressure, but can be restarted either by poking the finger into the drone end and sharply flicking it out again, or else by relaxing the air pressure, then restarting the whole bagpipe. Tuning can be a lengthy process, not because it takes long to adjust the drones in the first place, but because all four pipes must be blown into a steady state. The reeds tend to go flatter as they absorb moisture, but on the other hand they sharpen with warmth, and each one will respond differently. Prior to all this, the chanter reed itself must have been properly set so that the interval between top and bottom notes is just right. Then again, a particular reed may be 'off' on one note, but come into tune after five or ten minutes' playing. The piper will know this and will patiently play on, one short tune after another, with an occasional touch to the drones, until he is ready to begin on the main pieces he wants to play. If he is playing in a competition, the judges will allow him reasonable time for tuning, but they will expect him to have brought his instrument into shape well beforehand, so that only the finest adjustments are needed on the platform. Similarly, if he is playing in public he will have gone through lengthy preparation out of sight and hearing of the audience. Keeping the bagpipe in good order is a major part of the piper's life.

Experienced pipers often have certain favourite phrases or tune fragments which they will use when the instrument is nearly settled. As William Matheson has shown (1970), this is an old practice; harpers as well as pipers used to compose preludes called *deachinn ghleusda* ('a test of tuning'). Several of these preludes are noted in early collections of pipe music (J. MacDonald, 1760; D. MacDonald, 1822; A. MacKay, 1838). Anthony Baines (1957, 216) has written of the Spanish bagpiper 'completing the tuning and at the same time loosening up his reeds in an extended ... *tempradura* appropriate to the coming lay and drawing the audience into its mood'. Some Scottish pipers do suit their preludes to the mood of the piece, but most do not. When a piper in a competition is about to play a long pibroch, one might think it only prudent for him to test the prominent notes of the tunes before starting. But usually he plays a variation or two from some particular favourite piece — playing himself in, as well as his pipe.

To play on a 'good-going pipe' — as the Scots phrase has it — is one of the most satisfying experiences in the world. The sound is all-enveloping and self-sustaining. The drones not only harmonise with the chanter, but also somehow take away the hard edges of the sound, so that one could play for hours without tiring of it — if the reeds would allow. The blowing is not so hard as to distract attention from the music, but on the other hand there is enough resistance to give some sense of effort. With a good reed, the vibrations of the notes can be felt in the chanter, so that the piper is literally fingering the music.

Technical developments

If the bagpipe arrived in the Highlands as early as 1400, it must presumably have had only one drone, the bass drone. Unfortunately, there is no evidence for or against this. Two-drone bagpipes became common in various parts of Europe in the sixteenth century, and pictures of bagpipes in sixteenth-century Irish sources also show two drones, of unequal length[2]. The oldest really clear pictures showing Highland bagpipes are a portrait of the piper to the Laird of Grant, painted in 1714 (Plate 5), and a self-portrait sketch by the young piper Joseph MacDonald, done in 1760, and they both show the three drones. A tiny detail in a painting dated 1683 seems to bear this out (Plate 4). It is thus impossible to put dates to the additions of successive drones, as we have no evidence which is early enough, but we can guess that at least one of the tenor drones would have been added by the time we get our earliest notices of the pipes, in the mid-sixteenth century. If the pipes were used effectively in battle, they must already have been particularly loud, as they are today. Most writers comment on the loudness of the pipes even if they say nothing else about them. Such a loud chanter needs extra drone power to balance it, and this is presumably why the tenor drones were added in the first place. With softer-sounding pipes, such as the modern Spanish or Hungarian, the single bass drone is adequate.

The idea that the bass drone came first and the tenors were added later, which I believe to be the most likely, is not the view which has been taken by previous writers. It has frequently been stated that there were first one, then two tenor drones, and that the bass drone was not added until about 1700 (some have even said 1800). These statements have been copied from one writer to another at least since 1899,[3] but the ultimate authority for them is not clear. Most probably they result from the fact that two early writers — Thomas Pennant in 1774, and the author of an article in the

Encyclopaedia Britannica of 1778 — stated without qualification that the Highland pipe had two drones. It is now known that at that time some pipers did play two-drone sets with no bass drone, while others had the three drones, and that the matter was, or became, controversial. From 1781, pipers began playing in organised competitions (see below, p. 74), and the three-drone players objected that they were being placed at a disadvantage, as they undoubtedly must have been, since one of the major hazards in a competition is that a drone will wander out of tune. Another writer, in 1803, possibly replying to the previous one, claimed that it was the pipers of the North Highlands who played three drones, while those of the West (probably he meant Skye and areas to the south of Skye) played only two (P. MacDonald, 1803). He stated firmly that the three-drone pattern was the original, and that the pipers of the West had 'laid aside the use of the great drone'. It requires little experience of the nature of piping controversies to guess that the two-drone players asserted that on the contrary, theirs was the older, and therefore correct, way. Eventually, in 1821, two-drone pipes were formally banned from competitions (*NP 19*, No. 7; Dalyell, 1849, 7), and we can imagine that there must have been much bitterness. Several two-drone pipes exist in museums, but there is nothing to show that, as a type, they predate the three-drone ones.[4] It is also worth noting that Lowland bagpipes (of which a little more is said below) all seem to have had three drones, one bass and two tenor. This is a point in favour of the bass drone being original, and the absence of the bass drone being a local exception; but it is the comparison with the bagpipes of other countries already discussed above (p. 5) which makes this practically certain.

The major differences between the Scottish bagpipe and those of Spain, Brittany and elsewhere are the louder chanter, the extra drones, and the longer blowpipe. All these go together: the loud chanter, necessary in an instrument of war, the extra drones to balance it, and the long blowpipe to enable the player to stand upright and march while playing. The scale of the chanter also differs from the others in that the lowest note is a semitone flatter than required in a major scale. As we shall see later (below, p. 38), this is an essential requirement of the music. So we can be reasonably sure that all the distinguishing features of the Highland bagpipe were established at an early date, and that it has not changed significantly since the time of the earliest music that has come down to us.

At this point it would be natural to turn to an examination of old pipes preserved in museums, and to trace developments in construction, or to refer to differences between the work of different pipe makers. Unfortunately, this cannot be done at present. Old bagpipes certainly do exist, but none of them can be dated reliably. A bagpipe preserved at Dunvegan Castle is reputed to have been played by Patrick *Mór* MacCrimmon who flourished in the seventeenth century (F. Collinson, 1975, 188). Only the top joints of the drones are claimed to be original. These are exceptionally ornate, with bands of ivory let into the wood in addition to the usual ferrules and rings, earning it the name of *pìob bhreac*, the 'speckled pipe' (Plate 9). Possibly one of the oldest chanters in existence is the one said to have been played by the famous blind piper of Gairloch, Iain *Dall* MacKay, who died in 1754, aged 98 years. It was taken to Canada by Iain's grandson and is still kept by his family (J.A. MacLellan, 1980b; A. MacRae, 1982). On the other hand, a well-known bagpipe with the carved date 1409, which was first described in 1880 (R. Glen, 1880), has been proved beyond all reasonable doubt to be a nineteenth-century fake (J.F. Bryan, 1970).

Other famous relics include the *feadan dubh* ('black chanter') of Clan Chattan (W.L. Manson, 1901, 228), the 'Bannockburn' pipes of Menzies (D.P. Menzies, 1894–5; F.C. Collinson, 1975, 133–4) and the 'Strathy' pipes, a full three-droned set, still in good playing order (Anon., 1973). These are undoubtedly genuine, though impossible to date, and the same is true of several Highland bagpipes in the Royal Museum of Scotland, Edinburgh, well described in a recent catalogue by Hugh Cheape (1983). A point of interest about one of the Edinburgh sets is that they were apparently made on a pole lathe — that is, a lathe which turns the wood intermittently backwards and forwards — or possibly they were carved by hand without any lathe. This is the kind of technical detail we may hope to have for the other old sets when they receive expert examination.

One thing which can be said is that materials of construction have varied from time to time.[5] Early pipes in museums are made of local woods, especially boxwood, but also laburnum, holly, and fruit woods like plum and apple, all very close-grained. Mountings were of horn, lead or pewter. Imported blackwoods, and ivory mountings, came in about the same time as for other instruments in the 1780s. Ebony is sometimes used, but African blackwood became standard, with cocus wood, from Jamaica or South America, as a cheaper alternative. From 1781 onwards, the Highland Society of London offered newly made bagpipes as first prizes in competitions. They were proclaimed to be of the best possible manufacture, and may well have set new standards for makers throughout Scotland. At least one of the early prize pipes still survives (A.D. Fraser, 1907, 121) and is essentially similar to those of today. In Victorian times, the ivory mountings tended to be made heavier than before, and silver mountings became usual for the most expensive sets.

As regards the design of the instrument, pipers have fiercely resisted any innovation which in their view would affect the music. To this day, the chanter has no keys, it will not produce semitones by cross fingering, and it will not overblow to the higher register. Only the detailed measurements have changed gradually over the years. Modern chanters are lighter and thinner in the wall than older ones, and many do not have the ivory sole. They are somewhat differently tuned (see below, p. 29) and more evenly balanced for volume. The low notes are still louder than the high notes, but the contrast is not so great as it used to be. Another recent development is a chanter of moulded plastic instead of wood. As with other instruments, it is cheaper to construct and can easily be made to a reproducible standard. It has made considerable headway in pipe bands, but is felt to be not quite brilliant enough in tone for solo work. Otherwise, the only new device which has yet been accepted is a simple trap inside the blowpipe to collect excess water. Not long ago a ball-valve was introduced, but more recently a plastic version of the normal leather flap valve has become popular.

The fact that Spanish cane is used for reeds, and seems to be the only satisfactory material, raises the question of how the early makers obtained it, of if they did not, what material they used instead. Nowadays, supplies are regularly imported from growers in Spain and France who specialise in cane for various instruments, including specifically the Scottish bagpipe. Mr T. Pearston has pointed out (1951) that, previously, Scottish reed makers used to get cane from incoming cargo ships: it was used as dunnage or packing material. Earlier still, it is suggested, local canes such as *phragmites communis* may have been used. Experiments have shown that this material is not very durable, but it may have been better centuries ago, if the Scottish climate was then drier and sunnier than it is today. The same author makes the interesting comment that in the outer Isles, practice chanter reeds were made from 'a small tube of dried grass or hay, and the result is quite satisfactory'. This evidently means a single beating-reed, as in a pipe drone, an interesting link-up with the hornpipe or stock-and-horn of earlier times (see below, p. 25).

Bagpipe manufacture

Bagpipes of the West European family, like shawms and other conical reed-pipes, have always been made from wood, turned on a lathe. When first introduced, they would have represented a relatively advanced piece of technology, something to be manufactured by a specialist, rather than home-made by the piper. Lathe-working is a very long-established craft, and there must have been turners in many Scottish towns in the Middle Ages, making candlesticks, chair legs and the like, who could produce musical instruments when required, but nothing is actually known about instrument manufacture in Scotland before the eighteenth century. The assumption is that pipes may have been made in the Highlands, but that they would also have been bought from makers in the Lowlands like many other articles of Highland life (H. Cheape, 1983b). The oldest record of such a purchase is in 1765, when a set of pipes was ordered for one of the MacCrimmons in Skye. They were made by one R. Robertson, a turner in Edinburgh (I.F. Grant, 1981, 492). Ten years later, we hear of the pipe maker Hugh Robertson who was in business on the Castle Hill in Edinburgh (L.G. Langwill, 1980). It was he who made the first sets of prize pipes for the Highland Society's competitions in 1781. Later, Donald MacDonald was appointed pipe maker to the Highland Society. He too was in Castle Hill until his death in 1840. This area, convenient for the military establishment at Edinburgh, continued to be a centre of bagpipe manufacture for over a century. In 1840, the firm of Thomas Glen, established in 1827 first as a 'general dealer', then as a musical instrument maker, began making bagpipes, probably in direct succession to MacDonald, and Thomas' brother Alexander set up independently himself three years later.[6] The two firms continued, as John and Robert Glen, and David Glen and Sons, until 1980 and 1950, respectively. Other early families were those of MacDougall, who were in Perth, 1792–1834, and in Aberfeldy until 1928 (A. MacAuley, 1964); and Malcolm MacGregor, originally from Perthshire but working in London in 1810. MacGregor came of a family of pipers and other musicians known since the seventeenth century as the *Clann an Sgeulaiche*, 'Children of the storyteller' (A. Campbell, 1950b), but whether any of them were instrument makers before him is not known. I suspect that if we had the necessary information we should find that places near the Highland line, like Perth and Aberfeldy, were the main centres of Highland pipe manufacture, and that the focus shifted to Edinburgh as the bagpipe began to be taken up by the Army. By the mid- to late nineteenth century, however, Glasgow had overhauled Edinburgh. William Gunn, Donald MacPhee, Peter Henderson and Ronald Lawrie are the most famous names over this period, among many others.

The earlier makers — MacGregor, Robertson, MacDonald — were all noted for other instruments as well, in particular for Northumbrian and Irish bagpipes, and for military band instruments such as flutes. Thomas Glen indeed dealt in general band instruments much more than in bagpipes, as appears from an early account book of his which still survives (J. Glen, MS). But his brother Alexander seems to have specialised in bagpipes, and most of the Glasgow firms, like most pipe makers today, made Highland bagpipes as their main or only instrument. They also diversified their business, but increasingly they did so by making and supplying Highland uniforms and accessories, and publishing pipe music (R.D. Cannon, 1980). The trend illustrates the increasing popularity of the bagpipe from the mid-nineteenth century onwards.

There is obviously keen competition between bagpipe firms, and success is measured not only in volume of sales but in prizes taken by the players of their pipes in the solo and pipe band competitions. There is also a remarkably rapid turnover in prestige — at any one time, two or three names, if not one only, are in the highest fashion among the top competitors. As most of the firms in question are actively trading, further comment on this aspect is withheld!

Other instruments

Several other bagpipes have always been accepted as closely related to the Highland pipe. The instrument so far described is more fully known (in writing, never in speech) as 'the great Highland bagpipe', or formerly 'the great pipe', corresponding to the Gaelic *pìob mhór*. According to our earliest reliable informant, Joseph MacDonald (1760), the great pipe was used entirely for outdoor playing, and especially for pibrochs, but there was also a second, smaller bagpipe, 'the same in form and apparatus with the greater', for playing dance music. It was presumably not so loud, but it was at the same pitch, as we know from a collection of tunes which were noted from one of its players.[7] These 'reel pipes', as they came to be called, were offered by a number of makers throughout the nineteenth century. 'Half-size' pipes, popular in boys' bands from about 1900, also play at the normal pitch. They both sound somewhat shriller than the big pipe, however, just as a tin whistle sounds shriller than a recorder at nominally the same pitch. The reel size and the half size are often confused, but at least one firm (Henderson of Glasgow) maintained the distinction, with separate specifications for each (*NP 19*, No. 7).

The Lowland bagpipe is comparable to the reel pipe but is blown with bellows and has the three drones fixed parallel in the same stock. The piper normally plays seated, with the drones pointing horizontally across his lap (Plate 5). He could stand or march with the drones over his shoulder, but probably he did not, as the tenor drones would then sound directly into his ear. Lowland bagpipes are thought to have been played from about 1700 (A. Baines, 1960), but they were displaced to some extent by another type of bagpipe, the so-called pastoral pipe mentioned below, and also by the fiddle and concertina. Lowland pipes are sometimes called 'Border' pipes, but the term is a misnomer: they were played throughout the Lowland region, which includes the whole North-Eastern seaboard of Scotland. In 1821 a piper named James Budge came from Caithness to compete at the Highland Society's competitions in Edinburgh, but was not allowed to do so as he played the 'bellows pipes' — also noted in the records as 'the common bagpipe' (HSL ii 4; *PT 20*, No. 3). The last pocket of Lowland bagpiping was to be found, about 1900, not in the Borders but in Aberdeenshire (P. Roberts, 1983). Considering that the Lowland pipes continued so long, it is truly regrettable that we know almost nothing about the playing technique. All we can say is that the chanter and drone tunings are the same as the Highland pipe, so that any tune which goes well on one pipe will go well on the other. In the last few years there has been a revival of interest in the Lowland pipe. Pipe Major James Wilson was the pioneer of this effort: he owned and played a set as early as 1965. Since then the Lowland Pipers' Society has been formed with a new journal *Common Stock*; the pipes are again being manufactured, and collections of tunes have been published, selected from older Scottish collections on the basis of their suitability and historical associations (G.J. Mooney, 1982, 1983). Bellows pipes were still included in bagpipe makers' price lists as late as 1901,[8] but these were not Lowland pipes. They were a bellows-blown version of the Highland half-sized or reel pipes, the drones being tied separately into the bag and splayed out over the shoulder while playing. The last known player of such a pipe was the late Angus MacPherson who died in 1976, aged 96 years. He told me that as a young man he played the bellows pipe at weddings, and preferred it not because of any difference in sound, but because, being blown with dry air, it would stay in tune throughout the long night — a thoroughly practical reason, which may be our best clue as to why bellows were introduced in the first place. The music which Mr. MacPherson played was his usual repertoire of Highland pipe tunes.

As already mentioned, bagpipes were used by the Irish Gaels in much the same way as the Scots. It is clear from references in literature that some form of *pìob mhór* was played, but it died out in the early 1700s, and was replaced by a new bellows-blown pipe of quite different character, designed for indoor playing. No specimen of the old Irish bagpipe survives, but there are some indications that it was essentially the same as the Scottish. The most telling point is that the new 'pastoral pipe' which replaced it also had the major scale with the lowest note a whole tone below the key note. A book of music for the new instrument (J. Geoghegan, 1746) included a number of tunes which feature this note in just the same way as the corresponding note in Scottish pipe music (see below, page 39). Subsequently the Irish chanter was again redesigned, producing the Union pipe, or as it has since become known, the *uilleann* pipe, and the bottom note was cut out altogether.

Pìob mhór playing began to revive in Ireland from the mid-nineteenth century onward, but the old tradition had been entirely lost. Scottish bagpipes were used, until the revival became more self-conscious and some distinctive type was felt necessary. The oldest written descriptions of Irish pipes referred to two drones only, so the simple expedient was adopted of playing a Scottish-type with two drones, one bass and one tenor. This is what is often referred to as the 'Irish bagpipe', and it was adopted as standard by Irish units of the British Army (see Plate 6). Most Army and civilian bands have now returned to the three-droned pipe, as they must in order to take part in competitions with Scottish bands. In Ireland the *pìob mhór*, whether two- or three-droned, is usually known as the 'war-pipe' as distinct from the bellows-blown 'uilleann pipe'.

Mention has been made already of the possibility of extending the scale of the chanter by means of keywork. The first known experiment in this direction was made in the early 1800s by Malcolm MacGregor, the pipe maker already mentioned, who had experience of other instruments including Irish and Northumbrian pipes. He brought his new chanter to the competition in Edinburgh in 1810, but the traditionalists, incensed at the desecration of their instrument (or perhaps fearing that the judges would favour it in competitions), got hold of it and smashed it (Dalyell, 1849, 8). No details were recorded of MacGregor's chanter, but in the *Glasgow Herald* of 29th January, 1836, a Mr. Robert Miller of Montrose, 'a celebrated performer on the Northumbrian, Union and Great Highland Bagpipes', was reported as having invented a chanter, with extra holes or keywork, giving one extra note above, and two below, the usual scale, and with semitones. The result was said to be so 'harmonious' that it had been accompanied by a violin and cello with excellent effect. Nothing more was heard of keyed chanters until about 1906, when a London maker, Henry Starck (successor in business to Queen Victoria's piper, William Ross) introduced the 'Brien Boru' bagpipe, aimed at the growing Irish market. In size, shape and sound, the chanter is the same as the Highland, but the scale, like that of Miller's chanter, extends upward by one note, to b'', and downwards by two notes, to f' sharp and e'. The low G note is sharpened to the true leading note, *g'* sharp. With this chanter, many of the popular Irish tunes like *Rakes of Mallow* or *Londonderry Air* can be played without distortion. The arrangement of the keys, however, seems very odd to anyone accustomed to other wind instruments, since the fingers have to be placed one position higher than usual. That is to say, the note low A which is the key note tuned to the drones, has the fingering normally associated with B; B is fingered as if it were C, and so on: thus even tunes which fit the original nine-note chanter have to be re-learned. Any piper already trained on the Scottish pipes would be strongly deterred from transferring to the Brien Boru, and for this reason Starck introduced a second design, again with keys, but adhering to Scottish fingering as far as possible. He called the two chanters 'Irish system' and 'Scottish system' respectively. The Scottish system chanter never made any inroad into Scottish piping, however.

The Brien Boru pipe was protected by patents,[9] and for a time it was also manufactured by Hawkes and Son, also of London. The original patent bagpipe also had modified drones: three of different length playing *A*, e, *a* and set parallel in one stock. But most players seem to have bought chanters only, and used them in ordinary bagpipes, some with three drones, as shown in Plate 6, and some with two. The Brien Boru pipe has been played mainly in Northern Ireland, and until recently it was used by the Royal Inniskilling Fusiliers, who issued a recording shortly before they gave it up (Fontana SFL 13072, 1969). But now all Army units use the Scottish Highland chanter, and only a few civilian Brien Boru bands remain (J. Doran, 1971). The chanters are no longer being made in Britain or Ireland but they are still being manufactured in Pakistan.

An essential adjunct of the bagpipe is the practice chanter (Plate 10). This consists of a chanter only with the reed covered by a cap so that it can be blown without being taken into the mouth. Unlike the bagpipe chanter, the practice chanter has a cylindrical bore, so that, being about the same length, it sounds an octave lower. The reed is double but longer and much softer to blow than the pipe reed. The practice chanter is the only practicable instrument for learning finger technique and rehearsing tunes. The beginner always starts with it and is required to take a complete course of lessons and become fluent in several tunes before he is allowed to take up the bagpipe. There is so much more to learn in the way of controlling the bag and drones that he must not be distracted at first by trying to learn fingering as well. Sometimes the practice chanter is fitted to a bag with a blowpipe, but no drones. This arrangement is called the 'goose' — presumably from the shape of the bag which is indeed distinctly birdlike. Once the bag has been mastered, it is physically much easier to blow the goose than the practice chanter alone, and one might think that it could be used as a transitional stage before going on to the full pipes. Actually it is not worth the expense to do this, and in practice the goose is used not so much by learners as by teachers who give long hours of chanter lessons. It is also excellent for indoor practice of pibroch playing, where continuity of sound and of mental concentration are essential.

Considering the amoung of playing it gets, it is surprising that the practice chanter is not treated more seriously as an instrument in its own right. It can be made to sound pleasant, but only too often it does not. Chanters made even by reputable makers are often badly out of tune, especially being sharp on the high G — the most difficult note to control on any chanter or simple pipe. But this defect, if not too serious, can be cured by partly covering the hole with sellotape, or by judiciously blowing harder or softer on certain notes — a thing which other woodwind players have to learn. Some players — only a few — have mastered the art of tone control as well, using the diaphragm and chest in the way a trained singer does, to produce a surprising increase in volume (J.C. Laughter, 1977). With a good reed the practice chanter can sound rich and 'woody', like a stronger version of the Northumbrian pipes. It also blends very well with other instruments, but few if any pipers have exploited this fact. Indeed few teachers even pay attention to blending practice chanters with each other, and when teaching half a dozen beginners together, they will tolerate the most remarkable discords. Perhaps such teachers find that this enables them to pick out each individual pupil's faults. It certainly does nothing for ear training.

Plastic reeds have largely displaced cane for practice chanters. They are more durable, and if good they stay good for a long time. Conversely, if poor they are very difficult to break in, and usually have to be discarded.

Practice chanters have two disadvantages, one generally recognised, the other not. The first is that the holes are closer together than on the pipe chanter. This makes it easier to play, but it also means that the beginner who has just mastered a particular movement on the practice chanter will find he still has some work to do when he tries to play it on the pipes. The second disadvantage is more subtle. As already mentioned, the bagpipe chanter tends to be louder on the lower than on the upper notes, but the practice chanter, like other cylindrical-bore instruments, tends to be the other way found. Consequently the low grace notes, which are especially important in piping, sound weaker than they should while the high grace notes sound too strong. They come out with a bright chirping sound and can be heard as actual notes, which is not the intention. As long as the practice chanter is regarded as a mere tool and not an instrument, the problem is not too important, but I suspect that some of the argument and confusion which have arisen in the past over pibroch grace noting (see below, p. 86) have been compounded by pipers comparing effects on practice chanters, rather than on the pipes. Some makers have produced longer chanters with the appropriate spacing. The first chanters of this type came out lower in pitch by one tone, so they could not be combined with ordinary ones; but a more recent design (Plate 10) is not only at standard pitch, but has a much improved balance of upper and lower notes. The bore is in fact slightly conical, but in spite of that the pitch is still in the low, practice chanter register.

There is little to record in the way of earlier history of the practice chanter. Joseph MacDonald (1760) mentions it and stresses its importance as much as any later authority. He actually calls it by the English term 'whistle', presumably translating the Gaelic *feadan*. The oldest surviving practice chanters are probably later than 1800. They are essentially similar to those of today, though some are a little smaller. No doubt practice chanters were made in much earlier times, but it is also possible that some pipers contented themselves with cruder, home-made instruments. One of these would be the simple reed pipe which has been made by children in Scotland from time immemorial. At least one famous piper started out in this way. He was John MacKay, an orphan herdboy born in Raasay in 1767. One day, when playing on a 'home made reed pipe', he was heard by a local gentleman amateur piper, Malcolm MacLeod, who befriended him, gave him his first lessons, and later sent him to be taught by the master players of the day (A. Campbell, 1961a).

Another pipe which could conceivably have functioned as a practice chanter was the 'stock and horn' (Plate 11). This was one of the widespread class of instruments known to musicologists as 'hornpipes', which were remarked on previously (p. 3). It was apparently last played in the eighteenth century (L.G. Langwill, 1950). In its crudest form the stock-and-horn consisted of three separate parts: the pipe made from an animal bone, a cow-horn to prolong the lower end, and the 'oaten reed' — made of straw and loosely held in the top. But better versions were made by skilled instrument makers, and some of these are still preserved. They retained the horn, but had a wooden pipe with the same holes as the practice chanter, and a wooden cap or mouthpiece over the reed, as on a flageolet or practice chanter. It must be repeated that there is no evidence that the stock-and-horn was used as a practice chanter, but it clearly would have been suitable, and music played on it must have sounded like bagpipe music.

Continuing the list of alternative bagpipes, the *miniature pipes* are mouth-blown, and have the normal three drones, but narrower in bore and not so loud, and a practice chanter in place of the normal chanter. There are a fair number of sets in use, and some pipers take them seriously while others do not. This book is not intended to be a record of the author's likes and dislikes, but here I feel bound to say that I find the miniature pipe unsatisfactory both to listen to and to play. It can certainly be tuned well, and with a fairly strong reed (plastic seems better than cane) the chanter can be balanced up to the drones. But since the chanter is an octave lower than on the large pipe, while the drones are at the normal pitch, the drone background is wrong. The tenor drones are in unison with the low A of the chanter, so this note tends to be lost; the important note B becomes discordant, and the harmony in general is poorer (on this point see the discussion above, page 5). Finally, the undesirable chirping effect of the higher grace notes comes out even more. The miniature pipe is best played with much simpler gracing than the full pipe — but then it tends to sound like the Northumbrian pipe — so why not play the Northumbrian pipe instead?

This is the place to mention that a Scottish counterpart of the Northumbrian pipe was occasionally manufactured in the past. An instrument made by Thomas Glen, probably in the 1840s, is mouth-blown, but has Northumbrian-type drones and a chanter not unlike a practice chanter (A. Baines, 1960; H. Cheape, 1983b). I have never heard such an instrument played, but a recent modern development is a Northumbrian pipe with a Scottish-type chanter, pitched in D, a fourth higher than the standard practice chanter. Invented by Colin Ross, the Northumbrian pipe maker, it has been taken up by some members of the Lowland Pipers' Society. The chanter can be fingered in the Scottish fashion, and the sound is distinctly attractive.

Some enterprising manufacturers have introduced toy bagpipes. They are, of course, just that — toys; but some have certainly been designed with care. One now on sale has dummy drones but a good chanter like a practice chanter, with a specially designed plastic reed. The airway from the bag to the chanter is constricted so that the bag can be blown to a comfortably tight pressure without choking the reed.

Finally, we should mention the electronic bagpipe. Pipers who have not heard it may write it off as a joke, but it is in fact an interesting and useful device. Externally it looks like the ordinary bagpipe, but no blowing is required. The 'bag' contains an electronic synthesiser, while the chanter, instead of holes, has contacts so that when fingered in the normal way, the appropriate notes are produced. Both pitch and volume can be adjusted, which makes it a simple matter to play in concert with other instruments, and a number of folk and 'folk-rock' groups have begun to do this. The electronic bagpipe also appeals to pipers who are physically disabled from blowing, though a less radical alternative, an electrical air pump to blow the ordinary pipes, is also available.

NOTES

1. For further details see e.g. Grainger and Campbell (1971); J.A. MacLellan (1964a); S. MacNeill and T. Pearston (1968).

2. These include 'a rude wood carving of a piper, formerly in Woodstock Castle, Co. Kilkenny', thought to be late fifteenth or early sixteenth century, and 'a drawing of a youth playing the pipes on the margin of a missal which had belonged to the Abbay of Rossgael, Co. Kildare' (Breathnach, 1971, 69; not illustrated); the *Dinnseanchus* manuscript with a medieval-type illuminated initial showing a pig playing the bagpipe (illustrated, *ib.*, 70); and a sketch thought to show the Battle of Ballyshannon, 1595 (Collinson, 1975, plate facing p. 172).

3. See e.g. A. MacBain (1899); W.L. Manson (1901), 52; A.D. Fraser (1907), 396–7; W.H. Grattan Flood (1911), 128, 135; W.A. Cocks (1954); *NP 19* No. 7 (1967).

4. A reference to the purchase of '2 pypes bought to MacCrimmon', in the Dunvegan estate papers, dated 1711, has been interpreted as meaning a two-drone bagpipe (I.F. Grant, 1981, 377; cf. A. Morrison, 1967, 330); but recently another document has been discovered which makes it clear that two separate sets of pipes were involved (Anon., 1984). Occasional mentions of a 'pair' of bagpipes have also been taken to mean two-drone sets (I.F. Grant, 1981, 491), but in fact in the eighteenth and early nineteenth centuries a 'pair' was the common expression for a set of bagpipes, of any type (see e.g. J. Logan, 1831, ii, 305; A.D. Fraser, 1907, plate facing p. 144).

5. The materials, technical terms, and methods of present-day bagpipe making have been well described in an article by Hugh Cheape, (1983b) based on information supplied by leading makers. For other information, see especially J. Robertson (1928); D. Glen (1927); T.W. MacLeod (1949); Anon. (1950); T. Pearston (1950); R. Thomson (1955); F. Collinson (1975), 209–212.

6. For detailed references to the MacDonald and Glen firms, see R.D. Cannon (1969). The tradition was that the two Glen brothers separated after quarrelling over the correct colour of hemp to be used for binding the blades of chanter reeds. Alexander used the same yellow hemp for reeds as for lapping the joints of the pipes; Thomas insisted on red hemp for the former purpose, yellow for the latter! The story was told to me by the last proprietor of the firm, Mr. Andrew Ross Junior.

7. 'North Highland Reels or Country Dances', in P. MacDonald (1784), 33–37. MacDonald states (*ib.*, 7) that most of these tunes were taken from 'a bagpipe performer' and he implies that the smaller bagpipe was used, since he goes on to print four pibrochs as examples of music of the 'large or true Highland bagpipe'.

8. David Glen, for example, offered 'half-size or reel bagpipes' with a sub-category of 'bellows bagpipe', in an advertisement in D. Glen's Collection, Part 5 'Third Thousand' [1901–7] (cf. R.D. Cannon, 1980, 164).

9. Patent Nos. 19831 (24 Jan. 1907), 23839 (25 Feb. 1909), 24305 (24 Oct. 1910).

CHAPTER 3

Bagpipe Music — Introductory

The bagpipe scale

The notes given by the chanter are as follows:

Ex. 3.1. The Highland pipe chanter scale

These are the notes as conventionally named and written, with the key note called A; the actual pitch is a semitone higher. Unfortunately, in most published bagpipe music the key signature is omitted, so that anyone not realising this gets a completely wrong impression of the music.

A point to stress at the outset is that because of the restricted scale, many well-known tunes simply cannot be played on the pipes; and in fact the great majority of tunes, especially those which pipers actually play of their own choice, are composed specially for the pipe. Of course, there are plenty of familiar ones available, and when a pipe band plays in public, a fair number of these will be included in the programme — tunes like 'Highland Laddie', 'Cock o' the North', 'Scotland the Brave' and 'Bonnie Dundee'. These four have all been taken into the repertoire from songs, and slightly altered in the process, though hardly enough to cause offence. But although a piper will go some way to meet a modern audience by producing such tunes, he can do so only to a limited extent. Few non-pipers realise that even such familiar airs such as 'Annie Laurie', 'Loch Lomond' and 'Auld Lang Syne' are impracticable on the pipes. The real strength of the bagpipe is the music peculiar to itself.

Most people are aware that the pipe scale is somehow 'out of tune' — or to put it less provocatively, that the scale is not the same as that of modern orchestral instruments. There are two quite separate aspects to this matter. The first is that if we take the note A as the key note, most of the notes are those of the major scale, but the two G's are natural, so that in the context of A major they sound as 'flattened sevenths'. When pipers play a tune

28

which is composed for the modern A-major key, the G's sound wrong. Actually very few of the tunes played use the G notes in this 'wrong' fashion, but the few that do are adaptations of particularly well-known non-pipe tunes, and these are the ones that the non-piping listener tends to notice. In traditional bagpipe tunes, the natural G's are an essential feature, as we shall see below. The other aspect of the pipe scale is that certain notes apart from the G's are slightly different from the usual standards, and on this subject there has been a good deal of discussion and research. Early work has been conveniently summarised by S. MacNeill and J.M.A. Lenihan (1960–1). Most authors have said that the C and F sharp are not quite so sharp as they are written, while the D and the two G's are a little sharper. This means that the two intervals shown as semitones (C sharp to D and F sharp to G) are actually larger than semitones, and the intervals next above them are smaller than whole tones. Such a scale has been recognised in many traditions of folk music, and is sometimes called the scale of 'neutral thirds', meaning that most of the thirds are smaller than a major third but larger than a minor third. It seems that there is a general tendency for traditional singers to even out the thirds in this way. With 'folk' woodwind instruments the tendency is the same, and Anthony Baines (1960) has pointed out the simple explanation, that the maker bores the holes at equal distances so as to lie comfortably under the fingers. If some notes then come out unacceptably flat, he will sharpen them by undercutting or enlarging the holes, but not usually by resiting them further up the pipe. The modern Spanish pipe plays a normal major scale, and its holes are very unequal in size. Scottish chanters have the holes slightly unequally spaced, somewhat varying in size, and very much undercut. In 1954 Lenihan and MacNeill made careful measurements of the pitch of notes of a selection of good chanters. They did not confirm the flatness of the C sharp and F sharp. It turned out that these notes were very close to the major third and major sixth, relative to the low A key note, when judged by the 'just-tempered' scale, though slightly flatter than the 'equal-tempered' scale of the piano and of modern orchestral practice; but the D and G were somewhat sharp. The authors concluded that the nominal semitones were in fact carefully judged intervals, with a ratio of frequencies of notes of 27/25 instead of the just-tempered 16/15. Perhaps a better way of putting this is to say that each note of the scale is tuned to give a simple chord with the key note A (E. Cornish, 1952) since this is in fact how pipe makers have normally made the final adjustments to a chanter — by playing it in a bagpipe and making sure that every note sounds well with the drones.

These measurements, however, were made thirty years ago, and it would be unwise to assume that the same results would be obtained today; or that the chanters used then were the same as in earlier times. My own strong impression is that they were not. I have played chanters made in c.1880, c.1910, 1955 and 1965. I found a clear progression, each successive chanter being brighter, slightly sharper in its key note, and more 'true' in its thirds than the previous one, and this trend seems to be continued in the chanters of today. On the other hand a much older chanter (c.1820–1840) by the celebrated maker Donald MacDonald, who made the Highland Society prize pipes, was closer to my 1965 chanter than to any of the others. I am inclined to think that modern chanters are converging towards the modern diatonic scale, but that among old chanters there was much more variety than there is today. I suggest that until fairly recent times, one of the marks of a really good piper was the intonation of his chanter as well as his playing ability. Donald MacDonald's chanter would have sung out more sweetly in a pibroch than those of some of his rivals, simply because it blended better with his drones. He was an educated musician and may have understood the reasons when others did not. But this is speculation. What is needed in the matter of chanter scales is more research of the kind pioneered by MacNeill and his colleagues at Glasgow. This work will have to be done with considerable care and discretion. It will be necessary to ensure that old chanters selected for measurements had been considered good ones in their day and had not been thrown out as a result of wear or some defect; and to experiment with reeds specially made for the purpose, since these too have changed with time. It seems that in general old reeds were longer and broader in the blade than modern ones (F.C. MacColl-Botly, 1980).

Pitch

The actual pitch of the chanter seems to have risen appreciably over the years. The names of the notes were decided in the late eighteenth century, and all writers agreed in calling the key note A. In 1954, Lenihan and MacNeil found the average bagpipe A to be 459 cycles per second (cps), considerably higher than the International Standard A (440) and almost up to standard B flat (467). It was suggested at the time that 459 cps might be adopted as a pipers' standard. Actually, pitch has continued to rise, though in the last few years there has been some reaction against this. In early times, the question of a standard pitch would not arise. The bagpipe was primarily a solo instrument, and in spite of occasional reports of pipers playing together in twos and threes (or even a hundred together if the account of Prince Charles' entry into Carlisle is to be believed!), there is nothing to suggest that this was normal practice until the formation of pipe bands started in the nineteenth century. Unlike pipers of some other countries, Scottish pipers do not regularly play in combination with other instruments. Thus even today the main requirement is that pipe scales should be consistent with each other rather than with any wider standard. (For some considerable time past, pipe makers have offered sets of specially matched chanters for band use.) But in the last decade or so, combinations of bagpipe and other bands have become popular, and if this continues to be the case, we may perhaps expect that the pipe chanter will finally arrive at the diatonic scale, and at the standard pitch of B flat.

Finger technique

Most bagpipes share two basic musical characteristics which go back to their ancestral mouth-blown reed pipes. Since the chanter reed is not taken between the lips, the sound is constant, with no possibility of playing louder or softer for emphasis; and it is continuous, so that it is impossible to play two separate notes of the same pitch, in succession. Both of these limitations have to be accepted to some extent, but both can also be largely overcome, and the principal method of doing this is to use grace notes. A grace note is an extremely short note interposed between two notes of the melody, so short that it has negligible effect on the timing, and does not even sound at its true pitch. The listener perceives the grace note as a kind of non-musical click, or tapping sound, and once the tune is well under way, he probably does not notice it at all, but simply registers that two melody notes of the same pitch have indeed been played in succession in spite of the apparent impossibility of it. The term 'grace note' is of course a borrowing from classical music terminology, and is not perhaps quite appropriate, since the simplest possible grace note, as I have just described it, is not an ornamental flourish or 'grace' added to the music, but an essential part of the technique. An older and better name is 'cut'. The longer notes which actually make up the tune are generally called 'plain' notes, 'theme' notes or simply the 'main' notes.

In Scottish pipe music, however, combinations of two, three or more grace notes are also common, and these can fairly be described as ornaments. They are to some extent optional, and different combinations can be applied to the same phrase of plain notes depending on the tempo or the type of tune. This is one of the ways in which the piper achieves emphasis and points up the rhythm. Here we shall summarise the principal kinds of grace notes in use, and to do this we have to consider the basic fingering of the chanter.

The fingering generally accepted today is shown in example 3.2 (● denotes a hole closed, ○ a hole open):

Ex. 3.2. Fingering of the pipe chanter

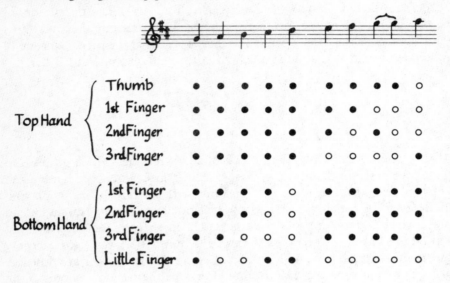

The two high G's are alternatives, and the reason why two different fingerings are used for the same note is a historical puzzle which has not yet been unravelled. It is possible that at one time the second fingering was adopted as an approximation to G sharp. The pipe maker David Glen did indeed state in 1881 that the second G was slightly sharper than the first, and that it should be used in places where conventional music would have the G sharp (see below, p. 40). On the other hand, Pipe Major John MacDougall Gillies, who managed Peter Henderson's pipe-making business around 1900, claimed to be able to adjust his reeds to give practically the same pitch with either fingering (A. Campbell, 1958). Modern pipers follow Gillies as nearly as possible. Fingerings of other notes have varied from time to time, particularly as regards the note C (or rather C sharp). Prior to the 1950s most pipers played this note with the bottom-hand little finger off the chanter. The earliest written finger charts (J. MacDonald, 1760; 'Amateur', 1818) gave the form shown here, and it seems that a few leading pipers preferred this form, at least in pibrochs. Today the 'closed C', as it came to be called, is preferred by virtually everyone. It sounds appreciably sharper than the open form, especially on modern chanters which are now designed to be played in that way.

Despite variations of this sort, the basic characteristic of the scale has remained the same since records were kept: that is, it is a *partially covered* system. To play each successive note up the scale, the next highest hole is opened, but certain lower holes are closed. If these holes are not closed, the note will be out of tune. This contrasts on the one hand with most classical wind instruments, which use completely open fingering, all holes up to and including the operative one being open; and on the other, with certain other types of bagpipe, which use entirely closed fingering, opening only one hole at a time. No doubt it would be easy to adjust the Highland pipe chanter to play either open or closed fingering, but the partial system which is actually used facilitates certain essential grace notes.

The simplest possible grace note is a single infinitesimally short note, as just described. It can, logically, be one of two kinds: either higher or lower than the pitch of the plain notes which it separates. Both kinds are used. Those of the higher pitch are made by momentarily opening and closing a higher hole, and this is always done by the movement of one finger only. This means that some grace notes involve false fingerings while others are true to the scale, but this is not considered significant since the sound is too short to show the difference. Of the possible high grace notes that can be fingered, three are particularly common, and sequences of grace notes such as the following often occur:

Ex. 3.3. Triplings on the low hand

The three grace notes are made by flicking three fingers in succession, respectively the index finger of the upper hand, the index finger of the lower hand, and the ring finger of the upper hand. The choice and order of the notes is partly musical, partly mechanical: the higher the note the brighter the sound, so it is felt that the highest note is the most prominent, and that it gives emphasis to the plain note which follows it. Hence the high G grace note is placed on the down-beat of the music wherever possible.

Grace notes of lower pitch follow a different principle. On the notes of the lower hand (pipers in fact do often refer to the notes of the scale as 'the low hand' and 'the high hand') the low grace note is generally the lowest note of the chanter, low G. So when it occurs on the plain notes A, B, C or D, the players must move one, two, two or three fingers respectively.

Moving these fingers together so that they strike the chanter simultaneously is one of the first and most important lessons for a beginner. On the upper hand, the low grace note is formed by moving one finger only. On the note D, there is also an alternative one-finger grace note, so the complete set is as follows:

Ex. 3.4. 'Slurs' or 'Strikes'

The sounds of these low grace notes vary from a dull tap, at the low end of the scale, to something which is practically imperceptible at the top end, and can only be described as a short break in the music, which is what it is intended to be. However, whether by accident or design, the fingering of each of these grace notes is true to the scale. The notes can therefore be lengthened to the point where they begin to sound out at their true pitch, and this is done to a considerable extent in pibroch playing (see below, p. 83).

Combinations of grace notes are basically of two types. One type consists of playing two single grace notes in succession, on the same plain note, for example, a high G grace note followed quickly by a D grace note, on the plain note B. The movement is called a 'double B' and the effect intended is a short B note followed by a long one, as shown here at (a) or (b). Usually the short B is also written as a grace note, as at (c), but when properly done it should sound as its name implies, the middle B being heard as a true, though very short, note. A more expressive notation, though not in fact used, might be as at (d):

Ex. 3.5. Double B

Doublings can be formed, as here, by playing two high grace notes in succession, or two low grace notes, or a high grace note followed by a low one (never in practice, the reverse combination): and since there are choices of high grace notes, the number of possible doublings is quite large. There is no need to discuss them any further here, as they are fully described in pipe tutors published over the past 150 years. From these books it appears that in the course of time the doublings used have settled down to a restricted set of standard types.

Three grace notes played on the same note in succession will produce various kinds of trebling, but except for an important movement on low A, these are not common (see below, pp. 142, 147).

The other basic type of combined grace note has been known at different times as a 'cutting', 'grip' or 'throw', and the last two terms are still in common use. In these movements the actions of low and high grace notes are sandwiched together. For example, after the note B, the fingers are moved as for a low grace note, low G; they are held in that position while a high grace note, D, is executed; the low G sounds again after the D; and finally the fingers are raised back to B (or to some other note). In slow motion, the movement sounds as at (a). At full speed it is noted as at (b):

Ex. 3.6. Throw on B

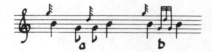

There is one such throw for each note of the scale, except for the bottom and the top notes. More complicated executions of the same type are done by playing more than one high grace note before opening the chanter to give the final melody note:

Ex. 3.7. Taorluath, 'bubbly note', and Crunluath

All these movements can best be described as producing a 'crackling' sound. The short, three note throws (Ex. 3.6) are done very crisply indeed and, like single grace notes, they are allowed no time in the music. The longer ones (Ex. 3.7) do take up appreciable time, although the notation does not indicate this. For example, the first of the three movements just quoted actually approximates to the rhythm of one of the following. The cluster of four grace notes fills out the time of the second note:

Ex. 3.8. Rhythm of the Taorluath

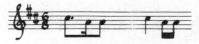

Grace notes are common to all bagpipe music, but the types used, and the extent to which they are used, vary greatly from one bagpipe tradition to another. The two types of single grace note seem to be well-nigh universal; some doublings can be heard in Spanish pipe music; particular forms of doubling and throw, known as 'roll' and 'cran' respectively, are used on the Irish Uillean pipes. No tradition exploits grace notes to the extent that present-day Scottish piping does, but on the other hand, some have effects such as vibrato and trills, more classical-sounding than the Scottish grace notes. There is also a considerable division within Scottish piping, between the grace notes of *ceòl mór* (see below, p. 45) and of other pipe music. The former relies much more heavily on 'throws' and the latter on doublings. But there has been no detailed study of any of these subjects, and this is not the place to go into further details.

Tonality

By this somewhat forbidding term I mean whatever it is that establishes the musical 'flavour' of a tune, apart from its rhythm and tempo: that which makes a Scottish tune sound Scottish, or which causes the listener to feel that a particular melody either is or is not suitable for the bagpipe. In classical music theory, tonalities are governed by the major and minor scales, and the emphasis is on harmony — the progression of chords in a natural sequence, and the feeling that certain chords are appropriate at certain positions in the tune. Early Western music admitted other 'modes' besides major and minor, and many writers have argued that these modes can be heard in folk music today.

Classical ideas of harmony have little to do with bagpipe music, nor is it at all clear that the older modes — 'Ionian', 'Dorian', 'Myxolydian' and so on — have directly influenced pipers. But these questions have never been thoroughly discussed, and again, this book is not the place to discuss them. Instead, we shall point out some features of Scottish bagpipe music which are generally agreed to be typical, and as far as possible we shall be guided by ideas which have been suggested by pipers themselves.

A great deal of Scottish music is founded on the pentatonic scale — the sequence of notes best known perhaps as those of the black keys of the piano. Many tunes, and not only the oldest ones, confine themselves entirely to this scale, while many more are not so strict but still have a strong pentatonic flavour which is an essential part of their 'Scottishness'. From the nine notes of the pipe chanter we can extract selections which

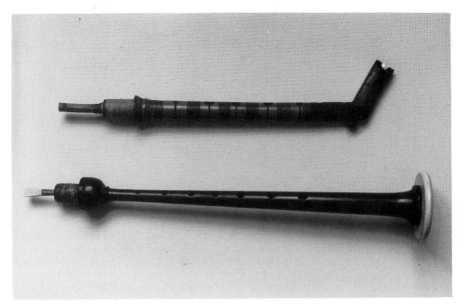

Plate 1. Examples of East- and West-European bagpipe chanters. (a) Rumanian *çimpoi*: cylindrical bore, with an additional lower joint carved from horn; single beating reed. (b) Scottish Highland bagpipe: conical bore, turned from a single piece of wood, with an ivory sole which has little effect on the sound; double reed. *Author's collection.*

Plate 2. The *pūngī* or gourd-pipe of India. Two pipes, one a chanter, the other a drone, each with single beating reeds, enclosed in the gourd. The piper uses circular breathing, contracting the cheeks while quickly taking in air through the nose, and so producing an unbroken sound as with a bagpipe. *Photo*: Dr. P. R. Cooke.

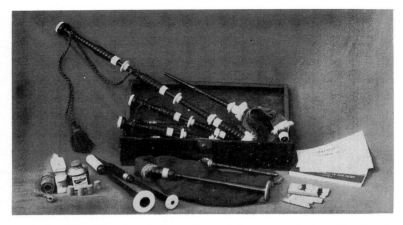

Plate 3. A piper's kit. The pipes in the traditional-shaped wooden box. Practice chanter and 'goose'. Spare reeds, seasoning for the bag, waxed thread for tying the bag, hemp for joints and tuning slides. When the pipes are not being played the chanter is withdrawn and fitted into a spare blind stock, to protect the reed from too much damp. *Author's collection.*

Plate 4. Detail from the painting of the Mole at Tangier, by Dirck Stoop, 1683. The painting actually shows the Mole being dismantled shortly before the British forces evacuated the fort of Tangier. The soldiers are lined along the edges of the structure, lifting the stones and throwing them into the sea. Four pipers are playing to encourage the work. Although the figures are very small, they can be seen to be wearing Highland costume, and the three drones of the third piper from the left can be made out against the pale background. *Photo*: National Maritime Museum, Greenwich.

Plate 5. (Left) A nineteenth-century Lowland piper. Engraved by Edwin Tyrrell from a painting by T. S. Good. The picture is actually entitled 'The Northumbrian Piper', but the arrangement of the drones of the bagpipe — two short drones equal in length, and one twice the length — is typical of what is now termed the Scottish Lowland or Border bagpipe. *Author's collection*. Plate 6. (Right) A piper of the 1st Battalion Royal Inniskilling Fusiliers, playing pipes with the Brien Boru chanter. The keys on the chanter can be seen, above and below the piper's fingers. Apart from the chanter, this is the normal Scottish Highland bagpipe. *Photo*: Imperial War Museum.

Plate 7. A company of the Royal Irish Fusiliers on a route march in Nijmegen, Holland in 1958. The men are in battledress, led by three pipers, who are taking it in turns to play, as is usual on long marches. The pipes are the two-droned 'Irish warpipes'. They are identical to the Scottish Highland bagpipe except for the omission of one tenor drone. *Photo*: Imperial War Museum.

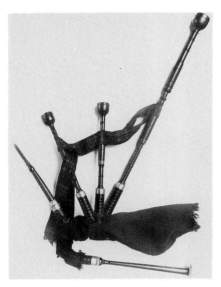

Plate 8. (Left) An old set of Highland pipes. The drones are probably eighteenth century. They are the same in number and length as modern drones, but less ornate, and they have the characteristic large bell ends. The stocks and chanter are more modern. *Photo*: Royal Museum of Scotland, Edinburgh.

Plate 9. (Right) The *piob bhreac* or 'speckled' pipes, reputed to have belonged to the MacCrimmon family, though only the top joints of the drones have ever been claimed to be original. The pipes now belong to the MacLeod family, at Dunvegan Castle, Skye. *Photo*: The Piping Centre, Boreraig.

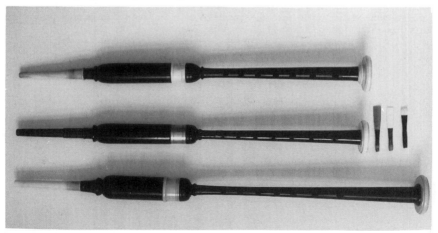

Plate 10. Three practice chanters. (1) Late nineteenth or early twentieth century, by P. Henderson, Glasgow. (2) c. 1960, by R. G. Hardie, Glasgow. (3) A practice chanter with holes spaced as on the full-size pipe chanter, and with a larger tenon at the joint so that it can be fitted into the standard bagpipe chanter stock to make a goose; by D. Naill & Co., 1975. Also shown are three practice chanter reeds: the traditional long-bladed cane reed; a plastic reed of similar size, and an improved design of plastic reed which has now largely superseded the second type. *Author's collection*.

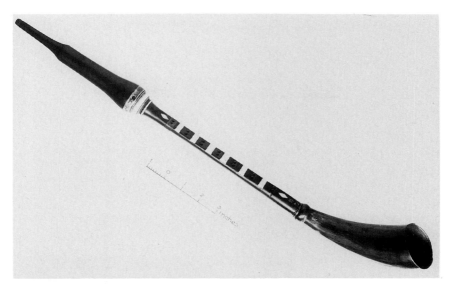

Plate 11. An eighteenth-century Scottish stock-and-horn. The wooden pipe is cylindrical, with finger holes arranged as on the bagpipe practice chanter. *Photo*: Royal Museum of Scotland, Edinburgh.

Plate 12. Pages from two Boys' Brigade manuscript pipe manuals, written by Charles Cannon, Band Officer of the 6th Manchester Company, Boys' Brigade, about 1912. *Author's collection.*

Plate 13. A page from Angus MacKay's manuscript collection of pibrochs, written about 1840. Angus has used symbols to show that the tune was known by different names to two informants, John MacKay (his father) and Ranald MacDougall. *Photo*. National Library of Scotland (MS 3753).

Plate 14. Donald Cameron, piper to the Earl of Seaforth. Among many other piping honours, he won the first prize at the Highland Society competition in Edinburgh in 1844 (the last year in which the competition was held), and the Gold Medal at the first competition at the Northern Meeting, Inverness, 1859. He was 'a shrewd, clever man, full of Highland lore and tradition', and the leading authority on pibroch playing in his day. *Photo*: National Library of Scotland (MS. Acc. 8662).

Plate 15. Highland dancing on the *machair* at Askernish; South Uist Highland Games, 22 July, 1981. *Photo*: Dr. P. R. Cooke.

Plate 16. A unit of the 7th Battalion, Seaforth Highlanders, marching to battle positions on 'D'-day, 25th June, 1944. *Photo*: Imperial War Museum.

Plate 17. Pipers, Drummers and Buglers of the 9th Battalion, Royal Scots. The band has ten pipers, four side drummers, who play the old rope-tensioned 'guards drum' and one tenor drummer. Back row: the drummers, wearing the broad leather drum slings; left-hand side, Pipe Major Thomas Porteous; right-hand side, Drum Major J. Small. Front row: the six buglers.

Plate 18. A modern outdoor piping competition. South Uist Highland Games, 22nd July, 1981. *Photo*: Dr. P. R. Cooke.

correspond to parts of the pentatonic scale, transposed to different pitches. One of them is as follows:

Ex. 3.9. The pentatonic 'A' scale

There is no universally accepted nomenclature for such scales, but it will be convenient to call this one the 'A-scale'. Many tunes built out of these notes emphasise the A, C sharp and E, and thus give, to a modern ear, the effect of the A major key. But a melody can also be made to start and finish on B, and to emphasise the F sharp, in which case it has the flavour of B minor, and this too is found in some tunes. In a true minor key, the scale would have a D to provide the third, and a G for the sixth, and the facility of varying the A to A sharp at certain points. But here we are not talking about keys in the modern sense of the word, and unless we are trying to harmonise a pipe tune, or taking a modern, harmonised tune and adapting it to the pipes, these considerations do not arise. Many of the tunes quoted in this book are built in or around the A-scale, and the reader who cares to play them on any other instrument, preferably with the addition of a low A drone, but with no other chords added, will soon grasp their essential flavour.

A second pentatonic scale available on the chanter starts one tone lower, and takes in seven notes, the 'G-scale':

Ex. 3.10. The pentatonic 'G' scale

In this scale, phrases with strong G, B or D notes will sound like G major, while phrases which emphasise A, B and E will have some of the effect of A minor. For phrases in G, the leading note F sharp is also available if required. What is not available is the fourth of the scale, since the C is sharp, and this tends to be avoided.

Finally, the following six notes make up the 'D' scale:

Ex. 3.11. The pentatonic 'D' scale

Here the 'major' effect is got by emphasising the D, F sharp and two A's, but it is different in character, since the tune will tend to lie above and below the key note, whereas in the previous two scales, the tune lies between two key notes — high A and low A, or high G and low G. (Some music theorists call this a 'plagal' mode, as opposed to an 'authentic' mode.) Again a minor effect can be obtained by stressing the E, F sharp and B, but a third possibility is to start or finish on A, stressing the E and B. In modern terms, this brings out the effect of the dominant.

Pentatonic tunes showing all these effects will be found among the examples printed in this book; likewise 'hexatonic' tunes using six of the possible seven tones. These may be composed of phrases from different pentatonic scales, or they may use the 'extra' note more fully.

The musical reader who is not accustomed to bagpipes may be surprised at the emphasis on the different 'keys' which are available on the chanter; or on the other hand he may be sceptical. There are two very widespread misunderstandings about bagpipe tonality, which I am anxious to correct. One is that since the bagpipe has a fixed drone, it can only 'play in one key'; the other is that since changing the key of a tune merely moves it up or down in pitch, the effect is trivial and not worth so much discussion. The answer to the first is that, whatever the case may be in other countries, Scottish pipers enjoy considerable freedom to play in different keys, simply because so many of their tunes are basically pentatonic, and the different pentatonic scales sound to a modern ear like different keys. The answer to the second is that, because of the fixed pitch of the drone, changing the key of a pipe tune completely alters its character. Notes which were consonant with the drone become dissonant, and *vice versa*, and the whole tune is heard in a new light. Actually, it is rare for the same tune to be played at will in either of two keys; more commonly, two keys will be available, but one is felt to be more appropriate than the other. Thus 'The Finger Lock' is always played in G though it could be played in A, and the 'Salute on the Birth of Rory Mor MacLeod' is in a kind of B minor though it too could be in A. (I have picked these two examples to show that in spite of the A note of the drones, it is not always the A key which is preferred.)

Mention of dissonance leads to another characteristic of many pipe tunes, the so-called 'double tonic' (F. Collinson, 1975; D. Johnson, 1984, 18). The tunes are made in two sections of similar general shape, but placed one tone apart in the scale, so that they give the flavour of two different keys. This construction is common in Scottish and Irish music, and also in older Northern English tunes (R.D. Cannon, 1972), and it is not confined to bagpipes. It gains special point on the bagpipe, however, since one of the two 'flavours' will be closer to the drone key than the other. This tune begins with a bar in B minor and then switches to A major:

Ex. 3.12. Strathspey: Struan Robertson

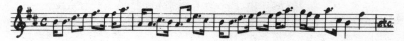

The following tune uses the same flavours the other way round:

Ex. 3.13. Strathspey: Highland Whisky

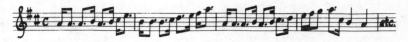

The most characteristic of all bagpipe modes, however, is the one which begins in A major, then switches one tone lower to G major:

Ex. 3.14. Reel: Thomson's Dirk

In this example the two sections are each pentatonic, and the second is an exact imitation of the first, in the lower key. But if the first section is not pentatonic, it will involve the note D, and the second section cannot imitate it precisely, but must use C sharp, where the G major key would require C natural. The piper never hesitates to use the C sharp in such a case, and it always seems to be effective:

Ex. 3.15. March: The Edinburgh Volunteers

It is tempting to suggest that the piper is merely glossing over an imperfection in his chanter, and that it works because in practice the wrong note is not much emphasised. Yet on trying the tune over on some other instrument, both with the C natural and with the C sharp, it will be found that the 'wrong' note is not wrong at all, but actually sounds the better of the two. Tunes of this type are pipe music *par excellence*. David Johnson has suggested (1972) that the style originated on some non-transposing instrument such as the stock-and-horn or bagpipe, and as for the recent tunes, they were certainly composed by Highland pipers. It is no exaggeration to say that the tunes were made for the pipes and the pipes were made for them. If they are to be played on any other instrument, the A drone is enough to bring out their character. Any attempt to harmonise them with extra chords is too much.

The same two keys are sometimes found in reverse — the G passage first, then the A; and the A passage complete with an emphatic C sharp. I believe that most, if not all, tunes of this type are adaptations from other sources, but a kind of natural selection has operated to ensure that only the best have survived. The pipe version of *Cabar Feidh* is of this type. The song and fiddle versions have the C natural. To succeed against the odds in this way, the sharp C's must be bold and unapologetic — the finest example of all is the pibroch, 'Lament for the Viscount of Dundee':

Ex. 3.16. Pibroch: Lament for the Viscount of Dundee

The true key of A major is theoretically not possible, since it requires the leading note, G sharp. In practice, however, this is not a serious limitation. Some tunes in A major happen not to use the G at all. The pibroch 'The Little Spree' and the quickstep march 'Atholl Highlanders' are of this type. Others have the G but only as a very short passing note:

Ex. 3.17. March: The Atholl and Breadalbane Gathering (2nd part)

Here the G marked * would be played sharp on any other instrument, but it is so short that it is doubtful whether anyone not deliberately listening out for it would notice the difference. Most commonly, this kind of false G occurs as the pick-up note to a phrase beginning on high A:

Ex. 3.18. March: Kenmure's on and awa' (2nd part)

Only the high G is affected in this way. The low G seems never to occur as a pick-up note, and the tunes in which low G is doing duty for G sharp all seem to be adaptations of non-pipe tunes:

Ex. 3.19. Reel: Speed the Plough

Usually when there are G's in a tune which has the overall feel of A major, they are fully and intentionally natural, and they have striking effects which can be quite different in different contexts. Low G's often occur in cadences along with B or D, so that in effect they touch on the key of G. High G's standing alone among the notes of the A major chord are also common, and are usually felt as 'flattened sevenths'. The following extract neatly illustrates both of these effects: the flattened seventh in bars 1 and 3, and the tonic G in bar 4:

Ex. 3.20. Reel: The Rejected Suitor

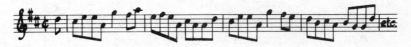

A third common situation is a high G as the topmost note of a rising and falling phrase, followed by F sharp:

Ex. 3.21. Reel: The High Road to Linton (2nd part)

Phrases like this recall the sixteenth-century convention of *musica ficta*, according to which a tune such as Ex. 3.21 would have been scored with a certain key signature (in this case three sharps) but the player would be expected to know that in some cases the G's were to be played sharp, as written, and in other cases they were to be flattened. Pipers today could be said to play *musica ficta* in another sense. They use the G note with different meanings, so to speak, even though they cannot modulate its pitch. It is noticeable that when a piper sings or whistles a pipe tune, he usually sharpens the high G when necessary. In older pipe collections we also find a number of tunes with C notes which 'ought' to be natural even

though they can only be played sharp, but in modern times these have
largely disappeared (for a surviving example, see below, p. 126).

The full diatonic major scale is possible only in the key of D. Tunes in
this key tend to alternate between tonic and dominant chords — that is,
they have phrases in the A, D, F sharp area, answered by phrases with A,
C sharp, E. 'The Barren Rocks of Aden' is one of this type. Other tunes
tend to steer clear of the C sharp and hark back to pentatonic feeling. The
really distinctive features of this class of tune, however, come in with the
note G, sometimes in typically Scottish cadences (Ex. 3.22) but ultimately
in its classical role as the note of the subdominant (Ex. 3.23):

Ex. 3.22. March: Colonel Robertson

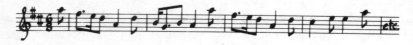

Ex. 3.23. March: Mrs. Lily Christie. D.S. Ramsay (1958)

To some extent, the different tonalities are connected with different classes
of pipe tune, and it seems possible that they were introduced at different
times in the past. As we shall see in later chapters, pibrochs are the oldest
form of pipe music still extant. Reels and jigs come later — that is to say,
although the oldest of them date back to the pibroch era, they have
continued to be composed in large numbers since then, and so as a group
they are more recent; in the same sense, marches come later again, and
hornpipes later still. It is among pibrochs that we find the greatest
proportion of pentatonic melodies. The double tonic effect is also used in
pibrochs, but it belongs more especially to reels and the older marches.
The full major scale is found mainly in late nineteenth and twentieth-
century tunes. As for keys, the key of G is mostly found in pibrochs, and in
some reels and jigs; the keys of A pervade all types of tune, but the key of D
accounts for a substantial proportion of marches, and for nearly all
hornpipes. It is interesting to note the opinion of one writer, A.D. Fraser,
in 1907. He disliked the key of D for pipe tunes, with the drone 'booming
along the while in A', though he admitted that there were some
outstanding tunes in that key. He suggested that the fashion for D tunes
was due to pipers composing on the practice chanter, without the influence
of the drones (A.D. Fraser, 1907, 376).

The choice of mode for a tune also involves technical factors. Tunes in D are generally easier to play than those in A. Certain grace notes, particularly impressive but also relatively difficult to play, occur on A but not on D. This is why competition marches are nearly all in A and not D, while on the other hand the first tunes taught to beginners are mostly in D. Again, one reason why the key of G, and also the double A and G mode shown in Example 3.14 above, continue to be favoured for jigs and reels is that these tunes tend to contain figures of repeated notes which can be played more easily on A and G than on D.

There is probably an element of tradition involved as well, in that a piper composing a new tune will tend to borrow ideas unconsciously from existing tunes, and thus perpetuate the key or mode. But the fact remains that pipers have undoubtedly given a good deal of thought to the strictly musical flavour of their tunes — in other words to tonality — even if, unfortunately for the historian, they have rarely expressed their ideas in public. Seumas MacNeill, who first explicitly pointed out the three pentatonic scales, is a leading piper, and his ideas have had time to spread among other pipers since he put them forward in the 1950s. We should also remember an earlier piper, E. MacDonald, who composed an excellent set of three jigs in each of the three pentatonic scales. They have been published together, without names, in the Scots Guards Collection (1954) simply as 'First Jig', 'Second Jig' and 'Third Jig', in the scales of D, G and A respectively. Pipers are also well aware that in slow tunes, pentatonic phrasing produces a characteristically Highland flavour, and this is seen not only in tunes arranged from old songs, but in new compositions which continue to appear regularly. Pipe Major Donald MacLeod sometimes used the Gaelic word *blas* ('taste') to describe the style of certain of his own tunes, such as a hornpipe set in the hexatonic mode of A minor rather than the more usual D major (see below, p. 149). In his last published work, a collection of original pibrochs (n.d.), he continued to follow 'traditional tonal patterns', as he himself said. An earlier player who may well have held decided views on keys and scales was James Mauchline (1817–1896). As well as the pipes, he played band instruments such as the flute and cornet. He composed pipe tunes in most of the modes described here, but his most famous ones are in the key of D. They include the strathspey 'Miss Ada Crawford' and marches, 'The Skye Crofters' and 'Barren Rocks of Aden' (S. MacNeil, 1951). If, as he claimed, he composed 'Barren Rocks' as early as 1843, he was breaking new ground in pipe music, and he may have been aware of the fact.

Turning back to the earliest writer on pipe music, we find that Joseph MacDonald, in 1760, had very clear ideas on the variety of modes available to pipers. He felt that certain keys (or 'tastes' as he called them) were appropriate to certain moods: A major for martial pieces, the pentatonic D-scale for 'rural' pieces and A minor and E minor (among others) for laments. But he did not restrict himself to the concepts of classical music, since he distinguished 'varieties' within the same key, which ordinary theory would consider together. A tune in the pentatonic scale of G which lies mainly on the low notes of the chanter has a very different effect from one which favours the high G, and MacDonald duly records them as different. Any modern player would agree with him, thinking of, for example, 'The Finger Lock' on the one hand and 'The Lament for the Laird of Anapool' on the other. It must be emphasised, however, that MacDonald does not suggest that these ideas are based in any way on traditional teaching. The first composers may have had some explicit musical theory to guide them — some Scottish counterpart to the *raga* system of Indian music — but if so it has disappeared without trace.

One idea, however, which is very prevalent among pipers today, and may have been so in the past, is the emphasis on the quality, not of scales, but of individual notes of the chanter, as they sound against the background of the drones. Learners, as they begin to master the techniques of good sound production, often declare a preference for certain notes. No doubt this in turn depends on particular tunes. The note F (or rather F sharp) is a common favourite, and this can be understood in view of the prominent, and very different, effects of this note in such tunes as 'The 79th's Farewell to Gibraltar', 'Barren Rocks' and 'Màiri Bhan Og' (in the keys of A, D and B minor). Some years ago (1973) Thomas Pearston, a well-known piper and teacher, put forward an interesting list of the feelings associated with different notes, as follows:

low G	the loudest note; the note of the Gathering
low A	the Piper's Note
B	the chiming note, or note of challenge
C#	the most musical note
D	the angry note; the note of battle
E	the echoing note
F#	the note of love
high G	the note of sorrow or lament
high A	like low A, the piper's note

These descriptions were not put forward as traditional, but pipers will understand them. Most of them are based on well-known pibrochs which emphasise the notes particularly strongly, and it is at least possible that the composers themselves had ideas of the same sort. For B and D one thinks of 'The Bells of Perth' or 'The End of the Great Bridge', for F sharp 'MacCrimmon's Sweetheart'. To call C sharp the most musical note may seem odd to a non-piper, but the exact tuning of this note is something about which pipers are particularly sensitive (see above, p. 32), and one has only to think of such varied tunes as 'The Little Spree', 'MacFarlane's Gathering' and (again) 'MacCrimmon's Sweetheart' to understand the feeling involved. To call high G the 'note of sorrow' is to echo what Joseph MacDonald said about varieties of the key of G major. The fact that low G, A and B are so much used in gathering tunes is no doubt partly due to their being the loudest, but the resonance of low A and the dissonance of low G also have a good deal to do with their expressiveness. A considerable number of pibrochs are composed entirely on the lowest four or five notes of the scale — what pipers call simply 'the low hand' — and the more traditional marches, reels, strathspeys and jigs also make much of these notes. There are more different sorts of gracenote on low A than on any other note, and it has often been noted that, in every type of tune, when the rhythm involves unequal timing of the notes, the low A is practically always arranged to be the longer note. Low A is truly 'the piper's note'.

The two traditions: *Ceòl Mór* and *Ceòl Beag*

In most countries where bagpipes are played, the staple repertoire consists of music for dancing, and to a lesser extent music which might be classed simply as 'music to listen to', mainly pipe versions of local songs. Scotland is an exception to this rule in two respects: one is that the bagpipe has become pre-eminently a military instrument, so that marches of various kinds have been added to its repertoire; the other is that the music now exists in two sharply divided categories, the ancient 'pibroch' which is regarded as 'classical', and all other music, considered, and sometimes actually referred to, as 'light music'. The distinction no doubt means different things to different people but all would agree that a good pibroch, while not so immediately appealing as a short tune, is ultimately more satisfying, more sophisticated in content, and in every way a 'bigger' piece of music.

The word 'pibroch' itself needs a few words of explanation. It comes from the Gaelic *pìobaireachd* which means simply 'piping'. In Gaelic contexts it has never denoted a specific type of music, but since the early eighteenth century it has been borrowed into English with its present restricted meaning, and the spelling 'pibroch' has become standard, at least in English dictionaries. This last qualification is important since most pipers today reject the 'English' spelling, which they feel has undesirable overtones, and insist on 'piobaireachd'. At the same time, some Gaelic speakers object to 'piobaireachd', however spelt, being used in the narrow sense at all. They prefer the expression *ceòl mór* ('big music') and pipers use this term as well, in writing if not in speech. It can be traced back to 1875 (T. MacLaughlan), and it seems to have been in current use at that time, though its ultimate origin is not known. The original composers do not seem to have had any special term for 'a pibroch': they used *port*, which has always meant simply a tune, played on any instrument. Nowadays *port* would be ambiguous, and some Gaelic writers such as Neil MacLeod (1841) and Alexander MacDonald (1934) have resorted to *port mór* ('big tune') to distinguish a pibroch from an ordinary tune. In this book I shall steer a middle course and use 'pibroch', with its plural 'pibrochs' when referring to actual pieces, but 'piobaireachd' or *ceòl mór* for the art or tradition of pibroch-playing in general. (In quotations, however, I follow the original spellings.)

Corresponding to *ceòl mór* is the expression *ceòl beag* ('small music'). Whether this is a traditional term or not is uncertain, and in any case it is not much used except in writing. *Ceòl aotrom* ('light music') is used still less, and is almost certainly a direct translation from the English. Whatever the name, *ceòl beag* is what most pipers play for most of the time, and it has grown into a complex and vigorous tradition expressed in many different types of tune.

The pibrochs we now have were almost all written down from tradition in the first decades of the nineteenth century, and they were mostly considered to be very old at that time. This makes it certain that as a group they pre-date nearly all other pipe tunes. It may be for this, or for other reasons, that they are utterly distinctive in character. Not only do they differ in the form of their melodies, and in their variations (as we shall describe in some detail later on), but the fingering technique is distinctive in many ways. One is tempted to think of old poetry, written in an archaic 'bardic' language. Most of the tunes are supposed to have been produced by a small number of highly trained pipers who were a class apart from ordinary players, and kept up their family traditions for many generations. Two members of these families, Angus MacArthur and John Mac-Crimmon, lived long enough to have some of their music written down directly (see below, p. 76) but the bulk of the music we have was notated by pupils of these men, or at one further remove, by pupils of pupils. We shall come back later to the question of whether and to what extent piobaireachd has been changed by transmission over the years. My conclusion is that there have been more changes than most pipers have so far been prepared to admit; but the point to be emphasised at this stage is that we do possess a large number of pieces, most of which are in a complete state, and that the playing has been handed down in an unbroken living tradition from the beginning to the present day. Some tunes have been corrupted in transmission, and the circumstances in which the tunes are played have changed radically, but the repertoire as a whole is in remarkably good shape.

The *ceòl beag* repertoire also began with tunes written down from oral, or rather 'aural', tradition. We have twenty-four 'North Highland Reels or Country Dances' published in 1784 by the Rev. Patrick MacDonald, and a number of other similar tunes scattered through collections of songs and fiddle music in the early decades of the nineteenth century.[1] But these collections were written for non-pipers, and do not include the grace notes. A bagpipe tutor published by an anonymous 'Amateur' in 1818 gives some details of fingering, but the first collection of tunes in full pipe notation was that of Donald MacDonald, the pipe maker already mentioned. In 1822 he included a selection of reels, strathspeys etc. in his pioneer collection of pibrochs, and in 1828 he followed this up with an album of 'Quicksteps, strathspeys, reels and jigs'. This was the first real pipers' manual, and though it sold slowly, it paved the way for a small surge of other books: William MacKay (1840), Angus MacKay (1843), Thomas Glen (c.1843) and William Gunn (1848). MacDonald, the two MacKays and Gunn were noted pipers, of Highland origin, and all four probably Gaelic-speaking. Glen was a pipe maker, but not a Highlander, and perhaps not much of a piper. Between them these first books contain about 400 tunes, but many tunes are common to two, three or four books, and the number of different ones is about 200. Some of the repetition is due to copying from one book to another, but by no means all: different pipers wrote down different settings of the same tune, and it is clear that much of what they wrote was simply from their own personal knowledge, and that between them they tapped the basic unwritten repertoire of the time.

The growth of written music

From about 1860 there is a considerable change in the literature of the small music. Composers' names start to appear frequently, and so do large numbers of tunes which proved to be short-lived; many of them printed once and never again. Behind this lies a revolutionary change in piping, as there emerged significant numbers of pipers who could read and write music. It is likely also, though it has not been proven as yet, that around this time the number of pipers began to increase dramatically, especially in the towns and cities, and in the Army, with the multiplication of pipe bands. Whatever the reason, piping quite quickly changed from an oral tradition to one which depended on books and manuscripts passed from hand to hand. From then on, anyone bringing out a new book would feel obliged to include plenty of new compositions. Although many of the new tunes were poor and unmemorable, some were excellent, and the stock of good tunes grew steadily. If a poll of tunes were taken today, the result would be much the same as in the time of Angus MacKay — a fringe of ephemeral tunes, mostly recent, a large number of good 'light' tunes, and a core of 'real pipe music', the last being defined as tunes which are technically demanding as well as being good strong melodies. But on tracing the good tunes back through the books we should find that they were by no means all equally old, and many were by known composers. The striking difference between today and the 1840s is that the *potential* repertoire is now much greater than any one piper can carry in memory alone. Nevertheless, the tunes are extant and alive: they can easily be found in up-to-date settings, and if one piper does not know some particular tune, some other piper probably does.

This leads to another point which is characteristic of pipe music today. Although written music is universal, pipers never actually play 'from music'. Indeed, by no means all pipers can actually sight-read at playing speed. For pipers, the music is the source from which they learn the tune, and to which they will occasionally return to refresh their memories, but once a piper has learned a tune he plays it 'from the fingers' so to speak, in much the same way as his distant predecessors. There is undoubtedly much greater uniformity than there once was: in a pipe band everyone must play exactly the same setting, and solo players also keep mainly to particular published versions. Settings of favourite tunes, 'as played by' some leading figure, are published; and since the 1920s, new compositions have mostly been played in their original settings. But all the time a slow evolution is going on, and new arrangements of existing tunes continue to appear.

Another result of the change to musical literacy, and the increasing number of pipers, was that publishing pipe music eventually became profitable — though never in a really big way. The earliest books seem to have been printed only in very small numbers — one case we know of, in 1841, comprised an edition of only twenty-five copies — and they sold at the rate of one per year (R.D. Cannon, 1980, 127). But by the 1890s David Glen was printing books of tunes in runs of one thousand at a time, and his tutor, the first really detailed instruction book, sold 24,000 copies between 1881 and 1951. The earliest publishers were all bagpipe makers, but about 1880 the Scottish music publishing company, Logan of Inverness, entered the field, and in the 1920s they were succeeded by Paterson's of Edinburgh, music publishers since the 1820s. Other well-known companies have produced occasional books, but the tendency now is for individual pipers to publish at their own expense, while Paterson's, still the largest single producer, deal mainly in officially sponsored compilations of Army pipe music.

I have possible over-emphasised the role of printed books as opposed to manuscripts. Every piper has in his possession a mass of dog-eared scraps on which he has noted tunes copied from books or from similar papers lent by friends, together with his own attempts at composing, or arranging some tune picked up by ear. Some have gone further and produced handsome manuscript volumes. But so far, unlike the prestigious pibroch collections, few such manuscripts have found their way into public libraries, and no one so far seems to have attempted to collect them. All too often, when a piper dies, though his pipes and his books may be preserved, mere pieces of paper are thrown away as rubbish.

One reason why manuscripts were written was simply that few pipers could afford to buy books. As long ago as 1872, Angus MacKay's small collection cost six shillings — about half a week's wages for a working man. At that time a piper would normally be a manual worker, a soldier, or if he was really well placed, a servant on some big estate in the Highlands. Possibly most books were bought by better-off amateur players, the class who provided the judges rather than the players in piping competitions. My grandfather was responsible for a Boys' Brigade pipe band around 1910. He owned a few copies of Glen's, Logan's and Henderson's publications, but at one shilling each there was no question of any of the boys buying them. Instead my grandfather wrote out small manuals, in the oblong quarto size which pipers have always favoured (it fits inside the pipe box — see Plate 3). He wrote them by a kind of mass-production, laying the books out in a semicircle on the table, writing a line of notes in each, then the tie-lines, the bars, and so on. I still have two of these books; they are practically identical, and as legible as print.

Music has become relatively cheaper as time has gone on, and printed books are now the order of the day. As early as 1900 some Scottish regiments issued privately printed manuals of duty tunes for pipers (see R. MacKenzie, 1901; London Scottish, n.d.), and beginning in 1936 with the Seaforth Highlanders, a number of regiments have issued comprehensive printed manuals for public sale as well as for internal use.

Individual pipers' collections continue to multiply, and although the spread of photocopying is causing concern among piping publishers as among others, there is no sign yet that the flow will diminish.

The impact of written music on *ceòl mór* has been equally great, but it has been slower to take affect. One reason for this is that, although the first printed pibroch collection appeared as early as 1822, such books were even more expensive than the *ceòl beag* collections. Also many pieces remained unpublished until the end of the century, and they circulated only amongst those few pipers who had the chance of copying them from the original manuscripts. But above all, there was the deep-rooted belief that written music cannot in any case be the whole essence of the music. This leads us into subtle and controversial questions to which we shall return in a later chapter.

NOTE

1. Unless indicated otherwise, the detailed references to facts quoted in this section will be found in my earlier *Bibliography of Bagpipe Music* (1980); see also R.D. Cannon (1976).

CHAPTER 4
Ceòl Mór

Historical background

As we have seen already, the bagpipe does not emerge into history, in the Highlands, until the sixteenth century, but already by that time it seems to have found a special place in daily life; and from writings of the seventeenth and eighteenth centuries we can put together quite a full picture of the status and functions of the piper. No doubt there were village pipers in the Highlands and elsewhere, but the pipers we hear most about, in Gaelic songs or in historical records, enjoyed much higher status. The leading clan chiefs had pipers as part of their domestic establishments. Two early examples of pipers named in this way are Robert MacIlwie, piper to the Laird of Buchanan, in 1604 (G.A. Dixon, 1983) and the piper to the Captain of Clanranald, in 1636 (*NP 23*, No. 4). In the days of clan warfare, pipers no doubt played on the battlefield, as they certainly did in the troubles of 1715 and 1745. They had a vital role, sounding the particular gathering tunes of their clans, to call the men together. It was said that at the Battle of Falkirk in 1746 the Jacobites failed to consolidate their victory because on that occasion the pipers had thrown away their pipes and gone in with the sword (W.R. Kermack, 1957, 131). In his domestic duties, the piper played in the morning, to waken the chief and his family, and at the arrival and departure of guests. In a famous poem, Mary MacLeod recalls her life at Dunvegan in the mid-seventeenth century, with 'the fiddle playing to put me to sleep, the pipe-playing to waken me in the morning'; and Captain Burt, travelling in the Highlands in the 1720s, noted that

> In the morning while the Chief is dressing, he walks backward and forward, close under the window, without doors, playing upon the bagpipe, with a most Upright attitude, and Majestic stride.

An earlier visitor, Morier, in 1679, reported that

> the nobility show themselves very great before strangers. At your departure you must drink a *dougha-doras* — in English, a stirrup cup — and have my

lord's bagpiper with his loud pipes, and his lordship's coat of armour on a flag, strut about you with a *loath to depart*.

There are traditions of particular tunes being composed in honour of important guests, and to mark special occasions such as the birth of a son, or a young chief's taking possession of his estate.[1] But it was weddings and funerals which attracted the greatest attention from outsiders. A wedding might begin with processions of young men firing guns and waving banners while pipers played, all in the manner of an army on the march; and even at funerals the warlike character of the bagpipe was well in evidence. In 1669, the body of Fraser of Foyers was conveyed in state across Loch Ness 'with many Grants, Cummings, Frasers . . . in four great boats, trumpets sounding, pipers playing, with echoes rebounding' (G. Campbell, 1962, 139). The burial of Campbell of Lochnell in 1714 was attended by two thousand men 'well armed and appointed . . . commanded by the famous Rob Roy MacGregor, carrying with them colours belonging to the Earl of Breadalbane and accompanied by the screams of thirteen bagpipes' (G. Campbell, 1962, 64). For peaceful indoor entertainment, softer music was preferred, notably the harp, played by a professional harpist, or passed from hand to hand among the gentlemen present (W. Matheson, 1970, 1ii-1iii). But harp-playing died out in the eighteenth century, and to some extent piping took its place. When Johnson and Boswell visited the Hebrides in 1773, pipers played to them indoors, at dinner, on several occasions.

The piper was a proud figure — close to the chief, in his own estimation. Burt noted the fact, albeit sarcastically: 'The piper being a gentleman, I should have mentioned him sooner'; and in fact the piper he saw had a servant of his own to carry his pipes. He would have clothes provided at the chief's expense (R.H. MacLeod, 1977) and would carry the chief's arms on a flag attached to his pipes. The portrait of the piper to the Laird of Grant, painted in 1714, now in the Royal Museum of Scotland in Edinburgh, shows what an imposing figure he could be.

There is overwhelming evidence that among pipers there were certain master players who were generally recognised, and of whom some at least regularly took pupils from distant parts of the Highlands. The earliest documentary evidence we have to show that a piper could enjoy a national reputation is provided in a well-known passage in what is now known as the Wardlaw Manuscript, written by the Rev. James Fraser in the late seventeenth century. It refers to an incident in 1651, when King Charles II held a review of the Scots Army at Stirling. There was a competition among the trumpeters, at which the King himself chose the winner, and then a competition among the pipers — or rather, there was no competition since

> the Earle of Sutherland's domestick carried it of all the camp, for non contended with him. All the pipers in the Army gave John Macgurmen the van, and acknowledged him for their patron in chiefe.

Then at the review of the Army the King noticed all the pipers gathered together — 'no less than 80 pipers in a croud bareheaded, and John M^cgyurmen in the middle covered', and on asking what was going on, he was told that the old man at the centre of attention was 'the Prince of Pipers'. Amused by this idea, the King called the piper by name, and allowed him to kiss his hand:

> and instantly [he] played an extemporanian part *Fuoris Póóge i spoge i Rhí*, I got a kiss of the King's hand; of which he and they were all vain.

It is thought that where the manuscript has 'part', the writer meant the Gaelic *port*, a tune. The title is that of a piece which is now known as a pibroch (see below, p. 56). The piper's name is somewhat puzzling. The most famous name in piping, according to later tradition, is MacCrimmon, and Macgurmen or Macgyurmen is not known at all. Most writers have assumed that the manuscript is in error, someone having either misheard the name when spoken, or misread it when written. There seems to be no easy solution to this problem at present.

Later in the seventeenth century another minister, the Reverend James Kirkwood, left a note of the importance attached to pipe music at that time: 'Pipers are held in great request, so that they are trained up at the expense of Grandees and have a Portion of Land assigned ... ' The assignment of land to a higher servant of the Estate was quite a usual custom in the Highlands. Harpers and poets, and in earlier times law officers, medical men and others, enjoyed this perquisite. They also tended to hand down their skills from generation to generation in their own families, so that they became recognised as hereditary office-bearers. The MacMhuirich bards and the Beaton physicians have been traced through a period of some 500 years (D.S. Thomson, 1963, 1969). No dynasty of pipers can match this, but the names of at least ten families of hereditary pipers have been identified, of whom the most notable seem to have been the Rankins, pipers to MacLean of Duart; MacKays, pipers to MacKenzie of Gairloch; MacArthurs, pipers to MacDonald of the Isles; MacIntyres, pipers to Menzies of Menzies; and above all, the MacCrimmons, pipers to MacLeod of Dunvegan (A. MacKay, 1838, 1–13). In the case of the MacArthurs and MacCrimmons, the fact that they held land wholly or partially free of rent has been confirmed by research in the eighteenth-century estate papers (K. Sanger, 1983; R.H. MacLeod, 1977).

The statement that pipers were trained at the expense of the chiefs implies that there were recognised teachers, and that pupils were sent to them from other estates. This too is borne out both by tradition and by historical records. Piping 'colleges' are said to have been run by the Rankins, MacArthurs and MacCrimmons, among others, and documents exist recording the arrangements for pupils to be sent to the MacCrimmons, in 1698 and 1743 (R.H. MacLeod, 1977; G.A. Dixon, 1980). Later writers undoubtedly exaggerated the prestige, size, and length of tuition in these 'colleges', and these exaggerations have provoked an even more exaggerated rebuttal (A. Campsie, 1980); but of their existence there is no doubt, as can be seen from the facts quoted here.

The MacCrimmon and MacArthur colleges had both ceased to function by 1772, when Thomas Pennant visited Skye, but the MacCrimmons at least had only just given up, for when Johnson and Boswell arrived in 1773 they learned that 'there was a college for the bagpipe in Skye, kept by the MacCrimmons, hereditary pipers of the Laird of MacLeod. It subsisted in a certain degree till last year; that an admirable piper went to America'. This was Donald MacCrimmon, known as Donald *Ruadh*, one of two brothers who are now considered the last of their famous line.

According to the Rev. A. Clark, writing in 1845, the MacCrimmons were remembered in Skye as 'well educated, inter-married with the most respectable families and . . . universally regarded as vastly superior . . . to the common class of the country people', and this estimate of their position in the eighteenth-century scheme of things is also borne out to a large extent by modern research. The farms held by different members of the family have been identified at various dates from 1664 to 1811 (R.H. MacLeod, 1977). From the value of the land it is clear that some at least of the MacCrimmons were wealthy, by the standards of the time, and that they employed a number of other families to work the farms. The farm at Boreraig, which was one of their last holdings, was claimed in 1838 to support no fewer than eighteen families. Donald *Ruadh*, who emigrated as just mentioned, joined in the American War of Independence (on the Loyalist side), and it is significant that he did so as an officer. His son, too, was to become a Captain in the British Army. Later on, Donald *Ruadh* was induced to return to Scotland, and efforts were made to set him up as 'professor' of a revived college of piping. Not much came of this, and the story (R.H. MacLeod, 1981) is a sad one, suggesting on the one hand that his would-be patrons found him an unsatisfactory person to do business with, and on the other that he found it hard to adjust to a world which had changed so much. It would be interesting to know the social standing of the other famous lines of pipers. Was there an elite 'caste' of leading pipers throughout the Highlands, or were the MacCrimmons literally a class apart? Whatever the answer, we can safely assume that many of the pipers who went to them as pupils were indeed 'of the common class of ordinary people', young men who distinguished themselves by their natural abilities and gained the patronage of the Laird. Such was a certain John Cumming who was sent to Skye in 1774, by his master Sir James Grant of Grant. He returned after training (we do not know who taught him) to be 'piper to the Family and likewise Servant in any thing they may find necessary' (G.A. Dixon, 1984). It was likewise the case with John MacKay, an orphan herdboy on the island of Raasay, who was befriended by Malcolm MacLeod of Eyre and sent for tuition 'to the MacCrimmons and the MacKays of Gairloch'. He later became piper to James MacLeod of Raasay, and one of the most eminent players of the immediate post-MacCrimmon era (A. Campbell, 1961a).

The musical tradition fostered in the piping colleges has come down to us as *ceòl mór*. In the rest of this chapter we shall look at the general nature of this music, with enough examples, I hope, to enable the general non-piping reader to appreciate its qualities. In the following chapter we shall see how the music has been handed down since the time of the first written records, and in a third short chapter, we shall set down what little is known of its earlier history.

The music[2]

A pibroch consists of an air with variations. The air, called *ùrlar* in Gaelic, 'ground' in English, is always slow and is often much longer than a typical march or dance tune. Some grounds have extremely simple melodies, made up from a few short phrases repeated in certain patterns, others are free-flowing and song-like. Many of them use fewer than the nine notes available on the chanter; almost all are in styles highly characteristic of the bagpipe, and in general they convey a feeling of antiquity when compared with the typical small tunes. The types of grace notes used differ from those of the short tunes, and the style of playing is very different. There is a great deal of *rubato*, so much so that the ordinary music notation can be quite misleading. Some pipers maintain that *ceòl mór* cannot in fact be properly noted on paper; others assume that the notation has been deliberately over-simplified so that the learner will be forced to go to a traditionally taught player in order to pick up the proper nuances. A third view is that styles of playing have changed since the music was written down, but for the moment we need not be concerned with these problems. This chapter aims to describe the music as it is played at present.

Here are the opening bars of the pibroch already mentioned as having been played by the piper at Stirling in 1651:

Ex. 4.1. I got a kiss of the King's hand. Ground

In this extract, I have omitted all grace notes and 'throws' (see above, p. 35). The E notes marked x are also regarded as grace notes, even though they take up substantial time in the music. They are not thought of as part of the basic melody and, as we shall see below, they are not taken up into the variations. They are usually called 'cadence — E' and are somewhat akin to the 'appoggiatura' of older classical music. To emphasise this, modern editors usually write them as small upturned grace notes, but with one tail instead of three. Examples of this notation are given below (Examples 4.23, 5.6), but for the present we shall keep to the more explicit notation which was used by the first editor of the tune (A. MacKay, 1838). The title of the tune contains the opening words of a Gaelic rhyme which is associated with it:

> Fhuair mi pòg, 's pòg, 's pòg,
> Gun d'fhuair mi pòg o làimh an Righ.
> Cha d'chuir seid nan croicionn caoraich
> A fhuair an t-urram a fhuair mi.

'I got a kiss, a kiss, a kiss, I got a kiss of the King's hand. No one who blew into a sheep's skin has had the honour that I had.' The words were printed by Angus MacKay directly under the music, but in fact they do not quite fit the rhythm. They would have been sung, not to the exact air of the pipe tune, but to a simpler form of it, shorter, and without the 'cadence E' grace notes. A good many 'pibroch songs' of this kind are known, and there are a few songs of similar character, which evidently belong to pibrochs now lost (J. Ross, 1957). Conversely, many pibrochs have names which are clearly the first lines of songs which are lost. These names often come out rather stilted, even comical in translation, but they are firmly fixed by usage —

'The Unjust Incarceration', 'Scarce of Fishing', 'Too Long in this Condition'. Very few pipers today speak Gaelic, and fewer still have inherited anything of these song traditions. Reuniting the songs and pibrochs will be a task for the next generation of Gaelic scholars.

The variations of pibrochs are basically of two sorts. One type consists of essentially the same melody cast into a different rhythm, or else merely 'doubled': that is, played over again with the pauses mostly ironed out into a regular rhythm. The other type takes a selection of the main notes of the melody, and plays them through in a regular rhythm, each one coupled into a conventional phrase featuring a constant note, such as the A or E which corresponds to the pipe drones, together with conventional flourishes of grace notes. Put baldly like this, it sounds unenterprising, and indeed the music looks very simple on paper; but the effect when well played can be highly impressive.

The free-flowing type of variation can be seen in this example:

Ex. 4.2. The Old Woman's Lullaby (from Campbell MS, ed. R.D. Cannon (1982a))

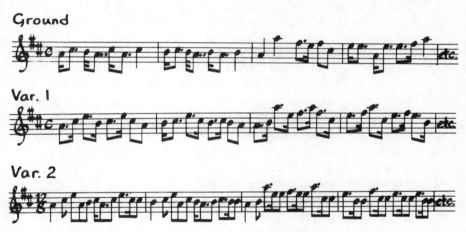

The characteristic of these variations is that they follow the ground very closely, but the short down-beat notes are largely smoothed out and, although not indicated here, the pauses for expression at the ends of phrases are not so pronounced. A feature of this example which is not typical is that Variation 2 contains more notes than Variation 1, and unless played unduly fast, it takes longer to play. More usually the variations become simpler as the tune proceeds.

The other type of variation, consisting of repeated conventional phrases, is found in several variations. The first variation of 'I got a kiss' is of a type which used to be called *Siubhal Sleamhuin* — the 'smooth movement' — because the effect is of a smooth passage from one note to the next; but nowadays it is called *Dìthis*, the Gaelic for a couple, the note groups being couplets. (Strictly, *dìthis* means a couple of persons: as a musical term it is probably not authentic.)

Ex. 4.3. I got a kiss of the King's hand (Var.1)

In this extract we have shown the grace notes as well as the principal melody notes. Their characteristic clicking sound is an integral part of the musical effect. The 'doubling' of the variation is quicker and in strict tempo:

Ex. 4.4. Var.1. Doubling

Next comes a much heavier movement, called 'Taorluath'. The meaning and even the spelling of this term are uncertain. The second part, more correctly written *lùth* or *lùthadh*, means 'movement' or 'turn' (W. Matheson, 1970, 138), and some writers have suggested that the whole word should be *Taobhlùth*, which could be interpreted as 'side-movement', although this does not seem to explain anything. The grace notes are written in different ways by different authorities, but they are always played as a full, round, crisp articulation, a kind of crackling effect leading from the melody note down to the low A or low G. The Taorluath 'singling' has long-drawn cadences at the ends of the phrases (Ex. 4.5); the 'doubling' is in strict tempo (Ex. 4.6):

Ex. 4.5. Taorluath

Ex. 4.6. Taorluath Doubling

Finally comes the 'Crunluath', or more properly, *Crùnlùth*. Again, the true meaning of the word is not known, but 'crowning movement' is not a bad description. The Crunluath beat is an extension of the Taorluath beat, a fast ripple of grace notes ending on the note E. The Crunluath variation always follows the Taorluath note for note, and if one has a doubling, so does the other:

Ex. 4.7. Crunluath

Ex. 4.8. Crunluath Doubling

In the doublings, the last Taorluath and Crunluath beats are different from the others. They have low G notes in place of low A, reflecting the momentary G-major flavour of the corresonding notes in the ground. In the Crunluath, however, it takes an attentive ear to notice the difference.

Next and last comes the 'Crunluath mach'. *Mach* or *a mach* means 'out', but it is not easy to guess the true meaning of the phrase here. The 'mach' is a real firework display: it sounds much faster than the plain Crunluath doubling, although the actual tempo is not much different:

Ex. 4.9. Crunluath mach

The characteristic 'mach' movement can actually only be played on three melody notes, B, C and D. On the other notes the ordinary Crunluath must be played instead, so that the Crunluath mach is always a mixture of the two types, and the rhythmical character of the variation can differ a good deal from one tune to another, depending on the patterns in which the relevant notes occur. Perhaps for this reason, the Crunluath mach was once regarded as optional, although it has now become virtually obligatory, at least in competitions. Some pipers, however, maintain that the 'mach' should not be played in a lament.

The crunluath doubling, or crunluath mach as the case may be, is the climax of the piece, but it is not the end, since after it the Ground is played through again. The earlier practice was to play the Ground after the Taorluath Doubling as well, but this was dropped some time in the nineteenth century. Modern players often do not play the whole Ground even at the end, but merely give a few bars.

Variations of a different type are found in the tune *Maol Donn*, commonly known as 'MacCrimmon's Sweetheart'. The name is thought to refer not to a young lady, but the tune itself; as it might be 'MacCrimmon's Fancy' or 'MacCrimmon's Favourite'. Certainly it is a favourite piece with pipers in general. The Ground begins as follows:

Ex. 4.10. *Maol Donn*. Ground

and continues for a total of sixteen bars. The rhythm is rather subtle, and no two editors agree exactly on the note lengths (P. Cooke, 1972). It is best considered as a series of syncopated beats, ♪♩♪ , with the last note shortened, and the whole complicated by the long E notes, here again marked x. The next variations, not shown here, follow the Ground very closely, first by replacing all the F notes with high A's, then by straightening out the rhythm into a relatively simple 6/8 time. Then we have a variation and doubling with two-note beats corresponding to the *Dithis* of 'I got a kiss', but with the accent the other way round. It is now called *Siubhal* ('travel' or 'movement'), though originally this was the term for a pibroch variation in general:

Ex. 4.11. *Maol Donn*. Var.3 singling (S) and doubling (D)

Next come 'triplings' based on the *Siubhal* with the running low notes divided into three rapid beats:

Ex. 4.12. *Maol Donn*. Tripling (S) and Doubling of Tripling (D)

Finally, the Crunluath and its doubling. This Crunluath is based on the Siubhal by adding a 'throw' on the note E. As with the Crunluath a mach, this can actually only be done when the melody note is itself lower than E. When the melody note is E or above, the ordinary Crunluath beat is used, so this variation is again a mixture of two types. The new type is *Crùnlùth Fosgailte*, 'Open Crunluath', because it involves raising the fingers of the lower hand off the chanter:

Ex. 4.13. *Maol Donn*. Crunluath Fosgailte Singling (S) and Doubling (D)

As already mentioned, these two types of variation differ in accentuation. The melody notes come on the down-beat of the music in 'I got a kiss' and on the up-beat in *Maol Donn*. A third basic type combines both features. These are *Taorluath Breabach* and *Crunluath Breabach* where *breabach* means 'kicking', or possibly 'shuttling' back and forth like the shuttle in a loom. The Ground of the 'Earl of Seaforth's Salute' begins:

Ex. 4.14. The Earl of Seaforth's Salute. Ground

and the variations are of 'breabach' type, as follows:

Ex. 4.15. Taorluath and Crunluath

Variations of the 'down-going' type, as in 'I got a kiss', are the most common. *Fosgailte* variations account for about a third of the known tunes, and *breabach* about ten percent. It would be possible to rewrite the variations of a tune from one type to the other, but this is never done. In general the variations played are felt to be the appropriate ones for the Ground (G. Moss, 1983), and in the case of the three tunes given here, the reader will probably agree that this is so. Sometimes it is possible to see a simple reason for choosing one type of variation rather than another, and a close study of this aspect of composition would probably reveal, if not hard and fast rules, at least some interesting pointers to the ways of thinking of the old composers.

There are other types of variations, some like these, consisting of a repeated figure attached to the theme notes, others more freely arranged. Some pibrochs have only one or two variations, generally of the free character; others have only the Taorluath and Crunluath. And to a limited extent, variations of different types can be mixed in the same tune. A fairly common mixture is Siubhal and Tripling, followed by ordinary Taorluath and Crunluath.

Besides the variations, the internal construction of the melody sets most of *ceòl mór* apart from the common run of pipe music. The tunes tend to be worked in intricate patterns, so precise that it seems that the composers must have been following definite rules which were known to them, although, if so, the rules have not been handed down, and they are now having to be rediscovered by scholars examining the tunes. Most tunes belong to one of a number of recognisable classes.

We will begin, however, with a type that is *not* different from other ordinary tunes. Here we have a four-bar strain, repeated, then a change of melody in the second strain, and a repeat of the original four bars:

Ex. 4.16. Struan Robertson's Salute. Ground (cadences and grace notes omitted)

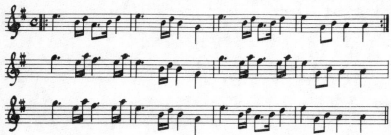

In this and the next two examples, the cadence E (see above, p. 56), as well as all the other grace notes, is omitted. We could call this type of tune the 'song' form since it runs AABA, A and B being the two four-bar strains, and the pattern is basic to all forms of Western music, from the smallest song to the fully developed Sonata. In classical composition, the first strain is in a certain key, which is defined as the tonic, and the second strain is in another key, the dominant. The dominant key may be fully established by sharpening one of the notes (as happens in an air like 'The Bluebells of Scotland'), or it may just involve emphasising different notes within the diatonic scale. The bagpipe composer cannot go so far as to define a new key, but he comes fairly close to doing so. Most often, his phrase B is built on notes one note higher in the scale than phrase A. For example, 'The Lament for the Children' begins with a flavour of the key of D, and its second strain begins and ends on the note E. 'The Company's Lament' begins in A major, and its second strain begins and ends on the note B. In the example quoted here, 'Struan Robertson's Salute', the first strain has the flavour of E minor, and the second strain touches on G, the relative major, which is another pairing of keys very common in music generally.

Rather different from the song form, and much more characteristic of *ceòl mór*, is an interlocked sort of structure, in which the first strain begins with two short phrases, related in one of the ways just mentioned, while the second strain begins with the same two phrases (or nearly the same two) in the reverse order. Thus, 'The King's Taxes' opens with a bar in G minor, then a bar featuring the higher note A; the second strain begins with this bar in A, followed by the original bar in G:

Ex. 4.17. The King's Taxes. Ground (cadences and grace notes omitted)

The arrows are put in here to show the characteristic reversal. Besides this, it will be seen that the last line of the tune begins with a repetition of the last part of the first line. This is a device which can be roughly paralleled in other traditions, and it seems especially appropriate in a work which was composed and handed on entirely by ear. A seventeenth-century English tune, 'The Derbyshire Hornpipe', has a set of variations, in which the first half of each one repeats the second half of the previous ones (Hale, 1690).

Many countries, including the Highlands, have lengthy ballads in which the first line of each verse repeats the last line of the previous verse — picking up the thread as it were.

Still greater economy of material is achieved in *Bodaich Dubha nan Sligean:*

Ex. 4.18. *Bodaich Dubha nan Sligean* (The Old Men of the Shells). Ground (grace notes and cadence-E's omitted)

Here the second line is not a repeat of the first, but line 3 consists of the two halves of line 1 played in reverse order, and line 4 also re-uses earlier material, though it is lengthened out by an extra bar. The letters A and B written over the different phrases point out repetitions of closely related phrases, and there are about a dozen other tunes, with quite different melodies, but with the same overall pattern.

The following type has features in common with 'The King's Taxes', though again it uses less material:

Ex. 4.19. Donald Gruamach's March. Ground (cadence-Es omitted)

The letters, a, b, A, B are inserted here, again to point out a pattern which is common to many tunes. The small letters a, b denote one-bar phrases, and A, B denote two-bar phrases, and there is a relationship, A being a kind of expansion or working-up of a, and B an expansion of b. Again we see the device of reversal, phrases a b at the beginning being turned round as b a halfway through.

   The simplest of all metres uses only two phrases, played four times each. The tune can therefore be set out as follows, with the instruction to play the phrases in the order A A B A B B A B:

Ex. 4.20. The Duke of Atholl's Salute (W. Ross Collection, 1885)

There has been a fair amount of discussion of metre since the subject was first raised by General C.S. Thomason in 1893. Thomason recognised what he called the 'Primary Piobaireachd', the last-mentioned metre above. Later the term 'Secondary Piobaireachd' was coined for tunes like 'Donald Gruamach's March' (A. Campbell, 1948). The metre of *Bodaich Dubha nan Sligean* was first clearly identified by Archibald Campbell in 1936 (*PS* 6, 167), and it has been thoroughly analysed by R.L.C. Lorimer (1962, 1964). The recognition of metre has been useful to modern editors, who have sometimes been able to restore corrupt versions of tunes by noticing where they deviate from the pattern. Undoubtedly, there is room for more such restoration, but the Piobaireachd Society, who are publishers of the definitive series of present-day books, and thus in effect custodians of the tradition, have tended to be very conservative in this respect, perhaps recoiling from the work of earlier, over-enthusiastic emendators such as Thomason and G.F. Ross (1926, 1929).

   Awareness of metre is also valuable to anyone trying to memorise a new tune, and to the player seeking to put in the proper expression. The more academic study, of the relationship of one metre to another, and the possible origins of metres, has been slow to develop, but some valuable research has been published in the last few decades. A point of controversy is, how should the structure of the ground be broken down into smaller units? With a simple tune like 'Struan Robertson's Salute' there is no problem. It obviously consists of four sections of four bars each — or if we prefer to say so, of three sections, the first being repeated. That is how the composer must have made it, and it is how every singer and piper has understood it. With the more characteristic metres, however, it is not so simple. The earliest writer on the subject, Joseph MacDonald, in 1760, said that all pibrochs were in four 'quarters' of equal length, and he made it quite clear that this covered all the different metres we have listed here. By this rule, the four quarters of 'Donald Gruamach's March' would simply be the four lines of music we have written above (Ex. 4.19); or, to put it more generally, the formula for a so-called 'secondary pibroch' would be written in four sections as follows:

a b A, B A, b a B, A B

On the other hand, all editors from Angus MacKay (1838) onwards have preferred to punctuate such tunes in three lines of 6, 6 and 4 bars:

a b A B,
A b a B
A B

The point of this arrangement is that every line ends with the same cadence, that of phrase B, which is certainly the more final-sounding of the two cadences used in the tune. The most recent suggestion, put forward by A. Haddow and J. MacFadyen (1973), is that there are only two lines:

a b A B A
b a B A B

This has the intriguing result that line 2 is, so to speak, the inverse of line 1: a is replaced by b and vice versa, and A by B and vice versa. Again, the metre of *Bodaich dubha nan Sligean* is usually described by the Piobaireachd Society editors as four very unequal lines, of 4, 6, 4 and 2 bars, but Lorimer (1962, 1964) has argued forcefully and, to me at least, convincingly, for the layout 4,4,4,4. And finally on this topic, although most writers accept the distinctions between the different metres, even though differing on how each one should be analysed, A.J. Haddow and J. MacFadyen have argued (1973) that the categories can merge into each other. They suggest that instead of sharp classes like 'primary' and 'secondary', it would be better to think of an extended family of tunes ranging by small degrees from one to the other. The problem is similar to that of an anthropologist who has to decide whether a collection of, say, fifty skulls consists of two groups with some variation in shape within each group, or a single group with rather more variation. These arguments are perhaps not very important, but if they could be settled we would have a clearer idea of how the original composers went about their work. Unfortunately, as with everything else in piobaireachd, opinions are coloured by the pipers' deep-seated feelings about the music. Arguments about metre tend to become emotional, and will probably continue to do so for some time to come.

If this account of variation and metre seems unduly formal, let us leave it and remember that the essence of the music is the tunes themselves. They vary enormously in character, and they can often be felt to be appropriate to their title — at least by the trained listener. There are haunting laments with long song-like melody lines, quite unlike anything in the small music — tunes like the 'Lament for Donald Duaghal MacKay', 'The Daughter's Lament', and perhaps the greatest of them all, the 'Lament for the Children'. Others are shorter and more formal, but still strong and tuneful. Others again, especially those called 'Marches' or 'Gatherings', tend to have short, memorable phrases, often repeated. Finally, some cannot be considered as 'tunes' at all in the ordinary sense of the word. They are worked patterns employing perhaps only two or three notes. They bear the same relation to the rest of pipe music as an abstract design does to a figure drawing. These are pieces like 'The Blind Piper's Obstinacy', 'The End of the Little Bridge' and 'The Red Speckled Bull'. Many pipers do not care for them, but each of them has its devotees. It needs a great player to bring out the music in them, but when this happens the result is unforgettable.

Canntaireachd

Before the days of written notation, *ceòl mór* was taught in a system somewhat like the modern tonic sol-fa. The piper sang the tune in vocables which had no meaning as words but which corresponded closely to the actual notes. The effect was similar to the vocables used in choruses of Gaelic songs, except that canntaireachd vocables had musical meaning, and conveyed fairly precisely the grace notes and therefore the fingering required for each note. The tunes mentioned above as having been collected from John MacCrimmon were actually written down and published in this form (N. MacLeod, 1828). A sample will show the strength and weaknesses of the system:

Ex. 4.21. Donald Gruamach's March (from N. MacLeod, 1828, cd. R.D. Cannon, unp.)

The low note A is represented by the nasal sounds 'n', or 'm', and the notes B, C, D, E, F are represented by vowels 'o', 'o', 'a', 'ie', 'ie'. The cadence E (written in the music here as a grace note) is 'i', and the other grace notes are represented by consonants, so that *tra* or *dra* means the throw on D, *botri* the longer embellishment on F, and *dirie* (probably with a long Scots trilling of the 'r') is the lengthy crunluath movement to E. Nevertheless, as the example shows, different sounds can stand for the same note, and the same sound for different notes, and it would not be possible to translate the tune into staff notation if we had nothing to go on but the *canntaireachd*. As it happens, the tune is well known, and the process of translation really consists of setting the known versions alongside the *canntaireachd*, and comparing the two in detail. In this way it is possible both to decode the system, and also to see in what ways MacCrimmon's version of the tune differs from others.

The sound of *canntaireachd* is remarkably expressive of the actual sound of the bagpipe. The piper who has been traditionally taught tends to sing through the nose as well as through the mouth, in a rather dead-pan style with no loud and soft effects. The recurring 'n' sounds of the low A forcibly suggest the bagpipe drone, and the vowel sounds as one sings up the scale change regularly from broad vowels at the bottom to the narrow 'i' sound (pronounced long, as in 'pibroch') at the top. The consonants also show some regard for pitch, with 't' and 'r' for high grace notes and 'd' for low ones. In fact I can think of no better way to explain the effect of bagpipe grace notes than to say that in the music example just quoted 'the first bar sounds like him-bo-tra-o hi-o-dro' and so on. The MacCrimmon system of *canntaireachd* has been much misunderstood by later writers, who have tried to decode it without allowing enough regard for its flexibility, nor for the inconsistencies and errors in the printed text, since unfortunately it is far from being as well presented as one would like. As a result, some have maintained that MacCrimmon's piping style was radically different from that of today, while others have decided that the book is of no value at all.

As with so many piping controversies, the truth lies somewhere in between the entrenched positions, and I have tried to show this in a full-length study, to be published elsewhere (R.D. Cannon, unp.).

A very different collection of written *canntaireachd* is the Campbell manuscript, compiled sometime around 1800 by Colin Campbell, a piper in Argyll. This contains no fewer than 160 tunes, presumably his whole repertoire. For comparison with the MacCrimmon system, here is the Campbell version of the phrase quoted previously:

Ex. 4.22. Campbell MS, ii, tune 18; arr R.D.C.

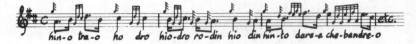

hin-o tra-o ho dro hio-dro ro-din hio din hin-to dare-a che-bandre-o

This has none of the inconsistencies mentioned above. Although the notes B and C still have the sound 'o', they are distinguished by the letters written in front of them. The letters used depend on the grace notes. When preceded by a high G grace note, B and C are written *hio* and *ho*; with a D grace note, *to* and *do*; with a throw, *tro* and *dro*. The system is so precise that it can be described fully in one page of the Preface to each of the Piobaireachd Society's current editions of pibrochs, and tunes can be translated even when they are not known from any other source. The translator has to exercise judgement over the time values of the notes, but the pitch values are clear. A closer examination reveals however that this *canntaireachd* cannot be exactly what Colin Campbell sang. It is an ingenious modification of sung *canntaireachd*, adapting it to the requirements of a written record. For example, the notes high G and high A are distinguished by writing the latter with a capital 'I'. Also Campbell uses 'm' for low G and 'n' for low A, while MacCrimmon seems to mix them up. But Campbell is then forced to write vocables such as *himto* which are contrary to Gaelic sound rules. MacCrimmon sings either *hindo* or *himbo*. But these are not criticisms of Campbell; on the contrary, what we find is that Campbell, working on the basis of the *canntaireachd* which he normally sang (and which must have been very similar to MacCrimmon's), has actually managed to invent a written notation for pipe music, independent of staff notation. We shall probably never know what led him to this invention, but we can agree with the judgement that he deserves 'to be numbered among Scotland's literary celebrities' (A. Campbell, 1961b).

Canntaireachd is by no means dead today, though no one now sings it as systematically as the old pipers did. Most pibroch players will croon their melodies in some such fashion, especially when teaching, or arguing a point about some tricky phase (M. MacLeod, 1974; C.K. Chambers, 1980). Some of the women members of piping families have been particularly adept, even to the extent of being able to teach the tunes when they do not play themselves. Captain Niel MacLeod of Gesto, who collected and published the MacCrimmon tunes, was also credited with this ability (R.D. Cannon, unpubl.). Many pipers hold that even now *canntaireachd* is a better teaching medium than the printed page.

Time and phrasing

Pibrochs are always played extremely slowly, with an enormous amount of 'expression' which is gained by lengthening out some notes at the expense of others, and by holding out some phrases far beyond the regular pulse of the music. Very little of this is indicated in the written music, a fact which causes much confusion to beginners. A few examples may give some idea of what is meant. Unequal timings are usually accentuated so that ♩ ♪ turns into ♩♪ , and ♪♩ into ♪♩ . Less commonly the process is reversed and the accent is softened. This, together with the practice already referred to, of writing long notes as grace notes, means that the written time signature can be quite deceptive. Here is the Piobaireachd Society's setting of Ex. 4.1 above compared, with what is usually heard in practice:

Ex. 4.23. I got a kiss of the King's hand

The endings of lines are often held out to great length, especially in variations, as was indicated above (Examples 4.5, 4.7, 4.11, 4.12), and there are many, other subtleties which have to be learned for each particular tune. Although few pipers may agree, I am inclined to believe that these effects are mainly due to successive generations of players, rather than to the original composers, but this is a controversial question, to which we shall return in the next chapter.

Sometimes it is no exaggeration to say that the tune itself can only be perceived by someone who is already familiar with it. Certainly if a listener compares *ceòl mór* directly with the ordinary pipe music, or with songs of the type sung by modern Gaelic choirs, he will not find it easy going. But if he knows traditional ballad singing, or *òran mór*, or the psalms sung in Gaelic church services, he will find the pipe music relatively clear. The sort of difficulty that arises can be seen from an experience of my own. The tune 'The Massacre of Glencoe' is printed by the Piobaireachd Society essentially as follows:

Ex. 4.24. The Massacre of Glencoe. Ground, bars 7–10

A piper who had learned the tune from the famous John MacDonald was anxious to convey to me a particular point of expression which MacDonald had taught, and he described it as a way of coming quickly off the third F note in the third bar and off the third E in the fourth bar. We went over the phrase many times on the chanter, but I could not satisfy my informant until I realised that the effect was approximately as follows, in effect a switch from 4/4 to 6/4 rhythm:

Ex. 4.25.

My friend was familiar with the printed text, and he remembered clearly the sound of the music as he had heard it, but he was not at all concerned to relate the two.

My attempt to rationalise traditional phrasing in terms of conventional time signatures would probably not be accepted by many pipers today. They would be more inclined to agree with a writer in the 1890s who argued that *ceòl mór* was different from other music in the way that prose is different from poetry (quoted, C.S. Thomason, 1893, v); or with Seumas MacNeill who has written (1971) that 'any tune which has a regular swing is not piobaireachd'. I must say from my own listening, however, that the best players, while certainly adopting very free rhythms, nevertheless usually do convey something of the underlying pulse — the line, so to speak, from which they are deliberately straying.

Some editors have tried to put down these irregular timings in writing. Archibald Campbell (1948) used ordinary note values, but added pause marks and distinguished two kinds of long grace notes, with one tail and two tails. Roderick Ross (1959) replaced the regular bars with phrases of different lengths. Seumas MacNeill (1968) used time signatures but gave much more explicit note-values than previous writers. All would agree, however, that ordinary notation is inadequate. Notation supported by explicit verbal comment is better, and for Archibald Campbell's book we now have this in the form of extracts from the compiler's personal diaries, edited by his son, James Campbell (1984). Tape-recorded lessons with musical illustrations are even better, but even today the only fully accepted method of learning is to memorise the tune from the book and then to relearn it from an established player, who will demonstrate each phrase on the chanter and in *canntaireachd*. The words in which pipers themselves describe this process are a pointer to what is going on. 'Putting the song into the tune' is one phrase which has been used (P. Cooke, 1972); expressing it 'like lines of poetry' is another (F. Richardson, 1968). The lengths of notes are varied subtly with 'lights and shades' (John MacDonald, 1942); 'hanging' a little on one note and 'cutting' another (J. Campbell, 1984). But once a pupil has learned the piece to the satisfaction of his teacher, he ceases to think in these terms. He plays what he has been taught to play, not looking at the book, and certainly not attempting to beat time. When a piper progresses from *ceòl beag* to *ceòl mór*, he becomes musically bilingual. He enters a different world where the conventional rules do not apply.

NOTES

1. Examples: 'The Marquis of Tullibardine's Salute' (N. MacLeod, 1828, 26); 'Salute on the birth of Rory Mor MacLeod' (D. MacDonald, 1822, 92); 'The Groat' [on the christening of Rory Mor's son] (D. MacDonald, 1822, 80); 'Salute to Alasdair Mor MacDonald, first of Boisdale' ('upon his taking possession of the Estate') (D. MacDonald, 1822, 56).

2. Unless otherwise stated, all the tunes quoted here will be found in the current series of Piobaireachd Society Publications, *PS* **1–13**. For a more detailed account, see S. MacNeill (1968).

CHAPTER 5

The Ceòl Mór Tradition

From patronage to preservation

Aristocratic professional piping entered into a steep decline around the middle of the eighteenth century. The reason usually given for this is the disastrous Jacobite Rising of 1745, after which Acts of Parliament abolished the traditional legal power of the chiefs and forbade any Highlanders — except soldiers — to carry arms or to wear Highland dress.[1] Even to possess a bagpipe became illegal — that is, if one accepts the ruling of an English court which in 1746 hanged a piper on the grounds that his pipe was 'an instrument of war' (F. Collinson, 1975, 170). But it seems that this interpretation was never enforced. Pipers continued to be trained in the 'colleges' for a decade or two more, and, as for total numbers, it has been claimed that in the late eighteenth and early nineteenth centuries as many as a thousand pipers were recruited into the Army from Skye and Sutherland alone (*NP, 19,* No.7). A more substantial reason for decline was simply that the times were changing, and the signs were there to be read even before 1745. The biggest landlords were adopting more modern habits. They sent their sons to England to be educated, some never to return. They found that Highland rents could not support their new lifestyles, and they felt that they had better uses for their money than maintaining old customs at home. The changes on the MacLeod estate, home of the MacCrimmons, were a pointer to what was going on everywhere. Iain *Breac* MacLeod was the last chief who maintained his own home entertainments in full with 'a fool, a bard, and a piper'. He died in 1693, and his successor was deplored by the bards for his lack of interest in them (W. Matheson, 1970, 131). From 1706 to 1724 the estate was managed by a cousin, MacLeod of Contullich. In this period, musicians feature in the Dunvegan accounts with various payments, but the pipers who held their lands free eventually became rent-paying tenants, and it was a dispute about this which eventually brought the 'college' to an end (A. Clark, 1845). In the main it was the lesser chiefs and tacksmen who encouraged the traditional arts: men like MacLeod of Talisker (W. Mathieson, 1970, lxiii), and the young Laird of Coll who entertained

Johnson and Boswell in 1773. And it was at Raasay, not Dunvegan, that Johnson declared he had found the 'patriarchal life' which he had travelled so far, and almost too late, to see.

By the 1770s there was concern that bagpipe playing was in danger of extinction, and it was this belief that led to the formation, in 1778, of the Highland Society of London, a body of gentlemen who incorporated themselves with various objects connected with the Highland way of life, but especially with preserving the Gaelic language, customs, and music (Anon., 1981). As regards piping, the means chosen was an annual competition, the first of which was held in Falkirk in 1781. As Dalyell records (1849), it was a three-day event, timed to coincide with the annual Falkirk Tryst, or cattle fair, and this in itself tells us something about the social position of pipers at the time. How many of the thirteen pipers who attended were actually cattle drovers is not known, but in any case the venue was soon changed, for in 1783, as a result of a dispute over the prize, the competitors 'resorted to Edinburgh' where another competition was held. From then on the competition continued to be in Edinburgh, managed by another body, the Highland Society of Scotland, which was set up for the purpose. The competitions continued annually until 1826, then triennially until 1844 (Campbell, 1948), by which time there was a regular round of competitions at various rural 'Highland games' (J. Logan, 1841, xlii).

The first prize winner in 1781 was Patrick MacGregor, from Glenlyon, in Perthshire. His family, the *Clann an Sgeulaiche*, had been well known as pipers and storytellers for many generations back (A. Campbell, 1950b), and tended to dominate the competitions in the first twenty years, though many other names occur as well. The records show that the areas of Perthshire and Breadalbane provided many players. Some came from further afield, but many must have been put off by the distance. Not many came from Skye, or from the far North, though one observer commented on the high quality of pipers from the MacKay country — 'almost as though trained in a school' (*NP*, *24*, No.2). Few, if any, came from the outer Hebrides, but in this case distance may not have been the only factor. Life there was even harder than on the mainland, and there may never have been much of the kind of patronage which encouraged first-class pipers. Certainly there are not many pibrochs associated with those districts. The names of the famous old piping families, also, do not appear in the competition lists. One of the MacArthurs appeared regularly in the early days, but not as a competitor. He was a celebrity, and was normally invited to play a special exhibition piece. He had settled in Edinburgh as a grocer, but he was styled in the records as 'Professor' MacArthur (J.G. Dalyell,

1849, 97), imitating what was then the usual designation for a professional music teacher (and implying presumably that he was still taking pupils). His position *vis-à-vis* the Gaelic community in the city must have been like that of Duncan *Bàn* MacIntyre, the famous Gaelic poet, who had come from Glenorchy and settled, as a member of the City Guard. He too used to appear regularly at the early competitions, and for several years he produced each time a new poem celebrating the bagpipe and the Gaelic language (A. McLeod, 1952).

Early written records[2]

A few pibrochs are found in early eighteenth-century fiddle collections, but they are either adaptations of the real thing, or as David Johnson has recently shown (1984), original compositions inspired by the pibroch form. Four actual transcriptions from a piper's playing are in the *Collection of Highland Vocal Airs* published by Patrick MacDonald in 1784, but they do not show the grace notes, and they need some editing before they can be played by a piper (R.D. Cannon, 1978, 1981). Patrick himself acknowledged this problem and said that in his opinion the only person who would be able to notate pibrochs properly would be someone who was a trained piper, and also versed in staff notation. He must have been unaware that his own brother Joseph had already begun just such an undertaking. Joseph's book, the first ever written on pipe music, is also one of the best. Although he was only 23 years old when he wrote it in 1760, he evidently knew his subject well. He describes the technique of piping in great detail, and gives an account of the general character of the music. He concerns himself almost entirely with pibrochs (which he calls 'marches'), and he gives short quotations from a number of them together with a wealth of Gaelic technical terms which would have been entirely lost if he had not recorded them. He also seems to have prepared a collection of complete tunes, but this unfortunately has disappeared. Indeed his surviving book was almost lost: he wrote it in the course of a voyage to India, and only a year after arriving there he died of some tropical disease. The book was found long after and sent home to Patrick, who published it in 1803. It was still the earliest book of pipe music to reach print, but it was soon lost sight of again, and not until it was reprinted in 1927 did pipers begin to appreciate its value.

The collections of full-length tunes which we now have are largely the result of the initiative of the Highland Society, who at their annual competitions began to offer money prizes to pipers who could produce written music. One of the earliest claimants was Donald MacDonald, the Edinburgh pipe maker, who had come originally from Skye. He was a good enough player to win the first prize in 1817, and he also had what he himself described as 'a tolerable acquaintance with other instruments'. In fact he manufactured, played and taught the Irish and Northumbrian pipes as well as the Highland. He is said, by one who knew him, to have acquired 'a correct knowledge of piobaireachd from the last of the MacArthurs' (Alexander MacGregor, 1878). This does not necessarily mean that he attended the MacArthur 'college' in Skye; his teacher could have been 'Professor' John MacArthur in Edinburgh. He received his first payment for music in 1806, and finally in 1822 brought out his *Collection of the Ancient Martial Music of Caledonia* containing twenty-three pibrochs and a few of the small tunes. He compiled a second and larger volume, which was never published, but which still exists.

The Highland Society also instigated the collection of tunes from Angus MacArthur, who was a cousin of the above-mentioned 'Professor', and was the last piping member of his family. MacArthur himself could not write, but John MacGregor, one of the Glenlyon family already mentioned, himself a piper, pipe maker, and player of other instruments, took down the tunes 'from Mr. MacArthur's whistling them'. This phrase in the manuscript may mean that MacArthur played them on the practice chanter, or it may mean just what it says, in which case the grace notes in the manuscript, which are in full detail, are presumably MacGregor's rather than MacArthur's. The collection contains thirty tunes, and although this makes it the smallest of the classical collections, it is probably the most accurate. Although MacArthur was a very old man, and bedridden at the time, his memory was clear and his helpers were meticulous. They noted down at one point only in the manuscript that there seemed to be some fault and that 'this was the only place where there seemed the least uncertainty'.

Several other manuscripts were compiled in the 1820s. Two which survive are the Hannay-MacAuslan manuscript, unsigned but thought to be another of Donald MacDonald's, and an interesting compilation by Peter Reid, an amateur piper. But the Highland Society's minutes record payments to other pipers, for manuscripts of which there is now no trace (A. Campbell, 1948), and as recently as 1940 Pipe-Major W. Gray described another, by one Angus MacSwayed, written in 1825 and containing both *ceòl mór* and small music. The important Campbell *canntaireachd* manuscript was apparently not commissioned by the Highland Society. When the owner brought it to a competition in 1817, the judges with amazing short-sightedness refused to accept it, and it disappeared again, not to be rediscovered until 1909 (A. Campbell, 1961). Another *canntaireachd* collection, of twenty tunes, was published by Neil MacLeod of Gesto in 1828. It was taken from the dictation of Iain *Dubh* MacCrimmon, and is remarkable as being the only first-hand record we have of the music of any of that famous family (R.D. Cannon, unp.). There has been much discussion of a possible larger collection, in manuscript, from the same source, but nothing really definite has emerged as yet.[3] The largest collections were completed later still, by Angus MacKay. He was born in 1813, son of John MacKay, the piper in Raasay already mentioned (above, p. 55). Angus first appeared at the Highland Society competitions in 1825, and he clearly gained the Society's confidence, for in 1836, the year in which he won the first prize for playing, a prospectus was issued for a book to be published by him, which was intended to be a definitive collection (J.A. MacLellan, 1966a). It appeared in 1838, with sixty-one pibrochs, a lengthy historical introduction, and historical and traditional notes on the tunes. Besides the book, Angus also compiled a manuscript containing some 180 tunes. Angus got most of his tunes from his father, but he also took material from other sources as well. In his printed book he does not name his informants, but in his manuscript (Plate 13) he sometimes does so: JMcK (his father), RMDll (Ronald MacDougall) and 'Mr. Reid' (the amateur player just mentioned). He also had access to the Campbell *canntaireachd*, though apparently not until after he had completed his manuscript (A. Campbell, 1961b). What is unfortunate from our point of view is that he usually gives only one setting of a tune, even if he puts more than one set of initials at the head of it. Presumably he conflated versions and tried to iron out discrepancies, and there are clear signs, such as erasures and crossings out, that he had to work over many tunes, and not merely write them down. He was the first great editor, as well as the last great collector, of *ceòl mór*.

The end of the collecting period

After Angus MacKay, the collecting of pibrochs from traditional sources practically ceased. Why this is so is by no means clear, but the fact is that, apart from modern compositions, nearly all the tunes contained in later books and manuscripts are essentially copies from Donald MacDonald or Angus MacKay, and especially from MacKay. The main exception is a manuscript compiled by Duncan Campbell who seems to have been a contemporary of Angus MacKay, and a pupil and friend of the MacKay family (*PS* **1**, iii). His music is very much of the MacKay school, but he preserved at least one tune, 'MacLaine of Lochbuie's Lament', which is not known from other sources,[4] and his settings are not always quite the same as MacKay's. Colin Cameron, son of Donald Cameron, another MacKay pupil, also preserved the tune 'My dearest on earth, give me your kiss' which would otherwise have been lost.

Why the sources of *ceòl mór* dried up so quickly is by no means clear, since there must have been plenty of other players in Angus MacKay's time, and even later, who had inherited other traditions, and could have communicated them if asked to do so. Indeed, we know of one piper, John Johnston from the Isle of Coll, who as late as 1900 produced several tunes from his own knowledge, which were published by David Glen in a collection of *Music of the Clan MacLean*. Johnson claimed descent from the Rankins, hereditary pipers to the MacLeans (cf. 'Fionn', 1911–12). One of his tunes, 'John Garve MacLean of Coll's Claymore', was previously unknown, and another, 'The MacLeans' Gathering', can be identified with a two-bar fragment quoted by Joseph MacDonald (1760) but is otherwise unrecorded. Even the appearance of these tunes did not stimulate anyone to collect any more, from John Johnston or from anyone else. Thus the classical repertoire of *ceòl mór* stems entirely from collections made in the period from 1800 to 1840.

It must be admitted that memory was fading even during the brief period when the collections were being made. We can see from the records that tunes were being forgotten, either wholly or in part. Of the twenty-one tunes briefly quoted by Joseph MacDonald in 1760, only fourteen were recovered in full by later collectors. In the next oldest source, the Campbell *canntaireachd* manuscript of c.1800, out of 168 tunes, some sixty are not found in any later collections. And in the last collections, the book and manuscripts of Angus MacKay, a considerable number of tunes are defective, with sections missing as compared with earlier settings.[5] Also noticeable in the early records is a decline in the art of composition. John and Angus MacArthur in 1790 and John MacKay in 1820 composed tunes which were published by A. MacKay (1838) and are accepted as classical. Some of John MacKay's are in the metre referred to previously (p. 65) as 'secondary pibroch', which shows that he had some grasp of the principles of construction, but later nineteenth-century compositions are simpler, being either four-lined airs like any march or dance tune, or else in the two-phrase metre called 'primary'. The variations in most of these tunes are 'correct' in that no obvious rules are broken, but rather dull. By the end of the century, composition had ceased altogether, and the one piece added to the repertoire then is the exception that proves the rule. It is 'The MacFarlanes' Gathering', not a new composition but an arrangement by

John MacDougall Gilles apparently from a violin pibroch. It contains a number of grace notings which would not have been used in the classical period, and the scheme of variations is unorthodox. Archibald Campbell of Kilberry, who wrote a detailed critique of the piece (1955c), went so far as to say that it should not be considered as *ceòl mór* at all. However, it is generally accepted as such.

It is tempting to try to guess how many pibrochs were in circulation when the tradition was at its height. We now have about 300, dating from that time. Perhaps there were once 500, but in any case one cannot be precise, as some tunes are clearly versions of others, and a certain amount of reworking of old ones seems to have taken place. What is more remarkable is the number of pibrochs that an individual fully trained piper was expected to know: Donald MacCrimmon in 1814 was said to be able to play some 200 (F. Collinson, 1975); others around that time guessed the total number to be 200 or 300, of which 'formerly an accomplished player should have been master of about 100' (J.G. Dalyell, 1849, 17). Figures like these remind us of the Highland bards who could recite thousands of lines of Gaelic poetry from memory. Like them, the hereditary pipers were true professionals.

Nineteenth-century players

In general it was possible for a man to be a full-time piper in only one of two ways: as a soldier in the Army, or as a servant on an estate with a Laird who was sufficiently interested, and wealthy, to have a personal piper. Several of the players in the early competitions were listed as 'piper to' various Highland lairds, and it is possible that such patronage may have increased along with the general build-up of Highland sentiment in the first half of the nineteenth century. Most of the really famous players held positions as 'Estate piper' — men like John *Bàn* MacKenzie, piper to Davidson of Tulloch, Angus MacKay, piper to the Laird of Islay and later to Queen Victoria; and Donald Cameron, piper to the Earl of Seaforth, whose portrait appears in Plate 14. The Queen's piper, and perhaps a few others, would be employed as a piper and nothing else, but most would have other duties as well. Even in Edwardian times there were still a few pipers in the relatively privileged position of private service. David Ross, writing of his teenage years in the early 1900s, recalled a number of such men: Donald MacPherson, piper to the Marquess of Bute; John MacColl, piper to Sir Arthur Bignold of Lochrosque; and some half-dozen others. He said that there was 'great rivalry by these Highland families to obtain the best possible piper ... they were usually drawn from the best competing pipers'. However, the impression one gets from reading biographical notices of pipers is that, as time went on, the post of Estate piper tended to become more often a brief interlude in a varied career, than a lifetime occupation. Although the Highland connection was as strong as ever, and most pibroch players were still Gaelic-speaking, most of them actually lived in Lowland cities. Robert Reid is reported to have said that piobaireachd as we know it was perfected not in the rural Highlands but in Glasgow (A. Campsie, 1980, 115, 120, 157). The statement has been taken to mean that important developments in the form of the music took place there, which is certainly not so, but it does seem that by 1900 most of the leading players were living in the poorer suburbs of Clydeside. Calum MacPherson worked for a time in the shipyards at Greenock; Sandy Cameron, son of Donald, lived in Glasgow; so did John MacDougall Gillies, who became manager of Peter Henderson's bagpipe-making business. Roderick Campbell, another noted teacher, lived in Edinburgh. Reid himself was possibly the first non-Highlander to become a leading player. He was born in 1895, the son of a miner in Slamannan, Stirlingshire. He once said, 'They claim you have to be brought up in the shadow of a towering mountain. Well'n, I was born in the shadow of a towering coal byng'.[6]

But if private service was one of the supports of piping, the mainstay was the Army. Most pipers seemed to have spent at least some time in the armed forces, whether in the Regular Army, or in various local units, forerunners of today's Territorial Army. (Nor should it be forgotten that the Army, and later, civilian pipe bands, provided the demand for instruments which supported the bagpipe-making trade.) The music generally required of Army pipers was not *ceòl mór*, but at least the Army provided employment and the opportunity to play. Seumas MacNeill argues (1980) that the very best players tended to stay out of the Army, and that may have been true. Even so, several distinguished pibroch players were in the Army, notably Ronald MacKenzie, nephew of John *Bàn* MacKenzie, Pipe Major of the 78th Highlanders from 1865. At some stage (we do not know when) it became the custom in the Highland Regiments for the Pipe Major to play a pibroch at dinner in the Officers' Mess. This seems to have led to the position where pibroch playing became one of the accepted qualifications for a Pipe Major. Army pipers were allowed — possibly even encouraged — to enter the main open competitions. No doubt the Officers would feel that a good showing in the pibroch competitions reflected well on the Highland character of the Regiment.

It is interesting to speculate on the attitudes which, at different times, have led enthusiasts to support, and pipers to play, *ceòl mór*. In the 1820s and 1830s most writers stressed the 'ancient' character of the music. The historical associations of the tunes were still strong, and the stories and songs that went with them were familiar to all the players. Many of the traditions were connected with the Jacobitism which, with its political force safely spent, had become respectable again under the influence of Sir Walter Scott. By the end of the century, rather different ideas were in evidence. Bagpipe music in general had enjoyed an enormous revival, especially in the cities, but *ceòl mór* had narrowed down to the pursuit of a tiny minority. It was rural and purely Highland, utterly different in character from the ordinary music, and acknowledged as superior even by pipers who did not play it. It was at this time that the term 'classical music' began to be used (for example by C.S. Thomason (1893) and in Dwelly's Gaelic dictionary, c.1901) for *ceòl mór*, as it still is today. The term is appropriate in some ways, though it has tempted apologists into drawing misleading analogies with the higher forms of Western classical music. A better comparison in many ways would be with the ancient and sophisticated classical traditions of some Asian and Oriental cultures, such as India or Japan — but that was not a view likely to occur to the typical British music lover of 1900.

An essential feature of the *ceòl mór* tradition is that it is believed to have been handed down by a small number of leading players, in a definite series of master-pupil relationships. One such line of descent (A. Campbell, 1948; S. MacNeill, 1968) is from John MacKay of Raasay (1767–1848), via John *Bàn* MacKenzie (1796–1864), Donald Cameron (1810–1868) and his brother Alexander (1821–1870), and son, also named Alexander (1848–1923). Another is from John MacKay to Angus MacPherson (1800– ?), his son Malcolm (1833–1898) and several later members of the same family. All twentieth-century players of note can trace their piping 'ancestry' either to the Camerons or to the MacPhersons, or to both. One of the greatest of the later figures, John MacDonald of Inverness (c.1868–1953) is reputed to have actually spoken of the 'apostolic' succession of piping (C.K. Chambers, 1980, 320), and several modern writers have published diagrams of the family-tree type stretching from the MacCrimmons to the present day (S. MacNeill, 1969; J.A. MacLellan, 1977; W. Connell, 1980). Whether the lines of connection were really so few — and so universally agreed — as modern tradition affirms, is perhaps open to doubt. What does seem clear is that the tradition became more exclusive as time went on and that, increasingly, it was defined in one way. To be accepted as an authority, a piper must have proved himself by repeatedly winning prizes

in competitions, and he was unlikely to do this unless he had in turn been
taught by a successful player.

The influence of the competition system is hard to assess, but it must
have been profound. Judges and players were, literally, classes apart. In
the earliest competitions, the judges were all landowners and gentry. They
may have been chosen for their knowledge of music in general, and some of
them could indeed play the pipes, but only a few. There were also only a
few who would nowadays be described as middle class. One such was Peter
Reid, apparently an excellent player, an educated man who worked as a
clerk in Leith. 'From the nature of his employment', we are told, he never
competed, though he often judged, and there is the significant comment:
'and his decisions were always looked on as completely satisfactory' (*NP*,
26, No.10). At one stage it was suggested that the Highland Society might
appoint 'persons of practical skill in pipe music, such as those who had
gained prize pipes', not to be judges, but to be in attendance for the judges
to consult as they wished. This was turned down on the grounds of 'the
jealousies that are usually found to exist among those of the same
profession and in the same rank of life as those competing' (HSL Notes,
58). It eventually became usual for the premier competitions to be judged
by men who were really knowledgeable, but still definitely of the
landowning or officer class; though at the smaller Games it seems that
entirely unsuitable people were often appointed. Even at its best, however,
one would expect that judging would favour uniformity of playing, and
this does seem to have been the case, as we shall see in the remainder of this
chapter.

Variety of traditions

Even a cursory examination of the old collections shows that, besides
differences in versions of the same tune, such as we would expect from any
oral tradition, there were overall differences of style, presumably reflecting
the teachings of different schools. Two examples will show how significant
these could be.

A very common movement is the 'echoing beat'. As described by Joseph
MacDonald in 1760, this consisted of a melody note divided into three by
two grace notes struck in quick succession. In the example (a) shown here
the melody note is E and the dividing grace notes are low A. Angus
MacArthur and Donald MacDonald in the 1820s give the beat in the same
way, and in the *canntaireachd* records of this time there are also three
syllables for the three E's, thus *che-re-de* or *hie-rie-rie*. But Angus MacKay

in 1838, and others since, timed the E's quite differently, and they also made the second A grace note long, as at (b). In modern playing the A grace note has become so long that it can exceed the melody notes, as at (c), though still conventionally written as (b):

Ex. 5.1. Echoing beats on E

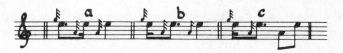

Another example is the 'cadence E' already mentioned. This is a falling sequence of grace notes, leading into a stressed note of the melody — in this example a low G:

Ex. 5.2. Cadence grace notes on low G

Joseph MacDonald (1760) writes the grace notes short and equal, as at (a). Donald MacDonald (1822) implies a similar effect, though he sometimes puts a rest mark under the E grace note. Angus MacKay (1838) always makes the E grace note long, as at (c), and to make his intention clear he often expands it into a full note as at (d).

In both these instances, and in others not mentioned here, it is Angus MacKay, the last of the 'original' sources, who differs from his predecessors; and it is also true that MacKay's style has subsequently displaced all the others. Undoubtedly, this is due to the publication of his book, which eventually became an absolute authority, accepted without question by all leading players. How and why this happened are questions which have not been adequately answered. The usual view is that it was because of the commanding reputation of John MacKay, Angus' father, the book being accepted as a faithful record of his teaching. This is undoubtedly part of the truth, but it is probably not the whole story. We cannot overlook the growing power of the competition system, and the probable attitudes of the judges. The prospectus issued in advance of MacKay's book (see J.A. MacLellan, 1966a) made it clear that one of the objects in promoting the work was to secure uniformity of playing. If it once became known — or merely believed — that the judges were judging by the book, then it could only be a matter of time before the successful players were playing by the book. Of course, there remained other tunes, not published in the book, but copies from MacKay's manuscript circulated among the leading players, and in any case, as time went on, the tunes actually played in competition became fewer, and those not in the book were rarely heard.

We do not know how quickly the 'MacKay revolution' took place, nor have we any traditions of what pipers at the time felt about it. Perhaps the MacDonald/MacArthur styles were out of date already by 1838. Equally possible, the change to a uniform style may have started then and continued gradually for a decade or two. We do know that the next printed collection of *ceòl mór*, William Ross's in 1869, followed MacKay's methods in nearly all respects. A few of MacKay's changes were resisted. Certain grace-note movements (for example the ones known in *canntaireachd* as *embari* and *hiobamdre*) have continued to be played in the older way. Some of these as they appear in MacKay's book have been assumed by the Piobaireachd Society editors to be misprints (*PS* 3, 83; 5, 144), but not all of them can be explained away so easily, and this is especially true of one curious example which eventually became controversial and where a sort of compromise seems to have been reached. The movement called *Crùnlùth Fosgailte* (i.e. 'open crunluath') was described in the previous chapter (p. 61). Two alternative forms of it are as shown here:

Ex. 5.3. 'Open' and 'Closed' Crunluath Fosgailte

In this instance, the beat is an embellishment on the basic two-note phrase, A-C#. In the older style, shown at (a), the two holes in the chanter which are opened on going from A to C are kept open while the E and F grace notes are played with the top-hand fingers, executing the 'throw' to the final E. This has the effect that two C grace notes are automatically sounded between the E and F notes. But in MacKay's style (b) the two fingers which were raised to open the C holes must be put smartly down again before the throw is played and, instead of the two C's, two A's are sounded. The *fosgailte*, 'open' beat has become closed, in spite of the name. William Ross in 1869–1885 printed different forms in different tunes. All pipers now play the closed form, but some retain the open form as an additional variation.

Further developments

Changes in playing style since the time of Angus MacKay have been less dramatic, and most of them can be seen as differences of interpretation within the limits allowed by the written music. Some changes seem to have crept in gradually without being noticed, while others have been fiercely resisted.

One of the less controversial developments has been the dropping of repetitions of the ground in the course of the tune. The last MacCrimmons were reported as repeating the ground regularly throughout (A. Campbell, 1814; N. MacLeod, 1828, 1); and Donald MacDonald in his book of 1822 usually prints 'D.C.' three times, after the doubling of the siubhal, taorluath and crunluath. Angus MacKay in 1838 usually has it twice, after the taorluath and crunluath only. His pupil Donald Cameron was still playing this way in the 1860s, but by 1900 only one repetition, after the crunluath, was normal (A. Campbell, 1948, 18; J. Campbell, 1984, 10). Another change seems to have been the addition of the crunluath mach to many tunes. It has been pointed out (A. Campbell, 1948) that Angus MacKay wrote this variation in only fourteen of the 240-odd tunes in his two collections, while today it seems to be played in almost every case where it is technically possible. Both of these changes are easily explained as being due to the requirements of the competition system: deleting the ground to save time, and adding the 'mach' to show off strong fingering.

More controversial was a change in timing of the so-called 'echoing beat' on low A. In the mid-nineteenth century this was being played in two ways, as at (a) and (b). By 1900, only the second form was to be heard, and this has now been ratified, so to speak, by a change in notation, (c):

Ex. 5.4. Beats on A

The E of the beat is actually a 'cadence E' grace note (see above, p. 83) which has gradually become longer until it now sounds like a full melody note. The changeover has been fully documented in a detailed study by Dr. P. Cooke (1978). It seems to have taken place around 1860–1870, to judge from recollections of a piper whose memories went back to that time (see C.S. Thomason, 1900; M. MacInnes, 1951), but the echoes of the controversy had died away in the present century. It was quite otherwise with another change which seems to have got underway in the last decades of the nineteenth century (P. Cooke, unp.). This is a revision in the method of playing the taorluath and crunluath beats which omits one of the grace notes. The old forms are shown here at (a), the new ones at (b):

Ex. 5.5. Old and new Taorluath and Crunluath beats

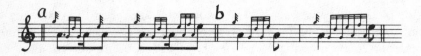

The difference is almost purely technical: important to the player, but hardly noticeable to the listener. The later forms are crisper and a little easier to play, especially in the case of the taorluath, and one theory is that the change came about with the increasing use of taorluath movements in quickstep marches. But it is characteristic of the pipe-music world that a fierce controversy arose which was conducted hardly at all in terms of musical merit, but rather in terms of 'right' and 'wrong'. The proponents of the new style claimed that their method had in fact been used all along by the best teachers, and that the written notation had been wrong throughout. The Piobaireachd Society took this view and in 1913 went to the length of drawing up a document in legal fashion to that effect, signed by three of its principal instructors. The document has recently been published by J. Campbell (1984). Pipers who remained in the competition system went over to the new style, cutting out the middle note which ever since has been called the 'redundant A'. A few remained unconverted, but they either played differently in public or else ceased to compete.[7]

Cameron and MacPherson styles

Today, the difference between different players' versions of the same tune are almost entirely restricted to choices between two recognised, but disputed, timings of the same notes. One of the more striking instances is the opening of *Cill Chrìosd* (Glengarry's March) which in modern notation is written as follows:

Ex. 5.6. Glengarry's March (*PS* **2**, 57, 1928)

The point of difference is, again, a matter of the handling of the long E grace notes. In one version they tend to occur before the beat, the following low G or low A notes being quite long, roughly as shown at (a); in the other, the E grace notes occur as strong beats, and the low G and low A are quite short; as at (b):

Ex. 5.7. Glengarry's March: alternative interpretations[8]

The two styles are examples of two basically different approaches to pibroch playing: the first style smooth and flowing (or round and featureless according to its detractors), the second bold and mannered (or jerky and un-Gaelic, as the case may be). At the present time the two styles tend to be described as the Cameron and MacPherson styles, in the sense that they are upheld by pupils, or more often, pupils of pupils, of the Cameron and MacPherson families already mentioned (p. 81). But it is difficult to be sure just how far back these differences really go. Pipe Major Robert Meldrum, whose professional career started about 1870, insisted that in his early days the flowing style, and in particular our Ex. 5.7a, was played by all leading pipers, including the founder of the MacPherson school, *Calum Piobair* himself (M. McInnes, 1951). Moreover, we also have on record, in *canntaireachd*, the version of the last of the MacCrimmons, which does not include the controversial E grace notes at all:

Ex. 5.8. Kilchrist (from N. MacLeod (1828); staff notation arr. R.D.C.)

I　hin-do ho-dro hin-do ho-dro

Tempo and rhythm

As was indicated in the previous chapter, *ceòl mór* today is played at an extremely slow tempo, with very free rhythms, especially in the ground — to the extent that most teachers actually forbid their pupils to think in terms of regular pulsed beats at all. Yet there are strong indications that this was not always the case. Joseph MacDonald (1760) says that the ground is played *Adagio*, and even *Allegro* in the case of 'Gathering' tunes, but never as slow as *Grave*. These are relative terms, but since MacDonald was trained in classical music as well as in piping, he was presumably using the words in their ordinary classical sense. Today no ground of any pibroch could possibly be called *Allegro*, and the usual tempo is *Grave* or even slower. MacArthur and MacKay also mark some tunes *Andante*, which would be quick by today's standards. Another sign of slowing down, as Kilberry pointed out (A. Campbell, 1953), is the gradual dropping of the repetitions of the ground. Some tunes, if played with all repeats at present-day tempo, would take more than half an hour to play, longer than any pipe would stay in tune. Kilberry considered that pipers seeking to put more expression into the music were generally apt to slow down and hold the long notes, and this may well be what has happened gradually over the years. As to rhythm, it has been pointed out (P. Cooke, 1972) that the earliest non-piping musicians who attempted to write down piobaireachd, while they confessed themselves unable to deal with the grace notes, had no qualms about using ordinary time signatures and equal-length bars. Pipers also used regular notation, and not until quite late did they start to apologise for the inadequacy of this system. Joseph MacDonald is again a highly significant witness. He gives considerable space to the discussion of 'time' and uses words like 'a species of Siciliana' to characterise rhythms. If pibrochs were played as irregularly then as they are today, his remark would have been quite misleading. And to underline this point, we know that when he came to write down the airs of Gaelic songs, he did in fact use highly irregular rhythms, 'without regard to the equality of bars', so that his brother Patrick, who published them in 1784, felt obliged to amend them for the sake of conventionally trained musicians.

A very general tendency seems to have been for tunes in 6/8 rhythm to be changed to common time. *Pìobaireachd Dhomhnuill Dhuibh* is quoted by Joseph MacDonald (1760), as shown here at (a), with a special sign over the C and B notes, and with the comment that the final low A is to be played particularly short. Nowadays it is usually played more along the lines of (b), and in other tunes of this nature care is taken *not* to shorten the low A's:

Ex. 5.9. *Pìobaireachd Dhomhnuill Dhuibh*

This can be seen as a consequence of the slowing of tempo, and if so it shows that the slowing was already under way in Angus MacKay's time, for he writes many tunes in common time which have a natural feel of 6/8.

Dissident players

I have tried to make clear that piobaireachd has not been a completely static tradition, even since the advent of written music. Many pipers today may find this hard to accept, in view of the sincere efforts which have undoubtedly been made to preserve the tradition from generation to generation. But it is only fair to record that in every generation we know of there have also been pipers who did see changes at work, and bitterly resented them. There was Finlay MacLeod (1783–1835) who won the first prize in the Highland Society competition in 1813 and who 'held that many of our compositions were being modernised to an alarming extent, even in his time' (A. MacDonald, 1914, 112). Unfortunately, we have no details of his complaints. Concerning Angus MacKay, Seumas MacNeill quotes (1978) a tradition that his mental illness and early death (1859) were brought on by the printing errors made in his book of 1838, which implies that he lived to see the traditional music being corrupted by the errors. John Johnston of Coll had nothing but scorn for the prize winners of his day. All that seems to be known of his playing is that he retained some of Donald MacDonald's grace notes, and that he played much faster than contemporary pipers. He also had a penchant for the old 'monotonous' gathering tunes like 'The End of the Little Bridge' (D. Glen, 1900; S. Gordon, 1923). More recently still, the change in Taorluath and Crunluath playing, eliminating the middle note A, was resisted by some players, notably John Grant of Edinburgh, Simon Fraser in Australia, and to the present day, George Moss of Inverness, whose views are set out in a recently published tape recording (1982) as well as in earlier letters to the piping journals. Other instances could be mentioned, but what all the protestors have in common is that their protests have been ineffective. Throughout the ascendancy of the competition system, pipers who deviated significantly from the prevailing orthodoxy have had to make a simple choice: to conform, or to retire. Some have conformed willingly, others unwillingly. Pipers are on record as having taught a particular variant setting of a tune to a pupil, with the warning that, if played in a competition, it might not please the judges (*PS* 5, 146).

The Piobaireachd Society

By the end of the nineteenth century, *ceòl mór* was seen by some observers to be in a state of terminal decline. Whether this was a fair view of the situation, it is now very difficult to say, but what is clear is that a number of well-informed connoisseurs were coming to the conclusion that unless something was done, the art would soon die out altogether.

One such person was Charles S. Thomason. He learned piping in the early 1850s, but thereafter he spent much of his life in India as an officer in the Royal Engineers (B.D. MacKenzie [1984]). He collected pibrochs from every source he could, and he compiled, edited, and finally — with his own hands — printed a definitive collection, *Ceol Mor*. One of his aims was to put the score of every pibroch into the hands of pipers at a modest cost; the other was more controversial. Thomason was one of those who believed that the complex rhythms of piobaireachd were a corruption of earlier, simpler styles. He also noted a number of tunes which were corrupt in the more obvious sense that there were parts missing, as compared with other tunes, and he set out to rectify both of these faults by amending the accepted versions.

A quite different aspect of the situation was perceived by Archibald Campbell, later known throughout the piping world by his title — Kilberry. He came of an old Argyllshire family which had long supported Highland music, especially piping, and was himself an able amateur player. To him the urgent problem was the small number of players who could be thoroughly relied on as having inherited the pure tradition of playing. Indeed, in a pamphlet which he published anonymously (A.M., 1903) he estimated that not more than twenty or thirty pipers could play even eight or ten tunes to gold medal standard, and as for the master players with really large repertoires, he maintained that

> there are four pipers alive in Scotland today, and if they should all, by some evil chance, die tomorrow, piobaireachd playing would receive a blow which might kill it outright, so slender is the thread which links our degenerate era with the golden days of past years.

Campbell did not say who his four pipers were. It is well known that he particularly venerated the Cameron school of playing. He might have included Malcolm MacPherson (*Calum Piobair*), but certainly not John Johnston of Coll, nor any of the other rural players who had stayed out of the competition circuit. Moreover, he was not worried by the irregularities and mannerisms which troubled Thomason. He held that the tradition had come down basically unscathed from the MacCrimmons, through the traditional lines of teaching.

If there were differences of opinion about what was wrong with *ceòl mór* playing in 1900, there was some agreement about what should be done. *Ceòl mór* had become 'classical music', and pipers would continue to provide it only so long as there was an audience sufficiently discriminating to want it. A discriminating audience, then as now, meant primarily competitions with truly knowledgeable judges. Also required were 'correct' published settings of the tunes, against which the competitions could be judged objectively. These considerations led to the formation in 1903 of the Piobaireachd Society (G. Campbell, 1944; J. Campbell, 1979). Initially it was a small body of gentlemen, nearly all pipers, some of them really good players, who set out as their principal objects: to publish music, to arrange competitions and provide the judges, and to finance instruction in piobaireachd, especially for Army pipers. In due course, books of tunes were published and Piobaireachd Society competitions were instituted, with the rule that only the versions of the tunes given in the Society's books could be played. With hindsight it is not surprising that this rule soon led to a crisis, the effects of which have lasted ever since. At the Society's second competition, in 1905, the problem arose of the timing of a variation of one tune, which the Society had reprinted from an early collection but which by then was usually accented differently. Some players in the competition conformed to the book, but one did not. He evidently played well, since he was awarded a prize, but almost immediately afterwards the judges' decision was overruled by the Committee of the Society on the grounds that the player had disqualified himself. It is easy to see the points of view of both sides, and not easy to see what should have been done, given the existence of the rule. What happened within the Society was that a number of members, including the Kilberry family who had been the prime movers, resigned; while in the piping world at large the Society gained a reputation for narrow dogmatism which, in spite of reforms which followed soon after, it has never quite succeeded in shaking off.

What followed can only be described as a coup, skilfully arranged by Kilberry and others, but especially by a new figure, John Grant of Rothiemurchus. The story has been told in some detail by James Campbell of Kilberry (1977), and it will be sufficient to say here that by 1913 the aims and constitution of the Society had been decisively altered. All matters relating to the selection and editing of tunes were placed in the hands of a small Music Committee. The published books were tacitly disclaimed, and a fresh series was started, based on much more thorough research. Instead of organising its own competitions, the Society began to operate through the two main established competitions at Inverness and Oban. Each year, lists of 'set tunes' are advertised for these events. From the lists, each competitor must select and prepare a certain number of tunes, and when he appears at the competition, he is finally told which one to play. The Society does not appoint the judges at these competitions, but in practice the judges very often are members. The set tunes are always taken from current Society publications, which for a considerable period of time were the only sources generally available. *Ceòl mór*, in Scotland at least, is thus firmly under the control of the Piobaireachd Society.

'Control' is not a word which would be accepted by many of the leading members of the Society, who undoubtedly see their responsibility as being to protect and support traditions handed down by previous generations. In its publications the Society itself has clearly and repeatedly expressed this view. In the main series of music collections, extensive editorial notes are attached to each tune, comparing the settings found in the oldest sources, and sometimes also describing variants which have arisen in more recent playing — all with the stated aim of enabling pipers 'to choose for themselves the settings they consider correct'. In keeping with this aim, the earlier rule as to settings allowed in competitions has been completely reversed. It now reads, typically:

> Competitors are not restricted to these settings and any other setting may be played although the judges may take into consideration the merits of these settings as well as their authenticity and the authority for them.

From this it would seem that the Piobaireachd Society was at pains to broaden the range of permissible interpretations of tunes, and it might have been expected that more variety of interpretation would have been heard. This has not happened. The differences between different players' versions of the same tune are minute compared with the differences which exist between manuscript versions. This may well be due to the style of presentation adopted by the Society. Faced with several versions of a tune, the editors have usually selected one as the principal basis, and have described the other settings by noting where they differ from it. The 'basic' setting is printed in full in staff notation, while the others can only be reconstructed with the aid of the editorial notes on the opposite page. Naturally the idea has grown up that the setting on the left-hand page is the approved one, and that players deviate from it at their peril. Only rarely have the editors printed two settings of a tune on an equal footing, so that one may hear, for example, 'The Battle of Auldearn, No.1' or 'The Battle of Auldearn, No.2'. More recently, however, the editors have begun to give much more detailed alternative settings, and it will be interesting to see to what extent these are taken up by the next generation of competitors.

Nothing that is said here can deny the importance of the cultural rescue operation which the Piobaireachd Society has achieved over the last sixty years. The standard of playing has been kept up. The number of players is greater than ever before, and so is the number of tunes regularly being played. It is noticeable how the set tunes tend to be heard at other competitions throughout the year. Those which find favour remain in circulation, and some become the personal hallmark of particular players. Most important of all, the tradition, though narrow, is still alive. This is shown by the fact that 'new' tunes, revived from old sources, have acquired the aura of tradition. As they have been introduced, players have cautiously experimented with the timings, fitting them into traditional ways of playing, and trying to sense what the judges are looking for. In this way, a tune is genuinely revived: and when a consensus has been reached, it is handed down orally like the older-established pieces. The tune 'MacFarlane's Gathering', which first appeared about 1900 (p. 78), is a case in point; but even more striking are tunes like 'Auldearn No.1' and 'Rory MacLeod's Lament', which have been reconstructed by the editors from the Campbell *canntaireachd* manuscript. The source gives only the melody notes and basic finger movements, so that time values and many grace notes have had to be added. What today's pipers play may well be very different from what the writer of the manuscript would have played; but it is probably a good approximation to what would be heard if the tune had stayed in circulation and had been handed down through the succession of MacKays and Camerons or MacPhersons. It is in this sense that the Piobaireachd Society can be said to have preserved the oral tradition.

NOTES

1. The full text of the Act of Proscription is printed in *Piping Times* **24**, Nos. 11, 12.

2. Unless otherwise stated, detailed references for this section will be found in R.D. Cannon (1980).

3. On this question, see especially B.J. Orme (1978). Earlier writers in favour of the existence of the MS include G.F. Ross (1926) and J.D. Ross Watt (1934–6); and against, A. Campbell, in *NP*, *21*, No.2.

4. All tunes mentioned in this chapter are published with editorial notes and details of original sources, in the current Piobaireachd Society publication, *PS* **1–13**.

5. For example, 'The Old Woman's Lullaby', 'The Lament for Donald Duaghal MacKay' and the 'Lament for Colin Roy MacKenzie', compared with versions in the

Campbell *canntaireachd*, A. MacArthur's MS and MacLeod of Gesto, respectively. For discussion of the first of these, see R.D. Cannon (1982a), for the second, see *PS* **13**, 434.

6. Sources: MacPherson, *NP, 24*, No.12; Cameron, *NP, 20*, No.4; Gillies, *NP, 23*, No.7; Campbell, J. Wilson (1978), 6; Reid, *PT* **18**, No.1.

7. An unusual revelation of a conversation between leading competitors at the time of the controversy was given recently by J. Wilson (1978, 21). Wilson clearly implies that some players who had played the middle note gave up doing so and warned him to say nothing about it in future. For a lordly (and amusing) dismissal of the whole matter, see F. Richardson in B. Seton and J. Grant [1975], vi.

8. The examples given here are the present writer's interpretation of instructions given by the Cameron School, as recorded by J. Campbell (1984), and of the playing of Malcolm MacPherson as transcribed by R. Ross, Vol.2, 18 (c.1964).

CHAPTER 6

The Origin of Piobaireachd

Questions

In this chapter we shall ask — when were the pibrochs composed? by whom? and what was the original purpose of the music? It must be admitted from the outset that we have no definite answers to these questions, and this needs to be stressed all the more for the reason that many pipers today have quite clear ideas on the subject. The orthodox view is that piobaireachd as a musical form was invented by members of the MacCrimmon family, in the Isle of Skye at least as far back as the time of Donald *Mór* MacCrimmon, who is asserted to have been born in 1570; that other schools of pipers learned their basic ideas from the MacCrimmons, although they added more compositions of their own; and that the pieces were composed in the form we have them today, for the purposes which their titles suggest: to assemble men for battle, to excite them on the battlefield, and to express appropriate feelings at births, weddings, funerals and other solemn occasions.

All of this may be true, but the point I am emphasising here is that we do not know it as historical fact, simply because there are no written records of pipe music during the period in question. The whole of the development of *ceòl mór* lies in the realm of *pre*history as far as we are concerned, and the task of reconstructing this development is more like archaeology than history. We do have sources of information, but they have to be used in special ways, and most of this research still remains to be done.

The stories of the tunes

Many tunes have more or less detailed 'legends' associated with them. At one time these stories were circulating by word of mouth, but now they are preserved in writing. Two early collections of pibrochs (A. MacKay, 1838; D. MacDonald, MS) have 'historical notes' attached, and separate books of such stories have been published ('Fionn', 1904, 1911). The earlier ones are tales of battles with much bloodshed and typical legendary matter; the

95

later ones tend to be more matter-of-fact. There is not space to recount any of them here in detail — and in any case many of them are readily available. The point is that, interesting and evocative though these tales undoubtedly are, they cannot simply be read as historical fact. They may contain fact, but this has to be extracted with care and discretion. Gaelic scholars have worked in this way on much of the traditional poetry which is extant — assigning the pieces to their authors, estimating dates, and putting them into the context of known history. The results of this work can be read in the splendid series of volumes published by the Scottish Gaelic Texts Society,[1] as well as in general works on Gaelic literature. But as regards pipe music, so far only one tune, *Cha Till MacCruimein*, has been adequately researched in this way (F. Blankenhorn, 1978). Some of the stories may well turn out to be legends common to many countries. Others will be found not to be legends at all in the true sense of the word, but actual fiction, invented by romantic writers, or theories put up by historians who collected the material in the early nineteenth century. But also there will be sober family history, handed down by the hereditary pipers themselves, and known only to them or their close associates. To distinguish these different strands is a task which will require judgement, and piping knowledge, but also — and this is what pipers have tended to forget — a wide knowledge of Gaelic culture and history in general.

Even when a story seems historical and can be dated, there is still a question of whether the story and the tune are actually contemporary. We know very little of how the stories of the tunes have been handed down, but I suggest that this has happened usually in one of two ways. When the story is actually about the tune as such, it may indeed be what it seems to be: a piece of information handed down from master to pupil. The story of 'The Pretty Dirk' tells how Patrick *Og* MacCrimmon was promised a gift if he could produce a new tune within a stated time, which he did. The story of 'The Half Finished Pibroch' tells how the same piper got stuck in the middle of a new piece, and John *Dall* MacKay, in a flash of inspiration, finished it for him (A. MacKay, 1838). These stories have the ring of truth. There is actually another version of the latter story told by J. MacKenzie (1841); but at least these are stories 'about' tunes, just as we have stories about the composition of more modern pipe tunes. When we come to the major 'historical' pibrochs, it seems a different matter. I doubt if a piper in the early days, teaching the tune *Lasan Phadruig Chaogaich*, laid down his chanter, and went on to tell in his own words the story of 'squinting Patrick' setting fire to his enemies' houses and burning the occupants (A. MacKay, 1838); or if he did, that was not the main way in which the story was handed down. More likely in this case there was a song, and the prose legend we have is a *précis* of the song, while the pibroch is a pipe version of the air. I cannot prove this example — or for that matter any other individual case — but if the general idea is accepted, it is easy to see that a pibroch is not necessarily as old as its legend, nor for that matter as old as its name. Indeed, one such case is already admitted by tradition. The Battle of Harlaw was fought in 1411, but a pibroch, 'The Desperate Battle, Harlaw', was reputed to have been composed by Angus MacKay of Gairloch, who lived in the mid-eighteenth century (R.D. Cannon, 1974).

This is not to deny that a pibroch may preserve some music which is very old indeed. This seems particularly likely in the case of certain tunes, classed as 'marches' or 'gatherings', which emphasise short and bold phrases, matching the known traditional words:

Ex. 6.1. Piobaireachd Dhomhnuill Dhuibh (Words and music from A. Campbell MS (1815))

Ex. 6.2. The End of the Little Bridge (Words from 'Fionn' (1904), music adapted from D. MacDonald (1822))

It is easy to imagine that these are mediaeval battle cries, and that they would have been played on the pipe as easily recognisable rallying calls. What is not so easy to believe is that a piper in battle would work his way steadily through the ground and variations of a pibroch as we know it today. The finished tune need not be as old as the basic musical elements of which it is made.

Early MacCrimmon history

The genealogy of the MacCrimmon family is usually presented in modern works with quite precise dates, and various tunes are ascribed to different members of the family. Nearly all of this material, as far as we are concerned, has a single source: Angus MacKay's book of 1838. Modern attitudes to this work range from unqualified acceptance to outright dismissal — but middle views between these are not much in evidence and, again, it has to be said, there has been very little detailed, critical research. MacKay must have taken his information from various sources, but he does not name them; and he must sometimes have been faced with conflicting stories, but we do not know how he decided between them. In these respects, MacKay is no different from many other important source-writers on Gaelic history, but until some sifting has been done, those who wish to base theories on him must be all the more cautious.

Returning to the genealogy, the sequence is Ian *Odhar*, Donald *Mór*, Patrick *Og*, Malcolm; followed by Malcolm's two sons, Donald *Ruadh* and Ian *Dubh*. The first of these is a name and nothing more; Donald *Mór*, Patrick *Mór* and Patrick *Og* are all credited with some compositions; Donald *Ruadh* and Ian *Dubh* had died not long before Angus MacKay was writing, and their descendants, though not pipers, were living in Skye at the time.

Working back from the most recent members of the line, Donald *Ruadh* and Ian *Dubh* are perfectly well attested. We know about their adult lives in some detail — where they lived and how much they were paid for their services as pipers (R.H. MacLeod, 1977). From Angus MacKay's statement of his age at the time of his death, we gather that Donald *Ruadh* was born about 1731. We also know from documents that MacLeod's piper in 1743 was named Malcolm, and that he held the farm of Boreraig, which according to Angus MacKay was the historic location of the MacCrimmon 'college'. Unless the documents in question were already known to MacKay, they can be taken as confirming the tradition. There is no similar confirmation of the earlier MacCrimmon ancestors, unless we call in evidence a song by Mary MacLeod, thought to be late seventeenth century, which mentions a piper named 'Patrick' as playing at Dunvegan (J.C. Watson, 1934, line 504); and a legal document of 1614 in which 'Donald MacCruimen', a piper, appears, but is not stated to be MacLeod's piper (A.J. Haddow, 1982; G.C.B. Poulter and C.P. Fisher, 1936). But the genealogy is not long by Highland standards. If it was collected all from one person, say from Donald *Ruadh*, it is not unreasonable that he should know the names of his ancestors back to his great-great-grandfather. Unfortunately, we do not know where it comes from.

By assuming reasonable lengths of time for each generation, it is easy to guess the birthdate of each member of the family. Presumably that is how the Clan MacCrimmon Society in 1936 arrived at the birthdates of Donald *Mór*, c.1570, Patrick *Mór*, c.1595, and Patrick *Og*, c.1640. But presumably they also took into account the fact that Angus MacKay (1838) ascribes three tunes to Donald *Mór*: 'MacLeod's Salute', 'MacDonald's Salute', and 'MacLeod's Controversy', and dates two of them to 1603, the year when a historic conflict between the two clans was settled. This looks like two pieces of evidence confirming each other — but can we be sure of this? Could it not be that a previous historian has already been over this ground, and linked up the tunes, the composer and the date? The only safe conclusion at present seems to be that the MacCrimmon 'history' stretches back to 1600, or perhaps earlier, but not much earlier. At this point some pipers may protest that I have muddled the MacCrimmon story by telling it piecemeal and backwards. But that is the state of our knowledge. The MacCrimmons are historical figures only from about 1700 onwards, and their music (if it is theirs) is on record later still. Before that time they are, quite literally, prehistoric and legendary, though it is highly likely that they were leading pipers.

Names and dates

After a lifetime's study, Campbell of Kilberry concluded (1948) that 'we have few if any piobaireachd much older than 1600 A.D.' He based this conclusion partly on the MacCrimmon dates just mentioned, but mainly on the consideration of names of tunes. Many of these imply dates, since they refer to battles, or to the births or deaths of known historical figures; and a good deal of research has been published on the historical backgrounds implied by these names, especially by Professor A.J. Haddow (1974, 1982). Kilberry suggested that 'There is no lament extant for any historical personage earlier or much earlier than that date ... nor have we any orthodox piobaireachd commemorating any earlier event, which we can say with certainty was contemporary with that event'. The second part of this statement sounds arbitrary — why should we accept some tunes as contemporary with the events named, and reject others? But when we do as Kilberry presumably did, and look at the whole range of tune titles (conveniently listed in the index of Thomason's *Ceol Mor*), it becomes less arbitrary. There is a very definite concentration of dates in the seventeenth century and early eighteenth century. Only a few tunes are dated much earlier, and they are not markedly different in character from the others. If their dates were accepted, it would follow that pibrochs had been composed in essentially the same style over a period of more than four centuries. It is more reasonable to look for some other explanation. There is no shortage of possibilities. If we take the case of 'The Battle of Bealach nam Brog', various dates have been suggested from 1249 to 1452

(Thomason, 1900; *PS* 9, 247). One possibility, to be sure, is that a bagpipe tune was composed at the time, but another is that a harp tune was composed, and taken over by pipers later on. Or again — and I think more likely — a song was made and the pibroch is based on the song. But songs can be fitted to more than one tune, and the present tune might not be the original one. As for the final form of the pibroch, with its Ground, Taorluath and Crunluath variations, we simply do not know if it was made in that form, or has been modified from time to time.

But to return to Kilberry's point: although arguments like this could be raised against any individual tune, the weight of numbers is significant. The preponderance of the dates certainly suggests that the period 1600–1740 was the principal period of pibroch composition.

Internal evidence

Another approach to the 'history' of pibrochs is to examine the tunes themselves to see whether they can be put in some sort of order, from primitive ones which could be early, to more developed ones which could be later. This possibility was advocated many years ago by R.L.C. Lorimer (1941), and his own subsequent studies of pibroch metre (1962, 1964) are valuable steps in that direction. The outlook is promising, but the work still has a long way to go, and at this juncture it would be unwise to make more than a few general comments. It would not be safe to assume that simpler tunes are, on average, older than more complex ones. The reverse could be true, since the simpler styles are easier to imitate. We see this clearly enough in the collections of small music. Plenty of reels and jigs composed in the last fifty years could be mistaken for eighteenth-century compositions. A more promising idea might be to look for signs of decline in composition towards the end of the piobaireachd era. If we could establish 'rules' of composition, and then show that some tunes contain 'mistakes' which cannot easily be written off as corruptions in transmission, we should know that the mistaken tunes were relatively recent.

The mere existence of rules of composition is important. It does seem that at one time composition, as well as playing techniques, must have been taught in the piping schools. Yet nothing of the sort has been handed down traditionally, and the rules we now know (see above, p. 62) have been worked out by latter-day amateurs, studying the published collections. The only source writer even to mention the subject is the earliest, Joseph MacDonald, and he makes just one remark: he says that the old pipers counted out the 'time' on the four fingers of the left hand, so that each

Ground consisted of four quarters, and each quarter consisted of four fingers. The finger generally corresponds to one or two bars of our notation, and sure enough, most tunes do have sixteen or thirty-two bars. MacDonald makes no distinction between the various metres which we recognise today. The four or five types illustrated above all conform to the sixteen-finger rule, but they are very different in character, and the composers must have had something more to guide them. Later writers do not seem to have perceived even the four quarters. In the Campbell manuscript, about forty years later than MacDonald, some tunes are set out in four lines, some in three, and others are divided in an irregular and misleading fashion even though the notes are correct. Donald MacDonald (1822) says nothing on the matter, but Angus MacKay (1838) favours the 6,6,4 and 4,4,4,4 divisions which are mostly used today. It seems clear that knowledge of metre was declining from the mid-eighteenth century, and eventually pipers were simply learning the tunes by rote. Can we make a guess as to when the theory was last fully understood? If we assume that it was a secret known only to a few pipers, then perhaps Malcolm MacCrimmon would be the last to hold it. He died about around 1769 (R.H. MacLeod, 1977). If the theory was ever common knowledge among professional pipers, it must have begun to die out earlier.

Harp music

The suggestion has been made that music of the pibroch type was formerly played on the harp, and that some pibrochs are actually versions of harp pieces (F. Collinson, 1966). The suggestion has also been ridiculed, for no very good reason. There is very little positive evidence either way. We do know that the harp was played from very early times in Ireland, Scotland and Wales, and that harpers were a professional class who underwent extensive training, especially in Ireland (W. Matheson, 1970; D.S. Thomson, 1983). Presumably their music included dignified formal pieces appropriate for salutes and laments. But we know very little about this music. The only living traditions of harping were recorded in Ireland in the 1790s, and most of the music is lighter in character than I have just suggested (Bunting, 1796, 1806, 1840). Scottish harp music is preserved only in a few arrangements for violin and piano. The idea that pipers took up harp tunes seems perfectly reasonable, just as in later times they have not hesitated to cull tunes from every available source — fiddle strathspeys, fife marches and folk songs. But can we recognise the harp tunes among the pibrochs?

The strongest case which Dr. Collinson has made out concerns the pibroch *Cumha na Chraobh nan Teud*, 'The Lament for the Harp Tree'. He suggests that the rather mysterious title should be amended by changing *Craobh* to *Crann*, i.e. 'Lament for the Harp Key'. There is indeed a ribald Gaelic poem, *Féill nan Crann*, concerning the loss of a harp key, which is attributed to the blind harper Roderick Morrison; and there is also a tale about the loss of a valuable harp key by an earlier Irish harper, Rory O'Kane (W. Mathieson, 1970). What has not been emphasised before is the musical character of the tune. It is a particularly long one, mainly in the pentatonic A-scale, but with a somewhat obtrusive low G which could be viewed as a 'wrong' note, due to adaptation from another instrument. Some of the presumed Scottish harp tunes also have extremely long melody lines and are pentatonic, but they also cover a wide range of notes — two octaves or more (D. Dow, [1771]; W. Mathieson, 1970). It is easy to imagine that a long free-flowing harp melody has been compressed to give the pibroch we now have. If so, the same might be true of some other tunes of similar character, such as the 'Lament for Donald Duaghal MacKay'.

Conclusions

This chapter contains no proof of anything, but it does indicate some of the limits within which we can speculate. Future research will no doubt give a clearer picture, but in the meantime I should like to offer my own suggestions on the way pibroch playing developed into its present form. We have already seen that pipers were playing at funerals and in battle as long ago as the sixteenth century, and they could have been doing so for a century or more before that. I take it that when the bagpipe first reached the Highlands it was used for playing short and repetitive tunes (as in other countries even to the present day), and that some of our 'gathering' tunes originated at that time. I presume that more elaborate tunes are of later date, and that some of the early seventeenth-century dates are correct, even if not all the tunes were pipe tunes at first. But the developed form of *ceòl mór* is, I suggest, a product of the more leisurely conditions of life that came into the Highlands in the later seventeenth century. This was the time when the chiefs began to build houses for comfort rather than castles for defence (W.R. Kermack, 1957, 142), to indulge in fine clothing, and to patronise other arts such as painting (C. Hesketh, 1961, 17). If so, pibroch composition would have reached its high-watermark towards 1700. From this time, the harpers were declining, and the pipers were taking their place; but already the leading clan chiefs were looking to Edinburgh and to

England for their cultural interests. Within a few decades their patronage disappeared, and piobaireachd was on the way to becoming a 'folk' art, rather than the old-style classical Gaelic tradition. As to the development of the music itself, I suggest that the variation form was used by harpers from early times. If the music recorded by Daniel Dow in 1771 is any guide, harp variations would tend to be of two sorts. One sort consists of restatements of the theme in different rhythms, and we have already seen that pibroch variations can be of this type also, as in 'Old Woman's Lullaby' (p. 57). The other type is less pibroch-like. It consists of reducing the melody to a steady rhythm, and breaking each long note into rapid repeated notes. If any of the pibroch variations was inspired directly by harp music, as opposed to being composed by a piper who was simply influenced by the general feel of the older music, it would I think be the Taorluath. Perhaps the actual word *Taobhlùth* had some meaning for harpers, and was inherited by pipers. But the Crunluath seems to be intrinsically a pipe variation, and it may well be a later addition to many of the tunes in which it now occurs. One reason for suggesting this is the way it grows naturally out of the Taorluath: it simply feels as if it had been invented on the chanter. Another reason, with which not all pipers might agree, is the musical effect of the Crunluath. It systematically adds the note E to every note of the tune, regardless of the key of the melody. On the bagpipe, this works well enough, since the E answers to the A notes of the drones, and to the strong harmonic E which the drones produce. But on any other instrument we might expect a Crunluath-type variation to lead to different notes — E when the tune is in A; D when it is in G, and so on. Taorluath-like and Crunluath-like variations for harp and violin do have different running notes, depending on the character of the piece. Pipe fingering no doubt developed gradually during the flourishing period of pibroch playing, and it may be that some of the excessively long grace-note figures which Joseph MacDonald described, and which no later writer has given, were recent innovations which rightly failed to catch on. The Crunluath a Mach, which has survived, may also be a late addition, which was still working its way into general acceptance during the period of writing music. Joseph MacDonald apparently did not know it at all. His near contemporary John MacCrimmon played it (N. MacLeod, 1828), but writers as late as Angus MacKay (1838, 1840) used it quite sparingly compared with the players of today.

As to the metres of pibroch, I can only hazard the merest guess as to the way they developed. The artistic purpose of the more complex metres is quite clear — it enables the piper to work up a reasonably long but satisfying piece out of limited material. When these tunes are associated with songs, the words do not follow the whole Ground. They have much shorter airs, using the same basic phrases but in ordinary four-square ballad form. It may be that the short form is the original, and the pibroch is the professional piper's working up of the air into something more substantial, on which to build his variations. Thus the words and the basic air may be older than the pibroch.

If any one metrical class is to be picked out as having, on average, the oldest tunes — as opposed to the oldest embodied fragments of simpler tunes — it is perhaps the metre of *Bodaich Dubha nan Sligean* (see above, p. 64). I suggest this simply because it seems to be the most subtle and the hardest to imitate. There are only about a dozen tunes known of this type, but they must date from a time when metre was thoroughly understood. Once this had ceased to be the case, the tunes could be handed down, but no more could be composed. Tunes like 'Donald Gruamach's March' come next in complexity, and similar comments would apply. But the more formula-like metres could easily be imitated, either by pipers who had learned the tunes and grasped the formula, or simply by imitating an older tune, phrase by phrase.

Finally, it is worth noting the great length of some pibrochs. One version of 'The End of the Little Bridge' has no fewer than twenty variations, and although it would doubtless have been played faster at one time than today (actually it never is played today), it would always have been a long piece. It has been suggested (*PS* 8, 241) that 'perhaps the purpose of the composer was to design a suitable accompaniment to hand-to-hand fighting', and of another such tune it was suggested (*PS* 10, 307) that 'the composer, "seeing red" in a battle ... wanted to give as long a blow as possible'. This seems unlikely. There are tales of tunes being composed on the spur of the moment, but never actually in battle; and for hand-to-hand fighting, the best music would be simple and stirring phrases already well known to the fighters. These long tunes would have needed care and thought; they are surely the products of long winter evenings, not hectic moments on the battlefield, and like much of the more modern pipe music, they would be played to excite the admiration — or envy — of other pipers.

NOTE

1. See, for example, J.C. Watson (1934); A. MacLeod (1952); W. Mathieson (1970); and, more generally, D.S. Thomson (1974, 1983).

CHAPTER 7

Music for Dancing

Early history

There can be no doubt that the Highlanders danced to the bagpipe from the very earliest time of the instrument, though actual records of the fact do not appear until the seventeenth century. We then find, in the Kirk Session registers, notices of pipers being convicted of playing on the Sabbath, and people dancing with them. Most of these records come from the Lowlands, but in towns like Stirling incoming Highlanders gave much the same kind of trouble as well (J.G. Dalyell, 1849, 32-35). Gaelic poetry also speaks occasionally of the pipes being used as an accompaniment to general merrymaking in the big houses of the West Highlands (D.S. Thomson, 1968, 71; F. Collinson, 1975). The music could be provided by a bagpipe, fiddle or jew's harp ('trump'), or the human voice, either singing *puirt a beul*, 'mouth tunes', consisting of short rhymes, partly nonsensical, or else 'diddling' or 'cantering' in entirely meaningless vocables. All these forms of music were common in the late eighteenth and early nineteenth centuries, although later largely displaced by the accordion. No doubt bagpipes predominated over fiddles in some areas, and vice versa in others, and one may have preceded or displaced the other. It does seem that bagpipes were commoner in the West Highlands, and fiddles in the East and Central Highlands (A. Bruford and A. Munro, 1973). We have already seen that the Highlanders favoured a special small-sized bagpipe for dance music, and perhaps it was one of these that was played by the piper at Armadale in Skye, when Johnson and Boswell visited in 1773, and which, as Boswell recorded, 'made us beat the ground with great force'.

Reels

The characteristic dance of the Highlands was the reel. The name is old, possibly of Norse origin, and is used also in Gaelic, variously spelled *ruidhle, righil* etc. The dance is performed by three people weaving in a figure-of-eight, or by four people in a figure with three loops instead of two (a 'reel of three' or 'reel of four', respectively). In more modern terminology, any dance done to the tune of a reel is called a reel, whether it contains reel figures or not. The best pipers cultivated reel playing to a high art, and in the early bagpipe collections, reels are the commonest dance tunes. A reel is in 'alla breva' time, 2/2, written ₵, with two beats to the bar. It is in short, four-bar strains, with a forceful driving rhythm, often characterised by three-note beats   ♪ ♫ .

Here is an example of a small reel — indeed that is its name, 'The Small Reel', otherwise 'Sir J.M. MacKenzie's Reel' or *Gun dh'ith na coin na ceannaichean*:

Ex. 7.1. Sir J.M. MacKenzie's Reel[1]

The Gaelic title is actually not a name as such, but consists of words fitted to the first two bars. It gives out the rhythm very aptly, contains a nice alliteration, and is something of a tongue-twister. It is a fragment of mouth music, and when the song was complete this line would have been sung three times, with a different line to finish it off; and then on to the next verse. It says 'the dogs devoured the pedlar' — but what happened next we shall presumably never know. Like most *puirt a beul*, many of which do survive complete, it probably made some sense, but not a great deal, and contained some broad rustic humour. The tune is very easy to play on the pipe. It has only these two measures, and it would have to be repeated many times before the dancers had done with it. Modern pipers, and dance bands, tend to string tunes together in medleys, but we do not know if that was the traditional practice. The fact that some *puirt a beul* run on for many verses suggests that it was not; as also does the fact that in the older printed dance collections the name of a dance is usually simply the name of the tune to which it is set.

A very different proposition is the reel 'John MacKechnie':

Ex. 7.2. John MacKechnie

This ranks as one of the first pipe tunes ever written down — by Joseph MacDonald in 1760 — and in MacDonald's original setting it is characterised by crisp but quite heavy grace-noting, much of it approximating to the grace notes found in pibrochs. MacDonald calls it 'one of the wild reels' and implies that these were a class of tune fit for the best pipers to play. Later tradition confirms this: the tune next occurs in William Gunn's Collection (1847) as *Port Mor Iain 'Ic Eachainn* — 'John Mac Eachainn's Big Tune', with an additional English subtitle, 'Jonn MacKay of Skerray's Favorite'. MacKay of Skerray, known in Gaelic as *Iain Mac Eachainn*, was a tacksman of Lord Reay who built up a sizeable business in cattle on the lands of Musal and Clasneach in north-east Sutherland in the mid-eighteenth century. He is remembered in poems by Rob Donn MacKay, as also is his daughter, Isabel MacKay (H. Morrison, 1899; I. Grimble, 1974). The tune is almost certainly a piper's composition. It occurs only in pipe collections and has always been highly regarded. We cannot be sure that it was originally composed in honour of MacKay of Skerray, but it may well have been, and it does seem to have been something of a local speciality. The most famous of all Highland reel tunes, and perhaps the oldest extant, is the 'Reel of Tulloch':

Ex. 7.3. Reel of Tulloch

This tune can be found in eighteenth-century fiddle collections, often with long sets of variations, and always under the same name, or a version of the name, like 'Hullachan', the phonetic rendering of *Righle Thulaichean*. Two different places called Tulloch have laid claim to it: a village on Deeside near Ballater (D. MacDonald, 1822), and a district in Strathspey near Nethybridge (J. MacGregor, 1801), and along with the latter goes the tradition that it was composed by Iain *Dubh Geàrr* MacGregor, a noted bard and piper of the *Clann an Sgeulaiche* (see above, p. 74), also an outlaw, who fled to Strathspey from his home in Glenlyon to evade capture, barricaded himself in a barn and finally killed all his pursuers, single-handed.

The story is told in a fine song of twenty-three verses. The chorus fitted to the second measure of the music has little to do with the text, but it rolls off the tongue very impressively:

O Thulaichean gu Bealaichean
'S o Bhealaichain gu Tulaichean
'S mur faigh sinn leann 's na Tulaichean
Gu 'n òl sinn uisge Bhealaichean.

'From Tullachan to Ballachan, From Ballachan to Tullachan, If we don't get beer in Tullachan, We'll drink water at Ballachan.' Today the tune is associated with the Highland dance of the same name, but the dance is thought to be of later date than the tune. It was developed around 1800 as a Highland ballroom dance, and was sometimes known as 'The Breadalbane Ball Reel' (J.F. and T.M. Flett, 1964, 134). One of the earliest reels to be attributed to a contemporary composer was 'Drive Home the Mainlanders' by Archie Munro of Oban, published by Angus MacKay in 1843. (Munro also composed the pibroch 'Glengarry's Lament' in 1828 (A. MacKay, 1838)):

Ex. 7.4. Drive Home the Mainlanders

Good reels have continued to be composed up to the present day, and although the trend now is more towards the elaborate competition style, simple airs suitable for dancing continue to appear. One thinks for example of G.S. MacLennan's 'Dancing Feet' (said to have been composed extempore when MacLennan, playing for an eightsome reel, went off the tune, but keeping the beat going, as every piper should, managed to evolve a new piece); or Archie Kenneth's 'The Back of the Moon', and many others.

Jigs

These are in 6/8 time, and like reels, are fairly rapid in tempo. In England and Ireland, the jig is a solo step-dance. This does not seem to have been the case in Scotland (J. Currie, 1800), but some of the old social dances had 6/8 tunes, for example 'The Reel of the Black Cocks', a two-couple reel done to the tune of the pipe jig 'The Shaggy Grey Buck' (J.F. and T.M. Flett, 1964, 167). There are plenty of other 6/8 tunes in the early pipe collections, some of them specified as jigs, but increasingly adapted as marches, like 'The Hills of Glenorchy' or *Gairm nan Coileach* ('The Cock-crow'):

Ex. 7.5. *Gairm nan Coileach*

This is a Highland version of a tune known elsewhere as 'Joan's Placket' or 'Jumping John' (R.D. Cannon, 1972). Donald MacDonald printed it in 1822 with the Gaelic name, but later it became better known as 'The Cock of the North'.

A few old jigs remained as jigs, but in the later nineteenth century jig-playing fell into abeyance. Books printed in the 1840s contain some twenty jigs among every hundred tunes; but by 1900 the figure was more like five per hundred. Jigs had ceased to be required for dancing, and they were not taken up seriously in competitions until much later (see below, p. 146). Only the best ones survived: tunes like 'The Shaggy Grey Buck', 'The Stable Boys', 'The Thief of Lochaber'. Some of the most traditionally minded pipers kept up jig-playing. The great pibroch master, Calum MacPherson (1829–1898), used to play small tunes on the practice chanter as finger exercises — but only jigs, as one of his pupils recalled (J. MacDonald, 1955). Eighty years later, I asked Calum MacPherson's son, Angus, what tunes his father had played, and he cited the two last-named. By that time, for most pipers, as for most English and Scots people, the word 'jig' had come to mean 'Irish jig', and titles like 'Paddy Carey' and

'Cork Hill' had entered the pipe collections, to be followed later by original compositions, also with something of an Irish flavour. 'Center's Jig', by James Center (1879-1919), is one of these:

Ex. 7.6. Center's Jig (from J.A. MacLellan (1966))

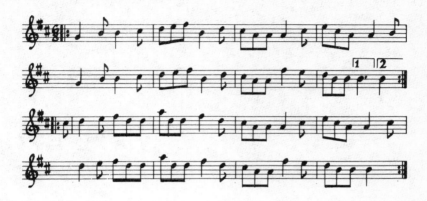

Strathspeys

While jigs declined, strathspeys flourished. Originally, the 'strathspey' was not a distinct genre, but was a style of reel-playing peculiar to the fiddle. It is thought to have developed in the mid-eighteenth century in the Central and Eastern Highlands. The word itself first appears in music in 1749 as an adjective — 'Strathspey reel' (G.S. Emmerson, 1971, 224). The strathspey style is characterised by extreme 'pointing': dotted rhythms played as if double dotted, and with a good deal of the reverse accent often called the 'Scotch snap'   , done by a special trick of the bow (F. Collinson, 1966, 221). The dances called 'strathspeys' are in the ordinary figures of reels and country dances, but done with a slow and especially springy step. Joseph MacDonald described the strathspey rhythm in 1760, but he did not use the term, and to him the rhythm denoted a typical violin reel as opposed to the rounder rhythm of the pipe reel. In other words, as far as he knew, strathspeys were not played on the pipes. Collections of Highland fiddle music published in the 1820s contain 'strathspeys' and 'pipe reels', but never a 'pipe strathspey'. Donald MacDonald published strathspeys for the pipes in 1822 and 1828, but they are mainly pipe settings of the best-known fiddle pieces ' 'Monymusk', 'Tullochgorum',

'The Bridge of Perth'. The dotted rhythms are present, but not much of
the reverse 'snap':

Ex. 7.7. Tulloch Gorum (from D. MacDonald (1822))

Among the earliest strathspeys attributed to a piper is MacBeth's
Strathspey:

Ex. 7.8. MacBeth's Strathspey

John MacBeth was piper to the Highland Society of London. He took
prizes for pibroch playing at the Society's competitions in 1825–1838, but
he was also a noted exponent of the lighter music. His tune was published
without a name in 1828, then under various names later on, and finally
attributed to him in 1889.[2] Whether MacBeth actually composed it, or
whether he made it popular, we cannot tell. It does however have very
much the feel of an original pipe tune, with its double tonic effect on the
keys of A and G (see above, p. 39).

In these early pipe settings of strathspeys, we tend to find unpointed
couplets ♩♩ . It is hard to tell whether they were actually played that
way — 'played round' as a piper would say — or whether the writer was
merely leaving it optional as between ♩♩ and ♩♩ . The really

sharp 'snap' , though perfectly playable, never seems to work so well on the pipes as on the fiddle, and I suspect this is because the short note really needs to be louder than the long one in order to produce the proper effect.

Like reels, strathspeys increasingly tended to be composed for competition rather than for dancing. Most of the really good simple strathspeys in circulation today are old ones which have stood the test of time — 'Cutty's Wedding', 'Munlochy Bridge', 'Loudon's Bonny Woods and Braes' and others to be found in any modern pipe collection. They generally have two parts only, and a considerable number of them are in keys other than A; especially D major. 'Orange and Blue' is one which has been arranged in many forms, including the best known of all Gaelic mouth-tunes, *Brochan lom, tana lom*:

Ex. 7.9. Orange and Blue (trad.)

Other dance tunes

Very few types of dance tune other than the three so far mentioned are found in pipe collections. The most important minority consists of jigs in 9/8 time. These are called 'slip jigs' in Ireland, and at one time they were 'hornpipes' in England (R.D. Cannon, 1972), but Scotland has no particular name for them. They have a long history as bagpipe tunes in England, and they may have reached the Highlands at an early date as well. It is noticeable that many of them seem to be versions of the same basic tune, and that many are connected with songs about weddings — usually bawdy songs unless they have been bowdlerised in print. The following tune belongs to an extended family which contains 'Drops of Brandy',

'Brose and Butter' and about twenty other variants from different parts of the British Isles (R.D. Cannon, 1972):

Ex. 7.10. Arlitrach, or The Faraway Wedding

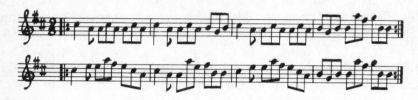

The intriguing rhythm presumably connects with a particular step in dancing (it is still used in one country dance 'Strip the Willow'), and it has tended to ensure that every piper knows a few of these tunes, though not usually more than a few.

Traditional dancing

During the nineteenth century the bagpipe was used less and less for ordinary social dancing, and by the time of the First World War it had practically been given up. But when J.F. and T.M. Flett undertook their researches in the 1950s they met a few old people in the Hebrides who remembered dances and pipe tunes from their young days (J.F. and T.M. Flett, 1964, 40, 42–5). A widespread dance was the 'Kissing Reel', or 'Babbity Bowster', in which the couples would kiss on a signal from the musician. In Barra and South Uist the dance was done to the pipes, and at the right moment the piper would play *pòg an toiseach* ('kiss first') several times:

Ex. 7.11.

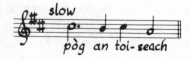

Piping held out in a few places under the influence of enlightened patrons, notably the family of Campbell of Kilberry. For many years up to 1914, the Kilberry Ball was an annual event. The servants of the house, and country people invited from miles around, danced all night, and the music was all pipe music. Reels were the main items, but by that date polkas and waltzes were in demand as well. Pipe Major Robert Meldrum, who played at Kilberry in the 1880s, composed or arranged several polkas, some of which are still played. The best known of these, now called 'Luberton Pipe Band' (unpublished), is a combination of two earlier ones, 'Mrs Captain Menzies' and 'The Kilberry Ball', which appeared in Logan's collection of pipe tunes (Books 4 and 5, about 1907), but both of them owe their inspiration to the favourite old polka, 'I have a bonnet trimmed with blue'. 'Mrs. Elder's Welcome' and 'The Pride of Scotland' are two examples of waltzes which had a short life as dance tunes before settling down as pipe-band slow marches (P. Henderson, 1900; Scots Guards collection, 1954).

Pipers often play at Highland Balls today, though only for a few dances. I have been unable to find out how old the practice is, or whether pipe music was once used more generally than it is today. The Northern Meeting Ball, held annually at Inverness from 1788, was not 'Highland' in character at first, but it became so as time went on. By the mid-nineteenth century, Highland dress was being worn (G.S. Emmerson, 1971, 110), and in 1859 the organisers of the Meeting took on the responsibility for a piping competition in addition to the Ball and other entertainments (W.L. Manson, 1901, 390). By 1870 or thereabouts, the pipes were certainly being played at the Ball, as we know from an anecdote of two pipers who got into trouble when they failed to turn up (M. MacInnes, 1951). At Balls today, the 'Gay Gordons' is often done to pipe music, the tunes being any selection of good familiar marches, but the dance for which the pipes are usually positively requested is the eightsome reel. The dance itself was created as a ballroom reel in the 1870s, and one of the venues mentioned for it is the Northern Meeting (J.F. and T.M. Flett, 1964, 134; G.S. Emmerson, 1971, 179). The tradition of piping the eightsome reel may well have continued unbroken from that time. Actual reels are usually played, though not invariably, and when a whole pipe band plays rather than a single piper, as at some Hogmanay extravaganza on radio or television, marches like 'The Barren Rocks of Aden' may be heard. The dance is a long one, about twelve minutes, and can be a major effort for the piper, especially as fast tunes are mentally more demanding than slow ones, and it is essential to keep track of how often each short measure has been played. It always begins and ends with the same tune, 'The Deil amang the Tailors', and in between come eight two-part reels played three times each. A good practice (or at any rate, my practice) is to use four tunes, one for each of the four men who dance the solo step in turn; then the same four tunes in the same order for their partners in their turn. 'The Deil' is not an original pipe tune, but it goes very well, and it can be traced back in pipe collections to a time well before the dance itself (W. MacKay, 1840).

Scottish country dancing

It is not generally realised that in many parts of Scotland the country dance is not an ancient 'folk' tradition. In their definitive study of the subject, J.F. and T.M. Flett have shown how country dancing came to Scotland from England about 1700 and spread mainly as a polite ballroom pastime. It reached the remoter Highlands and Islands only in the late nineteenth century, and never really took root there. The older reels gave place more or less directly to modern waltzes, foxtrots and quadrilles. Scottish country dancing today is a re-creation brought about by the efforts of the Royal Scottish Country Dance Society, founded in 1923. Most of the Society's dance groups use accordion bands (or recordings of the same), and pipe music in general is rather on the periphery, though by no means discouraged. In the Society's published books of tunes the music is set for piano, but alternative pipe tunes are also suggested. Dancers often claim that pipe music is difficult to dance to. In many cases this can be put down to the dancers' invincible inability to tell one tune from another: even when an accordion band is playing, many dancers listen to the beat alone, and not to the music. But pipers who play for dancing also often fail to appreciate what is wanted. Above all, the tune must sing out clearly with a real foot-tapping 'lift' to it; and if the piper is not quite in the Gold Medal class, and cannot keep a clear beat while still producing all the prescribed grace notes, then the grace notes must be cut down to what he can comfortably play. Collections of pipe music for dancing have been published (S. MacNeill, 1960, 42–48; J.A. MacLellan, 1966), but so far none of the instruction manuals gives any particular attention to dance music.

Competitive Highland dancing

What is now called 'Highland dancing' consists of certain step dances, mainly solo and (by tradition) mainly for men. Highland dances were featured as interludes in early piping contests, and by 1815, if not earlier, the dances themselves were being done in competition (J.F. and T.M. Flett, 1956). The idea that this kind of dancing originated as war-dances has not been confirmed in any way, though it does not sound altogether fanciful. Highland dancing has been and is encouraged in Highland Regiments of the Army, especially among the pipers, and the music is invariably pipe music. The steps are fully described in other books (*SOHBD*, 1955), but not much has ever been written about the tunes.

The 'Sword Dance' (or simply 'The Swords' to those who dance it) first appeared at a competition in 1832. Unlike some other Highland dances, it appears to have been a genuine folk dance (Emmerson, 1972, 245), and it was spoken of at the time as ancient (A. MacKay, 1838, 20). It is always danced to its own tune, *Gille Calum*, and in 1838 it was played by the champion piper 'to the high gratification of the audience, always enjoying this the most of any part of the whole [competition]' (J.G. Dalyell, 1849, 105). The champion on that occasion was John MacBeth, already mentioned (p. 112). The tune has appeared in many pipe collections since the 1840s, and could be found in fiddle books before that:

Ex. 7.12. *Gille Calum* 'The Ancient Sword Dance' (from A. MacKay (1843))

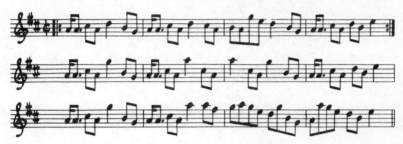

The name comes from the corresponding mouth-tune, of which the repeated chorus runs

Gille Calum dà pheighinn
Gille Calum dà pheighinn
Dà pheighinn, dà pheighinn
Gille Calum bonn-a-sia

'Gillie Calum twa pennies, Gillie Calum twa pennies, Twa pennies, twa pennies, Gillie Calum ae bawbee' (Fionn, 1896; K.N. MacDonald, 1901). Another verse is to the effect that 'I could get a wife for nothing ... a useless one for ae bawbee'. A suggestion which has often been made, that 'Gillie Calum' (literally, the lad Malcolm) was the eleventh-century King Malcolm Canmore, and that the money referred to was a tax introduced in his reign, seems to be completely without foundation. The words might be a corruption of some longer original narrative, but if so the narrative is lost. They do however fit the tune most aptly, and the 'l', 'm' and 'n' sounds, and the long 'a' of *dà*, even have the ring of pipers' *canntaireachd* about them (see above, p. 67). The sword dance begins in strathspey time, then changes to reel time. The strathspey part is actually one of the most difficult of all pipe tunes, and to judge from the written records it has been

E

getting stiffer as time has gone on. The full strathspey and reel form can be found in several modern collections (J. Wilson, ii, 1957; S. MacNeill, 1960; J.A. MacLellan, 1966b).

The 'Highland Fling', or simply 'The Fling', is usually danced to a strathspey called 'The Marquis of Huntly's Highland Fling', composed by one Thomas Jenkins, a teacher of Scottish dancing in London, in 1794. The dance also may be his invention. Previously the expression 'Highland Fling' referred only to a particular step used in a reel (J.F. and T.M. Flett, 1956). The tune is therefore not an original pipe tune, but it is a very fine one and has been printed in pipe collections since 1870.

The foursome reel seems to be a formalised version of the ordinary reels that were once the staple folk-dance of the Highlands. In its present form it is another of those which begin in strathspey time and then switch to a reel, in this case always the 'Reel of Tulloch'. *Seann Triubhas* is a solo exhibition dance with its own invariable tune, a version of 'Whistle o'er the lave o't'. In its song and fiddle forms this tune goes beyond the range of the pipe chanter, but the cut-down bagpipe version dates back to 1876 at least (David Glen's collection, Book 1), and is thoroughly naturalised.

More recent additions to the 'Highland' dance repertoire are the Sailors' Hornpipe and the Irish Jig. The hornpipe is a character-dance involving activities such as imaginary rope-climbing and peering out to sea, and is done in sailors' costume. The Irish jig is a solo stepping dance, often done in an eighteenth-century type of costume, in the Irish colours of saffron and green. Both are regularly danced at Highland games, to the music of the pipes, though how long it is since these admittedly non-Scottish dances came into the repertoire is not known. A few hornpipes and Irish (as opposed to Scottish) jig tunes have appeared sporadically in pipe-music collections since the 1840s, but both types of tune have taken on a new, and distinctively Scottish, lease of life more recently (see below, p. 146).

NOTES

1. Unless otherwise stated, all tunes in this chapter are quoted from one or more of the earliest five collections of pipe music D. MacDonald (1822 and 1828); W. MacKay (1840); A. MacKay (1843); W. Gunn (1847). Grace notes are omitted. Gaelic spellings are modernised.

2. *NP*, 22, No.6; D. MacDonald (1828), D. Glen, *Collection*, Part 4 (1889).

CHAPTER 8

Music in the Army

The Company piper

When Highland soldiers began to be recruited into armies, whether Scottish or English, pro-Government or rebel, pipers came with them. This seems to be quite certain, and if the records of the fact are patchy, it is most likely because the pipers existed on a semi-honorary footing, paid by individual officers, and not on the official payrolls (W.G.F. Boag, 1975). A Colonel of the Scots Guards wrote in 1671, 'With us any Captain may keep a piper in his Company, and maintain him too, for no pay is allowed him — perhaps just as much as he deserveth' (Scots Guards Collection, 1954, vi). Others were more enthusiastic, as in 1641: 'We are well provided of pypers; I have one for every company; and I think they are as good as drummers' (J.G. Dalyell, 1849, 23). It has been suggested indeed that Highland officers might simply have brought their own personal pipers with them (Anon., 1978). What is clear in all the early references is that the pipers were posted as individuals, to different companies, and this being so, it seems likely that for most of their duties they would have played solo, and not in organised groups. It is equally clear that the authorities, whether they liked them or not, accepted the pipers as essential, if Highland soldiers were to be brought under military discipline. Recruiting parties commonly went about with a piper playing; and there was a story told in the 1720s of a Captain who was ordered to add a piper and a drummer to his corps, 'as the men could scarcely be brought to march without them' (A.D. Fraser, 1907, 259).

The piper in battle

In clan warfare the piper had been a key figure. He played on the actual field of battle, and in the Army also the earlier accounts tell of the individual piper supporting the men in the actual fighting. At a battle in defence of Quebec in 1760, General James Murray commanded a mixed force of English regiments and Highlanders. It appears that at the outset he ordered the pipers not to play, but later, when the Highlanders were being beaten back, one of their officers went so far as to protest that the General had been wrong, and that even yet the pipes might be of use. Sure enough, 'the pipers being ordered to play a favourite *cruinneachadh*, the Highlanders, who were broken, returned ... and formed with great alacrity' (J. Ramsay, 1784). The pipes were a powerful weapon, but as General Murray must have known, they could be difficult to deploy in an orderly fashion. At the battle of Maya in 1813, the Pipe Major of the 92nd Regiment took it on himself to play without orders. 'The result was as anticipated. The Highlanders could barely await the word of command.' The General told him not to play again until ordered. He ignored this and played again. He was commanded to keep quiet on pain of death, but when a rival English brigade came into sight he started again. This time the Scots charged and the French ran, but it was a bloody and Pyrrhic victory (L. Winstock, 1970, 139). Most stories of the pipers are more favourable than this, and most of them are probably true. There was George Clark, at Vimeira in 1808, playing on the ground long after he had been wounded in the groin; and John MacLauchlan, the first man to reach the top of the walls at Badajoz in 1812, who was killed in the following year, while playing, at Vittoria. There was Kenneth MacKay who played the old pibroch *Cogadh no Sìth* around the outside of the British Square at Waterloo, and many more. They all knew that 'the paramount duty of the piper was indeed to play the men into battle and to keep playing as long as he was able' (L. Winstock, 138). And, under increasingly effective military discipline, pipers continued to fight in this way down to modern times. Not until well into the First World War did the authorities finally decide that pipers were too valuable in their supporting role to be risked in the front line. As late as 1918 an officer could write that not only were pipers too difficult to replace, but that also 'when the men heard the pipes they would lose control of themselves, and in their eagerness to get forward would be apt to rush into their own barrage' (B. Seton and J. Grant, 1920, 74).

Some writers seem to have assumed that the piper playing on the field chose a particular tune that would be known to the men; even a prescribed signal tune for the charge. In later times, regiments did in fact specify tunes for this purpose, but whether anyone remembered them in the heat of the moment is another matter. A story told after the Battle of Tel-el-Kebir in 1882 has the ring of truth. The Pipe Major was asked what tune he had played as the Highland Brigade charged forward. He said, 'I just played "The Braes of Mar", and then anything that came into ma heid' (D.J.S. Murray, 1975).

Duty tunes

On manoeuvres, or in camp, however, tunes were laid down for the various standing orders. The earliest known list of such tunes, dated 1778, contains five pieces, all of which can be identified as pibrochs:

Gathering	Coagive na Shea	(i.e. *Cògadh no Sith*, 'War or Peace')
Revellee	Glais Vair	(*A' Ghlas Mheur*, 'The Finger Look')
The Troop	Boadach na brigishin	(*Bodaich nam brìogaisean*, 'The Carles with the breeks')
Retreat	Gilly Christie	(*Cill Chrìosd*, 'The raid of Kilchrist')
Tatoo	Molly defshit Mahary	(probably *Moladh Mairi*, 'Mary's Praise')

The regiment concerned was the Argyll or Western Fencible Regiment, which existed only from 1778 to 1783 (A. Campbell, 1967). No doubt it was composed mainly of Gaelic-speaking Highlanders. It had two 'duty pipers', one of whom took the first prize for pibroch playing at the competition in Falkirk in 1782. A similar, longer list of tunes has been published (J. Logan, 1831, 11, 297), as taken from the 'orderly book' of the 72nd Highlanders, who were raised in 1778. The original of this has not been seen, and its authenticity has been doubted (D.J.S. Murray, 1975). In any case, even if pibrochs could have been used as call signs in a local Fencible regiment of Highlanders, Colonel Murray points out that they would hardly have been suitable in the greatly expanded Line Regiments of the Regular Army, during the Napoleonic wars. As early as 1815, in the nominally Highland regiments, more than half the soldiers were Lowland or English. Written lists of orderly pipers' tunes are lacking for the whole of the nineteenth century. They must surely exist somewhere, perhaps in private manuscripts written by soldier-pipers for their own use. Unfortunately, no such books have yet found their way into library collections. Early twentieth-century records are available, and it is interesting to find some degree of uniformity between regiments, at least as regards the most-used tunes. 'Reveille' is always 'Johnny Cope'; the call to a meal, especially breakfast, is 'Brose and Butter'; the March Past is often, though not always, 'Highland Laddie'; marching out of the Barracks, 'MacDonald's awa' tae the Wars'; Lights Out, 'Soldier lie doon'. It is noticeable that by no means all the tunes concerned are to be found in the earliest group of printed pipe collections — the ones before 1850 which enshrine so much of the original 'oral tradition' of piping. I suggest, tentatively, that most of them were adopted around the time of the Crimean War, and that they were picked by the officers on the basis of their titles rather than for their suitability or previous popularity as pipe tunes. Many regiments have a special 'Long Reveille', called by some of them 'The Crimean Long Reveille', which is played once a month. It is a medley of tunes of varied character, typically as follows: in slow time, 'The Soldier's Return', 'Granny Duncan', 'Erchless Castle', 'And sae will we yet'; then in quick time the reel 'Miss Girdle' and lastly the usual 'Johnny Cope'. It is thought to have originated when a brigade of three Highland regiments were at the Crimea, and to have been played ever since in memory of that time, though if so it has spread to other regiments since.[1] Another Crimean reference is the tune 'Robbie Ross', or 'Sir Colin Campbell's Farewell to the Crimea' (see below, Ex. 8.10), played as 'Lights Out' in the 93rd Regiment (J. & A. Campbell, 1908). Some of the tunes are now played only in these particular contexts. 'Granny Duncan' is a particularly odd one:

Ex. 8.1. Granny Duncan (from A.F. Cannon MS (1916))

It seems to be a slow air, borrowed from some long-forgotten song or fife tune. Probably the low G's were originally G sharp.

Marching

Today, the dominant function of the Army piper is to provide marching music. It may always have been so — we recall the account of Irish pipers on the march in London as early as the sixteenth century (above, p. 8). Whether the soldiers ever marched in step to the music in those early days is not known. Perhaps only the piper did so, strutting along in his accustomed way. We hear of pipes being used for marching in 1714, when the Highland Company of the Scots Guards marched through London 'arrayed in Caledonian Dress and preceded by their Pyper' (Scots Guards, 1954), and in 1739, when 'a very numerous body of sturdy Highlanders' from the far North of Scotland marched into Edinburgh, a piper playing before them (J.G. Dalyell, 1849, 23). Occasionally we are told what tunes were played. In 1716, 'when Argyle's Highlanders entered Perth and

Dundee ... every company had their distinct pypers, playing three distinct springs or tunes. The first played ... *The Campbells are coming, oho, oho*', the second *Wilt thou play me fair play, Highland Ladie*, the third *Stay and take the breiks with thee*', and the writer says that at one point the prisoners in the tolbooth of Dundee picked up the first tune and sang the words, 'which mortified the Jacobites' (Dalyell). As with all such early references, we cannot be sure that the writer has not just picked on three well-known song titles to make his political point; but at least we can conclude that he felt that such tunes might be heard on a bagpipe. Later sources are perhaps more trustworthy. In memoirs of the Peninsular War, pipe tunes are occasionally mentioned by name, and they include (again) 'The Campbells are Coming', 'Johnny Cope' and the 'Haughs of Cromdale' (L. Winstock, 138).

Also by the 1800s, we begin to hear of particular tunes being associated with particular units. The 'quicksteps' of the Sutherland and Breadalbane Fencibles, published by William MacKay in 1840, were the well-known 'Glengarry's March' and 'Stumpie'. These Fencible Regiments had only short periods of existence (1779–83 and 1793–1802 respectively; see D. Stuart, ii, 305, 315), so we have a good idea of when the tunes were played. Tunes associated with Line Regiments include 'The Highland Plaid' ('March of the 92nd Highlanders', *Celtic Melodies*, 1830) and 'Highland Laddie', named in connection with both the 42nd and 73rd Highlanders (W. MacKay, 1840; J. Aird, ii, c.1790). We cannot assume that these tunes were always played on the pipes when they were used for marching, but it is certain that by 1828, bagpipe marches were well established, as we see from the title and contents of Donald MacDonald's collection of 'Quicksteps, Strathspeys, Reels and Jigs'. Pipe tunes with purely regimental titles, like 'The 74th Highlanders March', begin to multiply after 1840. They are undoubtedly pipers' compositions, and would have been played on the pipes from the start.

It might be thought that each regiment would have its own marching tunes by which it might be recognised, but there is no clear indication of such a thing, and it is more likely that the tunes used were chosen by the Pipe Major, or the Commanding Officer if he was sufficiently interested. The names are best understood as dedications by the composer to his particular unit, possibly with, but more likely without, any sort of authority. Not until 1881 do we find lists of regimental marches laid down by Army orders, and even these were not necessarily followed for all time. From time to time, surveys have been carried out in the Army, enquiring what tunes are actually used in practice. These have revealed considerable variety, and one thing which is clear is that there is no relation between the historical associations of the tunes (whether real or fanciful) and the clan associations of the regiments, as defined by the regions where they were first raised, or the tartans which they now wear.

Quicksteps — 2/4 time

The classic tune of this type is 'Highland Laddie'. It was well known in the eighteenth century and served as the air to many songs, old and new, even including Methodist hymns (W. Chappell, ii, 748; G.F. Graham, 1908, 166). Its title made it a natural choice for a Highland march. Many of the songs had refrains along the lines of

> Where ha' ye been a' the day
> Bonnie laddie, Highland Laddie?
> Saw ye him that's far away
> Bonnie Laddie, Highland Laddie?

In the song versions, the second part of the melody does not fit the pipe chanter, but the version adapted to the pipes in Donald MacDonald's book (1828) is quite successful, and has been known to every piper since that time:

Ex. 8.2. The Highland Laddie

Tunes in this basic rhythm, with runs of semiquavers and the characteristic three-note beat at the end, had been well known since before 1700. They were called 'Scotch Measure' until around 1750, when they became 'hornpipes', replacing an earlier type of hornpipe in triple time (R.D. Cannon, 1972; G.S. Emmerson, 1972, Ch.14), and many of them can be found in military fife collections as 'Quicksteps'. It seems that the pipers took their inspiration, and some of the actual tunes, from the fifers.

The equally well-known 'Johnny Cope' is of somewhat similar character. It is the air of Burns's song 'Hey Johnny Cope are ye waukin yet?' and it too has had to be adapted to the pipes, in a different way. The original, one of the finest of all Scots melodies, is in a minor key, moving to the relative major at the beginning of the second measure, then back to the minor:

Ex. 8.3. Johnie Cope (arr. J. Johnson, vol. iii (1790))

The earliest printed pipe setting (William MacKay, 1840) is a barbarous distortion with all the C notes played as 'C' on the chanter which actually gives C sharp. Evidently MacKay felt it essential to preserve A as the key note: I suspect that he merely lifted a version that had been written out previously for the fife. A revised version given by Angus MacKay (1843) is somewhat better. It avoids many of the C's, and is the basis of what is played today:

Ex. 8.4. Johnny Cope (from A. MacKay (1843))

Later still, a much more tuneful version in B minor was published by W. Ross (1869), but it has not displaced the A version. The persistence of such a poor setting may well be due to its having been adopted early on as the Army Reveille tune and then handed down in writing instead of by ear. Besides such well-known tunes as these, Donald MacDonald's book contains a number of others in the same rhythm which give a strong impression of having been composed especially for the pipes. A minor puzzle is that they are all nameless, though most of them appear with names in later collections. They are mostly rather dull tunes, and none of them is played today. But they are interesting for precisely that reason, since they suggest that the habit of composing pipe quicksteps was still fairly new, dating perhaps not earlier than the beginning of the century. Here is a typical one:

Ex. 8.5. Murray of Harris's March (from D. MacDonald (1828); cf. W. Ross (1869))

Really good new pipe tunes in the 'Scotch measure' began to be composed from the mid-nineteenth century onwards. 'The Earl of Mansfield', attributed to John MacEwen of the 92nd Highlanders,[2] is a simple and attractive one, and 'The 79th's Farewell to Gibraltar' by Pipe Major John MacDonald, dated to 1848, must be one of the best pipe tunes of all time:

Ex. 8.6. The 79th's Farewell to Gibraltar (from D. Glen, ix (1899))

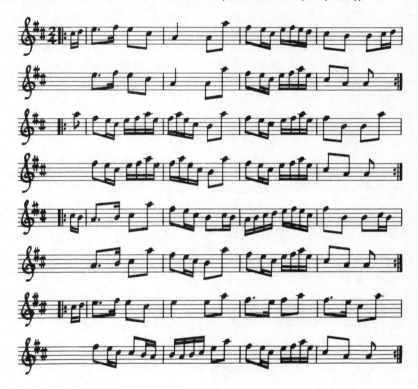

It is worth mentioning that there are very many tunes commemorating military events — well-known battles like the Siege of Delhi or the Battle of the Alma, or completely obscure troop movements such as 'The 93rd's Welcome to Parkhurst'. It should not be thought that these were in any sense commissioned pieces, still less that they were actually played at the time on the march or in the battle; nor yet that 'Welcomes' are cheerful tunes and 'Farewells' sad ones. It is purely a convention, which continues in full force to the present day. Pipers compose tunes, and name them after some place or person they know, or after some event in which (usually) they took part. A Pipe Major, however, might be asked to produce a tune in honour of some person or event, and he will often have something recently composed, waiting to be named.

Of the more demanding quicksteps, relatively few are adaptations from elsewhere. 'The Highland Wedding', 'The Duke of Roxburgh's Farewell to the Blackmount' and 'The Abercairney Highlanders' are arrangements by Angus MacKay, but his excellent march 'The Balmoral Highlanders' is apparently original (A. Campbell, 1958a), and so are most of the later ones, many of them by known composers such as Hugh MacKay (1801–1864; *NP, 24*, No.5, Feb. 1972). Simpler tunes in 2/4 time, not in the Scots measure, and in fact more suitable for marching, have accumulated gradually. Airs from songs like 'A man's a man for a' that', 'The Haughs o' Cromdale' and 'Duncan Grey' date back to the fife era. An early and outstanding pipe composition is 'The Barren Rocks of Aden' (c.1843, see above, p. 43):

Ex. 8.7. The Barren Rocks of Aden

Most leading pipers seem to have composed one or two pieces in this vein, such as 'Norman Orr Ewing' by Pipe Major William Ross. They tend to avoid runs of semiquavers, and the pointing or otherwise of the pairs of quavers (𝆕 or 𝆕) is essential to the rhythm, not merely an optional means of expression.

Quicksteps — 6/8 time

Entirely distinct as a class, and equally old-established, are marches in 6/8 time. The earliest ones have the character of Highland jigs, slowed down, such as *Bail' Inbhearaora* (The Campbells are Coming), which appears in all five of the earliest pipe manuals, and 'Over the Water to Charlie'

(W. MacKay, 1840), but one of the best is somewhat different, 'Pibroch of Donald Dhu':

Ex. 8.8. *Piobaireachd Dhomhnuill Dhuibh*

This tune is in many pipe collections, from William MacKay (1840) onwards, and it is in fact much older. A Northumbrian pipe setting was printed in 1805 (J. Peacock) and a Scottish fiddle version in 1760 (J. Oswald, xii). Before that, it was in circulation as a violin pibroch (D. Johnson, 1984), and its ultimate origin must have been the pibroch which is still played on the pipes, though nowadays regarded as a completely separate piece. Many excellent 'six-eights' have been composed by pipers, and they are popular with pipe bands. They lend themselves to the steady kilt-swinging pace of the Highland regiments, especially the more modern ones which tend to be less jig-like in character (see below, p. 157).

Retreats

A long-standing custom in the Army is 'beating retreat'. It had its origin in drum signals used to call the men back into camp at the end of the day, to be followed by posting of guards, meals and relaxation. From this it has developed into an evening performance by the Regimental Band, or the Pipe Band (R.J. Powell, 1985). Retreat marches are found in fife manuscripts, sometimes titled in the French spelling, *Retrait*. They are mostly more sentimental in character than quicksteps, and when retreats began to be played on the pipes, it was natural that slow or slowish Highland airs should be pressed into service. One of the characteristic rhythms of Gaelic song is 3/4, as in the well-known 'Mingulay Boat Song', and it seems to have become accepted that airs in 3/4 time are retreats, and

vice versa. One of the earliest tunes on record is variously called
'MacGregor's Search', 'MacGregor's Lament' or 'MacGregor of Rora':

Ex. 8.9. MacGregor's Lament (from W. Ross (1885))

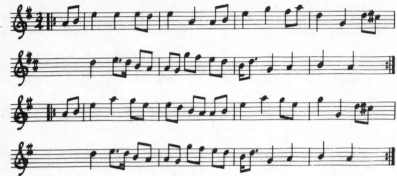

There are several versions of this tune, and they all seem (to me) a little
confused in the last three bars of each part. Possibly the reason is that this is
essentially a song air, which was not intended to be tied down to a strict
marching beat. Other 'three-fours' are more straightforward:

Ex. 8.10. Sir Colin Campbell (from R. MacKenzie (1901))

Two curious points arise concerning the notation of these tunes. One is
that the 'feel' of the rhythm is often closer to 6/4 than the 3/4 which is
usually written:

Ex. 8.11. Lochan Side (J. MacLellan (1905); arr. R.D.C.)

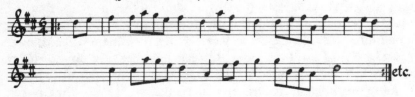

The other point is that there has been some disagreement about the placing
of the bar lines. The pulse of the music is usually ♫ ♩ ♩ ♫ ♩ ♩ ,
and it can be barred |♫ ♩ ♩ |♫ ♩ ♩ | or else ♫ | ♩ ♩ ♫ | ♩ ♩ .
The theoretical point in favour of the first barring is that the first beat

comes after the first bar line. The theoretical point in favour of the second barring is that the first *strong* beat comes after the first bar line, even though this beat happens to be the second beat of the tune. The practical point is that, in marching, by common consent, the beat immediately after the first bar line of any tune is the point where the left foot falls. Clearly when pipers play together the notation must be determined beforehand. The first of the two ways just mentioned now seems to be practically standard, but it was not always so; in fact, when the two books of the *Army Manual of Bagpipe Tunes* were published, the rule was changed from Book 1 (1934) to Book 2 (1936).

A few other tunes in 3/4 time are scattered through the nineteenth-century pipe collections, but the growth of new compositions really began about the time of the First World War. Many of these are outstanding, and some have found their way into circulation as song tunes, at least among modern folk singers, thus reversing the earlier pattern. An example is 'The Bloody Fields of Flanders' by Pipe Major John McLellan of Dunoon. If I have a personal favourite among these tunes, however, it is Pipe Major George S. MacLennan's 'Kilworth Hills':

Ex. 8.12. Kilworth Hills (from G.S. MacLennan (1929))

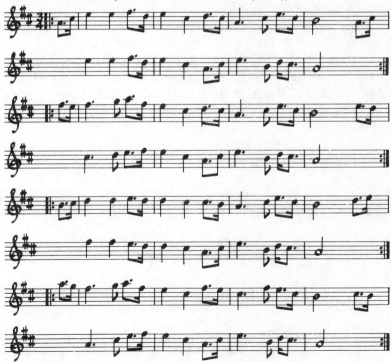

A few retreats are in 9/8 time. This is probably a development from 3/4 time, and indeed some 3/4 marches do tend to sound like 9/8, especially if they have a few tied triplets  interspersed with the dotted note-pairs ♩♪ . 'The Battle of the Somme', by William Laurie, is, however, unquestionably in compound triple time:

Ex. 8.13. The Battle of the Somme (from Scots Guards Collection (1954), cf. *NP 22*, No.2)

Slow marches

These are defined by Army orders as having sixty-five paces to the minute (see, for example, *Drill*, 1965) though in practice, sixty paces is quite common. In the older pipe-music collections, only a very few marches are actually designated as slow, and one is left wondering whether the pipes were ordinarily used for slow marching before, say, 1900. Some of these older slow marches are in 2/4 'Scotch measure', but since 1900, 6/8 time has become common. The tunes are mostly adaptations of Gaelic songs, such as the famous 'Skye Boat Song'. One of the best is 'My Home', a slowed-down version of the song *Mo Dhachaidh*, which was written in the 1890s to an older air which had originally been a vigorous dancing jig (R.D. Cannon, 1979):

Ex. 8.14. My Home

An alternative rhythm used in slow marches is based mainly on two-note figures, either in 6/8 time (♩ ♪) or 2/4 (♪♩). The classic early example is 'Loch Duich', said to have been composed by a piper, Christopher MacRae, as early as 1804 (R. Walker, 1967) but not widely known until about 1907, and a well-known more modern one is 'Loch Rannoch':

Ex. 8.15. Loch Rannoch (from J. Wilson (1937) and Scots Guards Collection (1954))

This is the work of Pipe Major John Wilson, and is usually considered to be an original composition, but the composer himself has explained in his autobiography (1978) how he took the basic idea from a Gaelic song, *Mo Ribhinn Choibhneil*. No doubt similar explanations lie behind a good many other pipe tunes. The distinction between a composition and an arrangement is often hard to draw.

NOTES

1. The medley is printed in W. Gray & J. Seton (1922) and W. Fergusson (1939); and more recently in the *Cabar Feidh Collection* (1983), from a manuscript of 1886. The present writer has a manuscript copy made by A.F. Cannon (Royal Scots), 1916. The history of the medley is discussed by J.M. MacKenzie (1970).

2. W. Ross, 1876, 200. D. Glen, *Collection*, Book 12, p.24; *NP, 23*, No.8.

CHAPTER 9

Competition Music

The idea of musical contests is very old, and it would be natural that the most skilled players, especially such individualists as pipers tend to be, should meet, when they met at all, as rivals. Angus MacKay (1838) recorded tales of jealousy, and even violence, among the early Highland pipers, which, if not specifically true, may well have been true to life in a more general sense. As far as organised competitions for pipe music are concerned, however, we have already seen how these began in 1781. The competitions run by the Highland Society were for pibroch playing only, then later also for dancing. The small music was not admitted, even though pipe music was used for the dances, and most of the dancers were pipers. Not until 1832 was it suggested that a competition for strathspey and reel playing might be included, and even then the idea was rejected by the organisers. It was even said that pibroch players regarded such music as beneath their dignity (A. Campbell, 1948, 7). This idea is not supported by anything else we know of pipers at that time. Joseph MacDonald (1760) makes it clear that reels and jigs were cultivated by the best players and played with grace-note technique not unlike that of *ceòl mór* (see above, p. 107). The tune 'Reel of Tulloch' enjoyed the designation *Rìgh nam Port*, 'King of Tunes' (D. MacDonald 1822), and the Highland Society records themselves show that the champion prize winners often provided music for the dances (see above, p. 117).

Competitions for reels, strathspeys and quickstep marches probably started at the rural Highland Games which began to proliferate in the 1820s. But little research has been done on the history of these, and so far we can offer only a few references thrown up incidentally in the records of the more prestigious pibroch events. Thus it is that we hear of a prize for reel playing at Muthill in 1831 (HSL Notes, 32), and for 'dance music', unspecified, at Glasgow in 1841, where the 1st, 2nd and 3rd prizes were won by John MacBeth, Duncan Campbell and William Gunn — all three well known in piping history (N. MacLeod, 1841). As for quickstep march competitions, one usually reliable authority places the beginning of these about 1830, though he does not quote his source (*NP, 19*, No.7).

Sooner or later it became the custom for strathspeys and reels to be grouped together in 'sets', one tune of each type, and in modern competitions this is invariably the case. Some Highland dances consist of strathspey and reel sections, and perhaps this is the origin of the custom. The major modern *ceòl beag* competitions include three types of event: strathspey and reel; march; and the full set of march, strathspey and reel.

The tunes of a set are played straight through without a pause and without any kind of extempore linking-up passage. The tempo and phrasing at the transition have to be managed very carefully, and they are keenly judged. The reel is faster than the strathspey, but most players today begin the reel a trifle slow and speed up within the first one or two bars. Less obvious, though sometimes effective, is a slight speeding of the strathspey just before the reel.

We might expect that certain sets of tunes would have become especially popular in time, but there is little sign of this. In 1869, William Ross published a collection of tunes with strathspeys and reels paired off in sets; but he abandoned the arrangement in his next edition (1876), and no other editor has followed suit. Three tunes linked by name — the march, strathspey and reel 'Donald Cameron', 'Maggie Cameron' and 'Sandy Cameron' — happen also to be particularly well matched, and are sometimes heard. There is also one tune, *Cabar Feidh*, which exists in all three forms, and which is sometimes played as a set, but these are exceptions. Nor has any composer ever designed new tunes in suites of any kind, though this might be a profitable way to build out from the existing range of pipe music.

Many competitions have a rule which actually prevents tunes being fixed into permanent sets. The competitors submit lists of a certain number of tunes of each type, and the judges pick one of each at the last moment. If the player has to put forward six strathspeys and six reels, it is no exaggeration to say that he must previously have thought out and practised all thirty-six possible combinations.

Competition tunes today are usually of four measures — four 'parts' as pipers always say — sometimes more, but never less. It seems unlikely that this was always so. Although multi-part reels do occur in older books, two parts was the common number, and it may be that a two-part tune played twice through was enough. Three-part tunes tend to appear in the mid-nineteenth century, and Ross said (1869) that they should always be played as four parts, in the order, 1, 2, 3, 2.

A fair proportion of competition strathspeys and reels are old tunes which have been extended gradually with extra parts. The reel 'If Charlie Comes', or 'Charlie's Welcome', is in Ross's collection of 1869 with two parts, no more difficult to play than any other. In MacKinnon's collection

(1884) it has four parts, and by the 1930s it had become a six-part competition piece with finger movements which make it one of the hardest of all to play, and one of the most exciting to listen to when well played. Sometimes the history of a tune is quite complex (R.D. Cannon, 1984). The strathspey 'Arniston Castle' originally had two parts, corresponding to parts 3 and 4 of the present version. Parts 1 and 2 came into being as 'J.D.K. MacCallum Esqr's Strathspey', composed by Pipe Major J. Paton, but the two tunes became associated. 'J.D.K. MacCallum' was renamed 'Arniston Castle'; a third two-part tune appeared, combining features of both; then the four parts were put together; and the final definitive version, published in 1899, incorporated features that could be traced back to every one of its predecessors. The whole tune crystallised over a period of twenty-five years.

Marches on the other hand have largely resisted elaboration. The older two-part ones have either dropped out of use or have been relegated to non-competitive playing, and most of the tunes played today are basically as the composers left them. A possible exception is the six-part march 'Donald Cameron'. It was printed in David Glen's collection (Book 3, 1886) with the last four parts separately titled as parts of other tunes. But Glen called his setting a 'new arrangement', and it is not clear that the familiar tune is the 'Hotch Potch' he claimed it to be.

All three types of composition tunes have evolved away from their original dancing and marching purposes to become distinctive kinds of music. Here is a typical reel, as heard in competition today:

Ex. 9.1. The Rejected Suitor (from Scots Guards' Collection, 1954)

Sixty years or so ago such a tune would have been printed without the alternate dots and semiquavers; whether it would have been played so at that time is not known. I do however feel safe in saying that originally it would have been played 'round' and much faster than today, since it was certainly a true dancing reel. The following settings of the opening bars show how it has been elaborated over the years:

Ex. 9.2. (arr. W. Gunn (1847))

Ex. 9.3. (arr. D. Glen, v (1890))

Ex. 9.4. (arr. W. Ross, i (1925))

Ex. 9.5. (arr. W. Ross (Scots Guards' Collection, 1954))

As the tempo becomes slower there is more room — and more need — for grace notes and unequal timings to point up the expression. Modern competition reels, of which excellent examples continue to appear, tend to have these features built in, and they cannot be simplified into dancing reels without violating the composer's intentions. One thinks here of tunes like 'John Morrison of Assynt House' by Pipe Major Peter MacLeod. John Wilson (1977) told the story of how he first encountered the tune in 1934. MacLeod was having difficulty in persuading pipers to play his new tune, and Wilson was equally put off by the 'new intricate fingering'. But he gradually mastered it and included the tune in his collection published in 1937, along with others which soon became competition classics.

'Arniston Castle' is a typical competition strathspey:

Ex. 9.6. Arniston Castle (from W. Ross, ii (c.1928))

Like all the best pipe tunes, it lies well under the fingers as well as being a
good melody. By this I mean especially that the pointings of pairs of notes,
long-short or short-long, are generally in the direction that the fingers are
apt to go. The long E and short A in bar 1 correspond to a quick tap of the
single E finger of the upper hand, while the short D, C and B of bar 2 are
done with a vigorous closing of the lower-hand fingers onto the chanter.
(Non-pipers may like to refer back to the finger chart, p. 32, at this point.)
The reverse-pointed couplets are essential to the tune. In older settings
they usually have minimal grace notes, as shown here at (a), but in
competition playing they have been elaborated with doublings (b).
Beginners practise the doubling slowly as at (c), but the final effect is more
like (d):

Ex. 9.7.

These movements have to be played particularly cleanly and smoothly to maintain the required 'lift' — the pipers' term of approval for the effect of a really well-played strathspey.

New competition strathspeys appear from time to time, but the peak of composition seems to have been passed in the last quarter of the nineteenth century. In present-day competitions, the variety of different strathspeys to be heard is generally less than the variety of other types of tune.

March playing has also developed considerably under the influence of the competition. In the 1870s, tunes as simple as 'The Earl of Mansfield' or various six-eights were regularly played, even by leading pipers (A. Campbell, 1968–9); but 'heavier' tunes were coming in rapidly. The four prize-winning marches at a competition in Edinburgh in 1886 were all tunes which can still be heard today: 'Bonnie Anne', 'The Atholl Highlanders' March to Loch Katrine', 'The 74th's Farewell to Edinburgh' and 'Abercairney Highlanders' (R.A. Marr, 1887). The following example, 'The Stirlingshire Militia', is also a standard piece. It can be dated to about 1860, since the composer, Hugh MacKay, was Pipe Major of the Stirlingshire Militia from 1852 until his death in 1864 (*NP, 24*, No.18):

Ex. 9.8. The Stirlingshire Militia (from W. Ross, i (rev.ed., 1950))

Typical features are the four parts, the large number of four-note runs, the very sharp pointing, and the key of A. Tunes in D, which may look equally complex on paper, are technically easier and are not usually heard in competitions. As with 'Arniston Castle', the pointing suits the fingers, as well as enhancing the melody.

There are probably more competition marches on record than strathspeys and reels together, but it must be admitted that many of them are extremely dull. They are preserved in print, but would not have survived in an oral tradition. There is general agreement among pipers as to which ones are really worth playing. Books like William Ross's collection (five volumes, 1925–1950) contain most of the best examples available at that time. Good tunes continue to appear, but in a present-day competition most of the marches will be old-established; less varied in number than the reels, more so than the strathspeys.

The formative period of the competition march was from about 1860 to about 1900, and the style of playing seems to have changed considerably over that time. The tunes are essentially 'Scotch measures' (see above, p. 125). When such tunes are played by fiddlers today, or used as reels by country dance bands, they are played at fairly fast tempo and with the semiquavers fairly even. This tempo is suitable for ordinary quick marching, and it seems to have been the normal pipe tempo. The designation 'quickstep' for these tunes continued to be used until the 1880s. My own earliest teachers, who played as taught by others who had played before 1900, always played this way. They played 'The Siege of Delhi', 'The 79th's Farewell to Gibraltar', or the '25th KOSB's Farewell to Meerut' at a round fast pace, almost interchangeable with 'The Barren Rocks of Aden' or 'The High Road to Gairloch'. When an uncle of mine joined the Army as a piper in 1914, he brought back home with him a different style, slower and more pointed. I have been assured by older pipers who were much closer to the centre of piping than my forbears were, that the round style was once normal. The style of today is very different. It is much slower. The piper does not so much 'march' around the platform as stalk around in a stilted manner, sometimes with an up-or-down motion exaggerated to the point of parody. The best players of course (and especially the military pipers) do contrive a manly, martial gait in spite of the tempo, but it is obvious that what we see today is a drastic slowing from the march tempo of early times. As we see in the tune just quoted, every semiquaver pair is pointed into ♩ or ♩ , and often the pointing is sharper still.

John MacColl was one leading player in the 'round' style, who retired from competition as the new style came in. The late David Ross, who remembered MacColl's playing in the 1900s, dated the change to that time. Non-competing players may well have lagged behind. A recording made as late as the 1930s by Henry Forsyth, piper to King George V, seems to preserve the old way (HMV B1820). It does not contain any of the 'heaviest' marches, but 'Murray's Welcome' and 'Niel Gow' are played round and fast. Forsyth served in the Scots Guards from 1887, became Pipe Major in 1895, and was piper to the King from 1910 to 1941 (*NP, 21* No.4). In playing ability he was a typical Army piper of the time, as I have been assured by the late Captain D.R. MacLennan. On the other hand, Pipe Major William Ross, who followed Forsyth as Pipe Major in the same Regiment, but was the leading player of his day, played his marches fully pointed in the modern style — though still a good deal faster than later players. A fine recording of his 'Abercairney Highlanders' proves the point (Parlophone, F3118). The late Archibald Campbell of Kilberry wrote (1968–9) an interesting critique of march playing as it had evolved over his lifetime. His recollections began with the late 1890s. He made no reference to the change of tempo just mentioned, except for a passing reference to tinker pipers, which suggests that they too were still playing the old style in his early days. He did however criticise the increased burden of grace noting which successive players laid on the tunes, especially under the influence of G.S. MacLennan who competed from about 1910 to 1928. Except in one detail, the MacLennan style has won the day, but in fairness it must be said that, according to the printed record, grace noting has been getting gradually more complicated ever since the beginning of the competition era.

The detail just mentioned consisted of the addition of one beat to the 'birl' or doubling of low A which occurs in the closing phrase of many marches. For example, the last two notes in bar 8 of 'The Stirlingshire Militia' are normally played as shown here (a), or in conventional notation (b). MacLennan's extra beat is shown at (c), conventionally written (d):

Ex. 9.9. The Birl (a, b) and 'G-grace noted birl' (c, d)

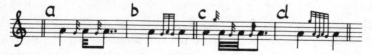

Several leading players were adding the high G grace note in the 1920s, but on one notorious occasion they were put out of the prize list by judges who held out for the simpler form. The resulting controversy has continued to the present day,[1] but the extended birl has ceased to be played, at least in public, in this particular context.

In the article already referred to, Kilberry noted a number of other points of style in competition marches, as opposed to what he called 'road quicksteps' meaning the ordinary march like 'Barren Rocks of Aden'. A tune like 'Barren Rocks' 'plays itself', he said, meaning that the dotting and semiquavering are integral to the tune, and could not be altered. But in the competition march the pointing is more discretionary, and Kilberry thought that certain rules of taste should apply. The note high A, for example, should never be cut short; and low A should only rarely be cut. In practice these rules are generally followed, though in my opinion it is as much a question of finger-movements as of purely musical judgement, just as in the strathspey already quoted. A more subtle point is that the closing phrase of a march can be enhanced by extra pointing of the notes before it, thus . These are only a few of the finer points which players have to consider, and they are mentioned here only to emphasise that march playing — and *ceòl beag* generally — today involves a great deal of the 'art that conceals art', while at the same time the styles have become conventionalised to a high degree. A poor, or merely fairly good player, can be overburdened with technique, but the best players combine superb fingering with a real flair for rhythm and style. A prizewinning performance can be an unforgettable experience.

NOTE

1. The *Piping Times* alone has printed the following articles and letters on the 'birl controversy', over a period of thirty years:
A. MacNeill, Letter, *PT, 1*, No.2.
'Veritas', "To 'G' or not to 'G'", *PT, 1*, No.4.
A. Campbell "The grace-noting of competition marches", *PT, 1*, No.5.
W. Gray, Letter, *PT, 1*, No.5.
A. MacNeill, Letter, *PT, 1*, No.8.
D.S. Sinclair, Letter, *PT, 13*, No.6.
D.R. MacLennan, "Where have all the birls gone", *PT, 17*, No.8.
T. Pearston, "The G grace note on the Birl", *PT, 20*, No.2.
S. MacNeill, "Birls and Blobs", *PT, 29*, No.9.
S. MacNeill, "Birls and Blobs, part 2", *PT, 30*, No.1.
J.A. MacLellan, Letter, *PT, 30*, No.4.
M. Forsyth; A.D.O. MacIntyre, Letters in *PT, 30*, No.6.
D. Forbes, Letter, *PT, 30*, No.7.
P. Taylor, Letter, *PT, 30*, No.9.
W.W. Elmendorf, *PT, 31*, No.3.

CHAPTER 10

Music for Pleasure

This chapter contains some of the oldest and newest pipe tunes, as well as the easiest and most difficult to play. All that links them is the fact that they are composed and played primarily for the pleasure of the individual performer.

Slow airs

In most countries where bagpipes are played, the pipers have a fund of slow tunes which are simply adaptations of the airs of well-known songs, and the Highland pipers are no exception. The first tune of this type on record is *An Còta Ruadh*, 'The Red Coat'. In one collection it has a title which is evidently the first line of a song, *Cha'n eil cailleach agam fhein* with the English 'I am alone since my wife died', and subtitle 'a pipe melody'. It is directed to be played 'slow, with marked expression':

Ex. 10.1. The Red Coat (from *Celtic Melodies* i (1823), arr. R.D. Cannon (1977))

It is given here with the original editor's time values (as far as possible, since it was actually written wrongly in 3/4). In Donald MacDonald's pipe-music collection (1828) it has more the character of a strathspey, but the grace notes show it to have been a slow strathspey, of the type which fiddlers tended to play for exhibition or for pleasure rather than for dancing. A good many tunes of this type seem to have been known to pipers but not written down. James Logan, writing in 1831, was puzzled by the fact they were not counted as pibrochs. In fact the distinction between pibrochs and other tunes was already firmly fixed by that date, and no piper could have had any doubt about it. Whatever might be felt about the musical character of the air, the grace notes alone were characteristically quite different. In 1909, an interesting collection of mainly slow tunes was issued by John and Archibald Campbell of Kilberry, under the title *The Kilberry Book of Ceol Meadhonach*. The Gaelic term, which the editors apparently coined themselves, means 'middle music', and it was put forward as a category of tune intermediate between *ceòl mór* and *ceòl beag*, or in other words 'such tunes as are neither constructed in the measure of Piobaireachd, nor adapted to the quick march or dance'. The term has not caught on, but music of this kind has continued to flourish. Arrangements of songs continue to be the main source, but they have mostly not been written down by pipers from their own oral tradition. They have been taken from songs arranged and popularised by urban Gaelic singers, such as those published by *An Communn Gaidhealach* and the collections of Margaret Kennedy Fraser.

Some of the tunes which would once have been played solely for pleasure have become retreats or slow marches, but others continue to be valued solely in their own right. Pipe Major William Ross's beautiful 'Loch Monar' (1943) cannot in any way be confused with a march, nor can some of the more recent adaptations of songs such as 'MacLeod's Oran Mor', arranged by Seumas MacNeill (1961) and retaining some of the pleasing irregularity of the sung version. Some of the twentieth-century slow airs have a flavour of *ceòl mór* about them, and one at least probably represents a pibroch that has come full circle. The song, variously known as 'The Seaforth Lullaby' or 'We will return to Kintail', has very much the character of a 'pibroch song', and it has been returned to the pipes:

Ex. 10.2. *Theid mi dhachaidh chrò Chinn t-Sàile*. Slow Air (from W. Ross, ii (c.1928))

Jigs and hornpipes

In spite of their exclusion from competitions, and from routine pipe-band work, jigs survived as pieces to be played for their own sake; and the 1930s saw the start of a considerable revival. A jig competition was instituted at Oban, and Pipe Major John Wilson has written of the consternation this caused to many able pipers who hardly knew any. But he himself composed some fine ones which he broadcast and published (1937, 1957), and since then many more have appeared. Some of the oldest ones are still highly regarded — 'The Shaggy Grey Buck', 'The Herring Wife', 'John Patterson's Mare' — but they have been extensively reset. Newer jigs include 'The Hammer on the Anvil', 'The Bobs from Balmoral', 'The Curlew' and others which are already classics. These three are in Donald MacLeod's collections (1954 — n.d.), the first two by MacLeod himself, the third by Donald MacPherson. A more recent notable selection is in the books of Duncan Johnstone (1979). Most leading pipe competitions now include a jig 'event', but it comes at the end of the day and is treated with a lighter touch than the rest. Jig-playing is still essentially ceilidh music: it demands the best that the player can give, but it is not yet in danger of being over-burdened with solemnity.

Hornpipes have come to the fore even more recently. Musically, a hornpipe is another form of 'Scotch Measure' (see above, p. 125), and the style of most of the old ones shows them to be violin pieces (G.S. Emmerson, 1971). They tend to be of wide compass, with lengthy arpeggios, easily done on the fiddle, but unsuitable for the chanter. The well known 'College Hornpipe' shows these features, and has never been arranged for the pipes. Later hornpipes have more of what Emmerson calls a 'jaunty' effect due to pointing of the semiquavers, just as do the pipe competition marches. A few hornpipes were printed for pipes in the earlier nineteenth-century collections, some as 'hornpipe or march'; and later the hornpipe was required as a set dance, as mentioned previously (p. 118). Really good new tunes did not appear until the 1940s, but since then the number has increased greatly. A considerable stimulus has come from the invention of a new grace-note movement. It is a trebling of the melody note, formed by striking three different grace notes in smart succession: two high grace notes and one low. It can be played in jig time as shown here at (a), or as a single ornament (b), to give a kind of light flurry of sound, which fits in well with the overall dotted rhythm of the modern hornpipe in phrases like (c):

Ex. 10.3.

In the following tune, the treblings come in the third part where I have notated them simply as triplets; and it should be mentioned that in this part the small differences between bars 1-2, 5-6, 9-10 and 13-14 are not misprints, but carefully contrived effects:

Ex. 10.4. Jim Tweedie's Sea Legs. By J.A. McGee (from S. MacNeill (1961))

Among other good tunes which use this effect are 'HMS Renown', in J. Robertson and D.S. Ramsey's collection (1953); 'St. Valery', by John Wilson (1959); and several more recent ones in Duncan Johnstone's collection (1978–9). To some extent these all preserve the arpeggio style of the typical English or Irish hornpipe. A rather different style with a more Gaelic flavour has been promoted especially by Donald MacLeod:

Ex. 10.5. Dr. MacInnes' Fancy. By D. MacLeod (from D. MacLeod, iii (1962))

We may conclude our 'music for pleasure' with a piece that defies classification. The tune which Donald MacPhee published (1876) as 'Yankee', and which has since been better known as 'The Banjo Breakdown', has not often been printed, but it is known to nearly every piper. No two pipers seem to play it the same way, and there is not even general agreement as to whether it is a strathspey, a jig or a hornpipe (some versions conclude with a reel setting for good measure). I show in Figure 3 a manuscript copy which has not appeared before. This tune belongs truly to the oral tradition of piping.

Figure 3. An eight-part setting of 'The Banjo Breakdown', written out by Angus F. Cannon, c.1940. *Author's collection.*

CHAPTER 11

The Pipe Band

The Army

In the Army there is an important distinction between the different forms of music making, which is known to every soldier, but not generally appreciated by the civilian. A 'military band', properly so-called, is the familiar ensemble of brass, woodwind and percussion, playing music specially composed and arranged for it. Bandsmen in the Army are officially listed, and paid, as 'musicians', and the Bandmaster is an Officer, with appropriate musical qualifications. In the early days of bands, the bandsmen, especially the bandmasters, were often not soldiers at all, but civilian musicians attached to the Army. Since 1874, however, band music has been on a regular military footing, bandsmen being trained at the Army's own music college, Kneller Hall. Quite distinct from the military band, and much older, is the Corps of Drums. Generally, when soldiers marched on ordinary, non-ceremonial duties, they did so to the beat of the drum. (The 'Scots March' which became famous in the seventeenth century was a particular drum beating, not a tune (H.G. Farmer, n.d.).) But melody instruments were added, especially the 'German flute' or fife. Fife and drum bands came into being, but they continued to be called simply 'the drums', and even today fifers are listed in official records as 'drummers'. A drum corps came under the direction of a drum major, and likewise the leading fifer was the 'fifer major' or 'fife major'. Drummers, fifers and buglers were always soldiers. They played in battle, or as near to battle as conditions allowed, and besides marching, they gave signals according to prearranged codes. In the German armies they were appropriately termed 'field music'.

The point of these remarks is to make clear that when pipers came into the Army they did so on the same footing as fifers and that the pipe band we know today is modelled on the earlier fife bands. How and by what stages pipe bands came into being is not known. An early reference to pipers playing in groups is in the Regimental Orders of the 93rd Highlanders, in 1805, directing that drummers are not to beat when the Regiment marches past in open columns, but 'pipers may play' (C.A. Malcolm, 1927). No doubt the practice was common, or became so, as James Logan in 1831 quotes an opinion that someone had expressed, that for a corps of pipers it would be a good idea if those marching on the left played the pipe on the left shoulder, and those marching on the right played the pipe on the right. (He rightly remarks that this would be about as sensible as requiring the two files of soldiers to carry their muskets on opposite shoulders.) After this, there is nothing until we come to an incident in 1848, when the 79th Regiment was embarked for Canada. As they were sailing up the Hudson River, they encountered fog, and the pipers were ordered to play on deck, so as to warn off other ships 'by their discord' (D.J.S. Murray, 1975). A more appreciative witness of marching pipers was Alexander Duncan Fraser, who as a young boy in 1853 watched Queen Victoria travel down the Crinan Canal by boat, while a bodyguard of the 93rd kept pace on the adjoining road. The pipers played 'The Campbells are Coming' 'as they marched gaily along' (A.D. Fraser, 1907, 38).

An important historical landmark is a War Office order of 11 February, 1854 which established '1 Pipe Major and 5 Pipers' in each of the Highland Regiments — the 42nd, 71st, 72nd, 73rd, 74th, 78th, 79th, 92nd and 93rd (G.A. Weatherall, 1854). Two years later the same arrangement was extended to the Scots Guards. This order has sometimes been assumed to mark the beginning of pipe bands, but there is no proof of this. It is equally possible that it merely confirmed what was already general practice. What it certainly did mean was that henceforth pipers could be paid legitimately out of public funds, instead of illegitimately by being listed as drummers, and they could appear on official parades without risk of censure from an Inspecting Officer (as had happened at least once — C.A. Malcolm, 1927, 144). One would also imagine that before 1854 the instruments played could vary from regiment to regiment according to the views of the Commanding Officer. There may have been a transitional period in which either fifes or pipes were played as preferred, and a recent writer has pointed out (Anon., 1978) that the situation must have been much like that in the present-day Army of Pakistan, who use native instruments in addition to the prescribed orthodox music (which in their case, ironically, is the Scottish bagpipe). Recent military historians seem to accept that 'by the time of the Crimean War, 1854, which is the date generally given for the instruction of the pipe band, it was in fact a good-going strong concern' (D.J.S. Murray, 1975). This suggestion is backed up by the fact that by the 1840s there were at least four pipe makers in business — Thomas Glen and Alexander Glen in Edinburgh, William Gunn in Glasgow, and Allen MacDougall in Perth, which suggests a much larger trade than at the beginning of the century; and especially by the appearance in 1847 of

William Gunn's collection of pipe tunes, which had among its professed aims that of standardising the conflicting settings of tunes. Twenty years later, in another edition of his book, Gunn duly claimed that he had succeeded in establishing 'a standard for both civil and military bagpipe music'.

No one knows when drums began to be added to pipes, though again the date 1854 is quite often assumed. The official term for a pipe band incidentally is 'Pipes and Drums' (or in the Gordon Highlanders, 'Drums and Pipes'), but most soldiers, in practice, refer to 'the pipe band' just as civilians do.

Civilian pipe bands

Mention of 'civil' pipe music emphasises that an important chapter of Scottish social history remains to be written. I presume that civilian pipe bands were inspired in the first place by the example of the Army, and that they grew up in the towns rather than in the country, first in Volunteer forces (the equivalent of today's Territorial Army), then in other uniformed organisations like the Police and Fire Brigades — but I have no proof of any of this. Of the bands in existence today, some have traced their history back to the 1880s. They include the Edinburgh City Police (1882) and the Govan (later City of Glasgow) Police (1885) (Anon., 1953a, 1953b). And just before these the 'Midlothian Amateur Pipe Band' gave its name to a tune which is still well known (D. Glen's Tutor, 1881). But there is nothing to show that these were the first.

Nowadays every town in Scotland seems to have a pipe band (always a private volunteer concern, never supported by the municipality), and most cities elsewhere in the United Kingdom have them as well; so also do industries, especially collieries in the Scottish Lowlands. The whole picture is very much akin to the National Brass Band movement. Youth organisations, notably the Boys' Brigade, have done much to stimulate interest in piping. The Boys' Brigade was founded in Scotland in 1883, but quickly spread to England, and it may have been this Scottish connection which first brought pipe bands to some places. The Boys' Brigade had a pipe band in Manchester as early as 1910 (R.D. Cannon, 1987).

Pipe-band competitions date back also to the 1880s if not earlier. The first one, it is claimed (Anon., 1953b), was promoted in Glasgow by Rangers Football Club. It was won by the Govan Police. Neil Munro, in 1906, wrote of the rise of band contests as a feature of the previous fifteen years. The World Championship is thought to have been started in 1897, at

Cowal, where it was won by the Edinburgh City Police (Anon., 1953a). The Scottish (later Royal Scottish) Pipe Band Association was formed in 1930, and one of its main activities has been to regulate band competitions.

Organisation of the band

As a minimum, a pipe band consists of one bass drum, a number of side drums, and a larger number of pipes. There is no hard and fast rule, but about six pipers is about the smallest practicable number. This was the number established for each regiment in the Army in 1854, but in practice there would be more, paid for as previously by the officers themselves, and twelve to twenty pipers would be more typical. In modern competitions, six pipers and three drummers are sometimes recognised as a separate category of 'miniature band'.

In a bugle or fife band, the side drummers march in front, but in a pipe band the pipers go first, followed by the bass drummer marching on the centre file, and the side drummers in one or more ranks, behind the bass. Tenor drummers — a more recent addition — sometimes march on either side of the bass. In front of the whole band goes the Drum Major, carrying his heavy ornamental staff or mace.

The musical director of the pipe band is the Pipe Major. In the Army, this is now a regular appointment. Before 1854, 'pipe major', or earlier 'piper-major', was merely a customary title, given on the analogy of drum major or bugle major, but without any rank. From 1854, the Pipe Major was recognised but paid, and indeed officially described, as a sergeant. Not until 1949 could he progress as far as Warrant Officer.[1] There will also now usually be a Pipe Sergeant, who is the Pipe Major's deputy, and may have specific responsibilities such as teaching recruits, and likewise a Drum Sergeant. Civilian bands use the same terminology and the same insignia of rank: four stripes for the Drum Major and Pipe Major, and three for the sergeants.

There is obviously no need for a conductor in a pipe band, but there must be a set of clearly understood instructions. The Pipe Major decides the music to be played, and directs the drill movements. He marches at the right-hand end of the front rank, or else one pace still further to the right, with no one else following behind. Pipe bands need to perfect a variety of drills such as marching and counter-marching, 'wheeling' to turn a corner, and changing from rank and file formation to a position with the pipers in a circle. This is the preferred position for playing at the halt. The pipers face inwards, and the smaller the circle, the better will be the blend of sound

when heard from some distance away. When not playing, the pipers carry
their pipes under the left arm, the bass drone pointing forward. On the
command 'pipes and drums, ready', the pipers raise their pipes to playing
position — in a practised and properly timed movement — and inflate the
bag, without however making a sound. The drummers raise their sticks
horizontally to upper lip level in the classic military posture. The signal to
play usually consists of two three-beat drum rolls, on the second of which
the pipers first sound their drones, then strike in their chanters on the note
E, and finally break into the tune. In full score, therefore, the opening of a
pipe band march goes as follows:

Ex. 11.1. Scotland the Brave (arr. RSPBA (1963, 1971))

For slow marches the procedure is similar, but a single five-beat roll is
often preferred. The command to stop playing is given by a kind of nod and
wink by the Pipe Major to the bass drummer, who then signals the
'knock-off' by two sharp beats, delivered off the main pulse of the music,
and repeated. The pipes stop at the end of the measure in which the signal
is given, and it is a point of discipline that the stop must be absolutely clean,
chanters and drones together.

Tuning a pipe band is a major problem, though one would hardly think
so when listening to the well-nigh perfect unison of the top bands of today.
Every piper must have brought his pipes to a good stable condition
beforehand. Each one then tunes his chanter to that of the Pipe Major,
resetting the reed if necessary. But this will only work if the chanters
themselves are tuned in the same way to start with. All high-grade bands
will use a set of matched chanters, supplied as such from the same maker.
(The fact that this still needs to be done shows of course that even today the
pipe scale is still not completely standardised.) Once the Pipe Major is
satisfied with the chanters, each piper tunes his drones, subject to checking
by the Pipe Major. One of the finer points is that if it is impossible to get

chanters in perfect unison on a particular day, the drones should all be tuned to one set of drones, and not to each individual chanter. Then the drone background can still give the required all-enveloping sound, even if the chanters are slightly off on some note.

Music

The settings of tunes used by pipe bands are generally the same as in solo playing, including all the characteristic grace notes. The effect of these is, of course, largely lost, since not even the most perfectly drilled band will play the ornaments exactly together; but certainly the better the band, the more clearly the grace notes can be heard. A modern, Grade 1 civilian or military pipe band comes close to playing literally as one man.

There is no type of tune which is exclusively reserved for pipe-band use, but some tunes are certainly more suitable than others. Marching is of course the *raison d'être* of the band, and the simpler 2/4 and 6/8 quicksteps may well have been played in bands from the earliest days of organised playing. Besides these, however, 3/4 and 4/4 marches go very well, and are in fact played more by bands than by soloists. The common-time march could perhaps be claimed as a species of true pipe-band music. With military bands, common time, four paces to the bar and not more than two melody notes to the pace, is quite normal. Tunes like 'Colonel Bogey' and 'The Garb of Old Gaul' are well known examples. 'The Crusaders' March' is one of the first of these to have been printed for the pipes, by Donald MacPhee in 1876, though if MacPhee was right in saying that it had been composed in 1784, it was presumably not originally a pipe tune:

Ex. 11.2. The Crusaders' March (from D. Glen, *Collection*, iv, enlarged ed. (1899); cf. J.&.A. Campbell (1909))

In the nineteenth century this piece was mostly used as a parade-ground slow march, and the same may have been true of others like 'And sae will we yet' (now also known as 'The Wearing of the Green') and 'Lord Lovat's Lament'. But others like the 'Badge of Scotland' and 'Scotland the Brave', which appeared about the turn of the century, are good, rolling quick marches. There are not many tunes in this category, but every piper knows some, and the numbers are increasing.

A number of the more modern 2/4 and 6/8 marches also seem to have been composed mainly for bands. They tend to have fewer notes to the beat than the older ones. In 2/4 time this means avoiding demi-semi-quaver runs and introducing full crotchet beats, as in 'Captain Norman Orr-Ewing', composed by Pipe Major William Ross in 1912 (Scots Guards Collection, 1954); while in 6/8 time it means more two-note crotchet-and-quaver pairs, and single dotted crotchets. 'John D. Burgess' by George Cockburn is an outstanding 'six-eight' of this kind:

Ex. 11.3. John D. Burgess. By G. Cockburn (from D.S. Ramsay (1953))

The distinction between tunes like this, and earlier quicksteps like 'Highland Laddie' and 'Kenmure's on and awa'', is not sharp, but it can be felt quite clearly. The whole tune has a more spacious feel to it. The trend has continued in the last twenty years, and some tunes have single notes sustained over more than one beat, which may be punctuated with a kind of counterpoint from the drums. A good example of a march which can only be properly played by a band is 'The Cockney Jocks':

Ex. 11.4. The Cockney Jocks. By J. Haynes (from Gordon Highlanders Collection (1983))

In the opposite direction, pipe bands have sought out more flamboyant pieces for exhibition playing. An early one was the 'Black Bear Hornpipe'. The second part has relatively long phrases, during which the drumming builds up to a climax, then suddenly stops, leaving the pipes to carry the melody on and back to the obligatory repeat of the first part:

Ex. 11.5. The Black Bear (from Scots Guards Collection (1954))

It is also a custom in this tune (though deplored by some) for the drummers to punctuate the first part with a loud shout on the fifth beat.

In band competitions the usual sets of march, strathspey and reel are played. The tunes used for competition have grown steadily more complex, and by the 1950s and 1960s the Grade I bands regularly played the same tunes and settings as the solo competitors. But since then there has been something of a reversion to simpler tunes, and towards more varied medleys of slow and fast tunes. The trend has not been without its critics, however, who feel that individual playing technique has suffered as a result.[2]

Drumming

Most tunes are in repeated measures and, as with fife and bugle bands, the traditional procedure is for the leading drummer to play through the first time, and all the drums to come in together on the repeat. Drum settings vary from simple beatings with the appropriate time signature to elaborate ones composed for each individual tune, and they tend to be determined by the drummers independently. One device, which was in use by 1914, is for the drummers to leave off for a bar or two while the pipes play on, then to come in together with dramatic effect. The second part of 'Green Hills of Tyrol', where the pipes play a slowly descending phrase in thirds (see below, p. 161), seems to have been a favourite place for this device. When pipe bands were limited to the simpler marches like 'Barren Rocks' and 'The 79th's', a selection of stock beatings in appropriate time signatures was enough, but as the pipe tunes grew more ambitious, so the drum settings became more elaborate (A.D. Hamilton, 1947-8; 'J.D.B.', 1969). It is difficult to follow the history of this development, since until quite recently the drums were learned and played entirely by ear. Mr. W.G.F. Boag, a leading authority on military drumming, considers (1976) that the civilian pipe bands led the way, and moreover that the distinctive music of the bagpipe led to new discoveries in drumming, which in turn have influenced modern military band drumming. Syncopated effects were tried out, using accented strokes on unusual beats; the basic movements of drumming — the rolls, paradiddles, flams and drags — were joined up in new ways; and grace notes corresponding to the pipers' doublings were introduced: all entirely foreign to the old standard Army drum beatings. It became usual to devise specific settings for specific tunes, and written notation gradually came into use. The first printed drum music for pipe bands appeared as long ago as 1922, and since then a fair number of pipe collections have included drum settings. The Royal Scottish Pipe Band Association *Tutor and Textbook* gives as much attention to drumming as to piping.

Along with changes in the music came changes in the construction of the drums. In the late nineteenth and early twentieth centuries, Army side drums were of two main types, the deep 'Guards drum', tensioned with ropes (Plate 17), and the newer shallow type, nicknamed 'cheese drums', tensioned with rods and thumb screws. Modern orchestral side drums have evolved from the shallow type, but the deep type was retained by marching flute bands and by many pipe bands (W.G.F. Boag, n.d.). It produced a 'fine resonant sound' but it needed constant adjustment. Rod-tensioned deep drums were introduced into pipe bands in 1931 and they quickly swept the field. They produced a harder and crisper beat, allowing the new ornamentation to be heard more clearly. The trend was parallel to the tendency of pipe chanters to become sharper in pitch and more brilliant in tone.

Drum beatings continued to be elaborated to the point where, by the late 1950s, some drummers were complaining that the clear rhythmic lift which is the basic function of the drum section was being lost.[3] Since then there has been some reaction, with more care to match the beating to the tune, and more sensitive use of loud and soft effects. Arguments about style, however, do not alter the fact that pipe-band drumming has now reached an extraordinarily high standard, and has excited the admiration of drummers outside the piping world altogether (J. Blades, 1961).

Ensemble playing

Nearly all pipe-band music is played on pipes alone, in strict unison. The practice of harmonising tunes in different parts got off to a very slow start in the mid-nineteenth century, and even today it is restricted to a small number of tunes. In the course of a newspaper correspondence on this subject in the 1880s, it emerged that the 78th Highlanders had started playing 'duets' when they returned from the Indian Mutiny (i.e. about 1857) and that they performed some in Edinburgh in 1860.[4] Probably what was meant was not duets but music in two parts, some pipers playing the ordinary melody, and others playing one third below, as far as the chanter permitted. We are not told what tunes were treated in this way, but one of the earliest was undoubtedly the retreat march, 'The Green Hills of Tyrol'. This tune was originally not Scottish at all, but is an air from Rossini's opera *William Tell*. It is said to have been first arranged for the pipes by

Pipe Major John MacLeod, of the 93rd Highlanders, who heard it played in the Crimea by a band of Sardinian soldiers in 1855 (J.&.A. Campbell, 1909). In the original opera the first measure of the tune is sung in unison, but the second measure, which has a gradually descending passage, is harmonised in thirds. I suspect that the pipers first confined their harmonisation to this second measure, but when the tune came to be printed, in 1888, the 'Secondo' part (subsequently always called 'seconds') was extended to the whole tune:

Ex. 11.6. The Green Hills of Tyrol (from P. Henderson [1888])

Seconds are now quite commonly played with retreat marches and slow airs. The style seems to have changed slightly as time has gone on. At first they followed the melody, one third lower as just mentioned, except on the notes B, low A and low G, when they reverted to unison. Later the melody note B was harmonised as well, using low G. It has been pointed out that when the tune is in the key of A, the low G natural is inappropriate, but the arrangers do not seem to have responded to this criticism. (For that matter, one might add, the prototype tune 'Green Hills' is inappropriate, since the melody itself uses the high G natural where it 'should' have a G sharp — see above, bars 9 and 13.) Also in recent years, 'seconds' have tended to go above as well as below the melody, as convenient. Intervals other than thirds now sometimes occur, but they are still rare, and regular descant parts do not seem to have been attempted yet. Harmonisation of tunes in quick time has only just begun, and whether it will catch on is hard to say.

A recent recording contains a very fine setting of Donald MacLeod's jig 'The Glasgow City Police Pipers', harmonised as follows:

Ex. 11.7. The Glasgow City Police Pipers

Attempts to combine the bagpipe with other instruments tend to be frowned on by traditionalists, but the trend is growing, and is unlikely to be stopped. The late Archie MacNeill recalled (1958) that he occasionally played in public on reel-sized pipes, in duets with an accordian. This was as long ago as the First World War. Some forty years later recordings were being made of pipers or pipe bands with an organ, the sounds being appropriately balanced by the engineers. The resulting controversy ran through several issues of the *Piping Times*.[5] One of the arguments against such experiments is that for proper tuning it will be necessary to modify the pipe chanter so that it will lose its distinctive character. On the other hand, as suggested above (p. 31), it may be that the chanter is already being gradually brought into line with other instruments and, so far, solo players have raised no objections. In the Army it is now quite usual for the pipes and the 'military band' to play together in public entertainments such as tattoos, so presumably the problems of tuning are being faced and overcome somehow. Again it must be said that not all connoisseurs of piping approve of such practices, but they are certainly popular with the listening public.

NOTES

1. Today, although the Pipe Major is '*musically* in charge of the pipe band', it is the Drum Major who is 'administratively in charge of all pipers and drummers' unless the Pipe Major has the higher rank, in which case the reverse is true (Anon., 1978–9). See also *Piping Times*, editorial Vol.2, No.5 (Feb. 1950); and letter from Capt. D.R. MacLennan, *PT, 2*, No.8 (May, 1950).

2. *Piping Times, 2*, No.5; *3*, Nos.1, 4, 8; *28*, No.6.

3. See *Piping Times, 10*, No.4 (Jan. 1958); *10*, No.7 (April, 1958); *The Pipe Band*, No.4, July–Aug. 1979.

4. Reprinted in *IP, 1* (1), p.10; *1* (2), pp.6, 22.

5. *PT, 8*, No.7; *9*, No.3, No.9.

CHAPTER 12

Piping Today

The average visitor to Scotland will receive much the same impression of piping as the average resident in the country: pipe bands playing in parades, or in open spaces on summer evenings; piping on television in the Military Tattoo at the Edinburgh Festival; the odd piper playing for money in the car park at Gretna Green or Glencoe. Few people realise that behind these occasional appearances there lies an entire musical world.

The players

It is impossible to say how many pipers there are in the world today, but a few published figures show clearly enough that piping is a thriving culture. The most popular College of Piping Tutor tuition book has sold more than 140,000 copies in the past thirty-five years, while at the other end of the scale the Piobaireachd Society's collections of *ceòl mór* sell roughly 700 copies per year. There are more than 400 civilian pipe bands affiliated to the Royal Scottish Pipe Band Association (Anon., 1985), and there must be many more besides. The bagpipe manufacturing trade appears to be flourishing, with at least ten firms in business at present. There must, at the very least, be tens of thousands of active players, ranging from novices to master players of international repute.

Among this large population, the proportion of pipers who actually make their living from their art is quite possibly less than at any time in the past; but if so, this is probably more to do with the rise in general standards of living than with any decline in public support of pipe music. Few if any pipers are now in private service. The Army employs fewer than before, and in most regiments piping is only a part-time addition to ordinary military duties. Nevertheless, among the leading players there are still those who can justly claim to be full-time pipers. Some are recently retired from the Army, and still active in playing, teaching and judging. Some are pipe makers, and some are full-time teachers. But many more have some non-piping occupation, yet still contrive to devote much of their life to piping. The energy which many pipers put into their art is indeed astounding. For it should hardly need saying — though perhaps it does need saying — that the standard among the leading players is such that no one who is not completely dedicated could hope to maintain a footing. The contrast, in technique, in quality of sound, and in general musicianship, between the acknowledged masters and the general run of good players is just as great for the bagpipe as for any other instrument.

It will have become clear from other remarks in this book that the piping world has long been divided socially into amateurs and professionals, just like many sporting activities. A professional piper is not necessarily one who plays full-time: he is, technically, one who is paid to play, and in practice this means any Army piper, or anyone who has ever accepted a money prize in a competition. 'Open' competitions are professional. Others, which offer only trophies as prizes, are amateur. There are amateur piping societies, such as the Royal Scottish Pipers' Society (founded in 1881 — see N.A. Malcolm Smith, 1984), which exclude professionals from membership, although they may retain professional pipers as instructors, just as golf clubs retain professional players as coaches. An argument often put forward in defence of the system is that in general the amateur player cannot hope to compete successfully with the professional, and must therefore seek the shelter of the closed contest. But a full account of social attitudes in piping would go far beyond the limits of this book, and would probably end up by showing that pipers are no different from other people. The system is rooted in the past. As we have seen, in the early competitions judges and players belonged to different 'ranks' of society, and the transition to the Army world of officers and other ranks followed naturally. The rise of organised amateur piping perhaps reflected the growth of middle-class interest. Since the last war, distinctions have begun to break down, although they have by no means disappeared. 'Middle-class' players have entered the professional arena, proving that a man or woman can be a successful lawyer, doctor or teacher, and also a consistent winner of the highest prizes. Some piping societies have always succeeded in avoiding the professional/amateur distinction, and in a significant change of policy since 1970, the Piobaireachd Society has admitted professional pipers to membership.

It is beyond dispute that the number of pipers has increased dramatically in the last few decades, and that the increase is continuing. The most obvious sign of growth is the spread of piping overseas. In the former British Dominions, the nucleus of interest consists naturally of expatriate Scots and their descendants through several generations. In India and Pakistan, the Highland bagpipe is an Army instrument, again a legacy from British times (R.J. Powell, 1980). But piping has spread beyond its historical roots, to England, where there are pipe bands in most major cities; to Brittany, where there is now a large community of pipers; to the USA; and increasingly to Western Europe and Japan. Leading Scottish pipers regularly conduct summer schools abroad. French and American pipers are now competing successfully in Scotland, and pipers from other countries will certainly do so as well.

While numbers have risen, so too has the general standard of playing. Most judges who have watched the piping scene for fifty years or more seem to agree that if the top players of today are not better than those of their youth, they are as good, and more numerous, while the 'second eleven' has changed out of all recognition. Poorly tuned pipes and woolly fingering are simply not tolerated. Any local pipe band will contain at least a few strong players, and others will be working seriously to emulate them.

It would be very interesting to know what it is that draws people with no previous family or cultural connection so firmly into the world of piping. The obvious reasons are not necessarily the right ones. Bagpipes are not cheap, nor are they easy to play. The colourful pageantry of the pipe band excites the onlooker a good deal more than the piper. Closest to the mark perhaps is the recent comment of an American piper (and also orchestral musician) who confessed to 'a kind of addiction' to the sheer physical sound of the bagpipe (P. Cooke, 1976–7). Certainly a well-tuned set of pipes has a special quality of richness which is matched by few other combinations of instruments. Added to this, the technical difficulties both of playing and of sound production present a challenge which is perhaps its own reward.

Performance

The system which maintains such high standards is that of competition, and, today, public performances of bagpipe music are still predominantly competitions. Traditionally, these are held in the open air, at various Highland Games through the summer, but the main solo events are nowadays held indoors to avoid problems of weather, and this is true also of the competitions organised at various dates throughout the year by piping societies, mainly in Glasgow, Edinburgh and London. *Ceòl mór* competitions are held at most games, but not all. The other solo competitions are for a march, and a strathspey and reel, or for all three types of tune in one 'set'; and less commonly a jig or hornpipe as a more light-hearted event to finish off with.

Pipe-band competitions are held at many Games, though in Scotland (unlike elsewhere) these are not generally the same Games as hold solo competitions; and they also take place at suitable city arenas such as football grounds. The great Games at Cowal in August are a major venue. There is also the World Pipe Band Championship, held in a different centre each year, usually in Scotland, but sometimes in Northern Ireland and in England.

The number of competitors in a solo event can be anything from less than a dozen to close on a hundred, but it is probably true to say that in any one year there will be twenty or so pipers systematically working round the games and collecting the majority of the prizes. These are the potential gold medal winners and leaders of the future. Many others will know that they have little chance of a prize, but they are working their way up, or else have reached their personal limit but continue to compete because they enjoy it, and because it focuses their efforts. No doubt there are some players equally good who choose not to compete, but they too will attend the competitions when they can, and enjoy agreeing or disagreeing with the judges.

What is noticeably lacking in the piping world is any visible audience of non-players. At an open-air competition there will be a sprinkling of casual listeners attracted by what is going on, but at the indoor competitions there will be few, if any, knowledgeable non-playing enthusiasts, and in either case the bulk of the audience will be pipers themselves. They will not all be competitors or have any ambitions in that direction, but nearly all will have handled a chanter at some time or other. Even among pipers, formal recitals of a non-competitive kind are rare: pipe bands meet together for practice; piping societies hold members' nights and ceilidhs where pipers (usually the better players within the club) can play in a relatively informal atmosphere; a group of friends will get together 'after the games' or on other convenient occasions. But it is rare for an audience to assemble and pay to hear a pre-arranged performance.

This situation has been much discussed and generally deplored, but efforts to change it have not had much success. Piping societies and the College of Piping do from time to time arrange recitals, with a guest piper, but again the audiences consist mainly of pipers. The Scottish Arts Council has supported piping recitals in the rural Highlands, as well as in urban areas.[1] Special competitions designed to attract a wider audience have had more encouraging results. The first of these to be established was the 'Silver Chanter' competition, held annually since 1967 at Dunvegan Castle, and to this has been added the Grants' Championship, held at Blair Atholl, the residence of the Duke of Atholl, promoted by William Grant and Sons Whisky Distilleries. The detailed arrangements have varied from time to time, but in general only pipers who already have won other leading competitions take part. The attraction for the players may be judged by the fact that in recent years pipers have appeared by invitation only. These events show piping at its best, in an atmosphere which partakes of the informal ceilidh as well as the competition. The players and their tunes are introduced with remarks by some well-known authority on piping. The proceedings are usually recorded, and selections are broadcast on radio or television shortly afterwards. Even so, it is significant that a further step away from the competition system was unsuccessful. As an experiment, one year the Silver Chanter event was renamed a 'recital competition', and comparable sums were paid to all the pipers who took part, not just the winners. But it was felt that the standard of playing dropped as a result, and in the following year the original format was restored; though in general now, all those who play receive expenses and a token prize at least.

Another innovation which has proved popular in piping clubs is what might be described as free-style competition. The piper is not restricted to a prescribed set of tunes, but makes up his own programme, which may continue for five or ten minutes, and the prizes are awarded for the arrangement, as well as for technical excellence and expression. The medleys offered will often include light tunes not usually heard, as well as the traditional 'heavy' marches, strathspeys and reels, or the brilliant modern hornpipes and jigs. Extracts from pibrochs may be included as well. At some such events, the judges may be instructed to abandon the usual criteria, and simply mark up the performances they enjoyed the most; or there may be no judges at all, in which case the audience votes for the prize winners at the end of the evening. These are some of the ways in which piping organisers have been trying to 'break the mould'; but still it remains true that competition is the backbone, and the only effective route to the top of the profession.

Education

Before the last war, the only teaching manuals generally available were Logan's, Henderson's and David Glen's tutors, all still in print but unchanged from the nineteenth century. They printed the fingering of the scale and described the grace notes more or less adequately, and they gave a bare minimum of advice on setting up and tuning the pipes. A tutor for pipe bands, by Pipe Major W. Gray and Drum Major John Seton (1922), was somewhat better but still basically the same. These books served their purpose only because everyone knew that piping had to be learned directly from a teacher. The better teachers evolved their own courses, taking the learner step by step through the movements, and through simple tunes, and carefully correcting faults as they occurred. But anyone who had no access to a teacher — and this included many learners in Scotland as well as elsewhere — had little hope of becoming a good piper. Shortly after the war, a few young players started the College of Piping in Glasgow. It was endowed with premises in Otago Street, the gift of Captain Charles Hepburn; and under Seumas MacNeill and Thomas Pearston as joint Principals it began classes for beginners, and later for pipers at all levels. The College has continued ever since, relying mainly on part-time teachers. Its influence expanded greatly with the publication in 1953 of the first part of the *College of Piping Tutor*. This work clearly embodies years of practical teaching experience. Designed for self-tuition, it assumes no previous knowledge of music, and besides giving the fullest instructions yet published, it anticipates the common faults in playing and shows how to correct them. Subsequent volumes have dealt with the tuning and maintenance of the pipes, and with music up to competition standard. It has proved to be the best-selling of all pipe-music books, and there can be few pipers who have learned in the last thirty years who have not been exposed to it. More recently, the long-running *Logan's Tutor* has been revised, indeed rewritten, by Captain J.A. MacLellan, and is now available with an accompanying cassette. A similarly thorough manual of *ceòl mór* was started by John MacFadyen and Pipe Major Donald MacLeod, but sadly both authors died before more than one volume (1977) had appeared. Piobaireachd tuition tapes are available from several leading players. Mention should also be made of the older School of Piping run by the Army at Edinburgh Castle. Between the Wars, the School was supported by the Piobaireachd Society, who paid the salary of the resident instructor, Pipe Major William Ross, while the Army provided the premises (D.J.S. Murray, 1975). All types of pipe music were taught, but the speciality was pibroch playing, which was a required qualification for an Army Pipe Major. Since the last war, the School has expanded and flourished under a succession of distinguished Army pipers. It moved to new premises in the Castle in 1959, and although the number of pipers in the standing British Army has decreased, the fall has been offset by increasing numbers sent by the armies of overseas countries, notably Canadian and Gurkha regiments.

A more recent development which holds great promise for the future has been the recognition of piping by the Scottish education authorities.

Beginning in 1972, children in schools, studying for the Scottish Certificate of Education, have been allowed to offer bagpipe playing for the practical element of the examination. The written part of the examination remains the same as before, covering general music theory and history, but there is also an oral examination related to the instrument. The full story of how this change was brought about has not yet been told,[2] but the vital consequence has been that, since the subject came into the syllabus, teachers have been required. A considerable number of schools, mostly in the Highlands and Islands, now employ piping instructors, most of them covering a round of peripatetic teaching. One of the first to be appointed was Iain MacFadyen, who has given (1975) a valuable first-hand account of his work. The instructors have been professional pipers of the highest reputation — leading in musical terms to a situation equivalent to Daniel Horowitz or Yehudi Menuhin spending his time teaching absolute beginners! But on the credit side this means that young players are exposed from the start to the very best musicianship; and first-class pipers are found a niche in which they can operate professionally, with nothing to prevent them taking advanced pupils privately, or teaching in summer schools. Moreover, most of the new teachers are prominent pibroch players, and increasingly *ceòl mór* is being taught to pupils from the start, rather than as a kind of top-dressing to a long course in marches, strathspeys and reels. Today, ten years later, young pipers are emerging and taking good prizes in competitions. More significantly perhaps, piping has been reimplanted in parts of the country, such as Skye, from which it had disappeared for a century. But very little has been done so far in schools in the main urban areas where, in fact, most pipers are found.

There also remain serious anomalies which have been discussed but not yet settled. It is difficult for a piping instructor to show formal proof of his qualifications. Diplomas and teaching certificates are available from the Army School of Piping (for Army pipers only); from the Royal Scottish Pipe Band Association; and, more broadly based, from the Institute of Piping, a body which was set up jointly with the College of Piping, the Army School, and the Piobaireachd Society.[3] But there are no teacher-training courses accepted by the education authorities as being on a par with those offered by Universities or Colleges of Education, and as a result pipers in schools are classed not as teachers, but as instructors, in a lower salary range. Equally if not more serious is the lack of suitable school-level textbooks on the history and theory of piping. Not surprisingly, therefore, these aspects are omitted from school music syllabuses, and are not formally examined. This at least is a matter which it is within the power of pipers to remedy.

Literature

Books about piping have never been plentiful, and until recently good ones were rare indeed. Some of the older classics, like Joseph MacDonald's *Compleat Theory* and Angus MacKay's *Ancient Piobaireachd*, already mentioned many times in this book, have been reprinted and are now again generally available; and the same is true of W.L. Manson's valuable and long-underrated book *The Highland Bagpipe, its History, Literature and Music* (1901). But books which could be recommended without reservation to the general musical reader hardly began until the appearance in 1948 of Archibald Campbell's *Kilberry Book of Ceòl Mór*. This is primarily a collection of pibrochs, but it also has a lengthy introduction setting out clearly the origins of the main music collections, the histories of some piping families and the descent of *ceòl mór* through the competition system to the present day. Not everything which Kilberry wrote can still stand unamended, but the great virtue of this, as of all his writings, is that it is firmly based on detailed and critical research. Moreover, the Kilberry Book has been widely read by pipers, and must have done much to encourage the higher standard of writing of the next generation.

Of other books available today, Seumas MacNeill's *Piobaireachd* (1968) is a thorough descriptive account in terms which should be clear to any musically educated reader. Francis Collinson's *The Bagpipe, the History of a Musical Instrument* (1975) is of wider scope. In some respects it is insufficiently critical, and pipers have also faulted it on points of detail (not always fairly), but it contains a great deal of valuable material presented with an enviable flair for picturesque detail.

New additions to the range of piping literature are pipers' auto-biographies. The reminiscences of Angus MacPherson (1955), though in rather sentimental vein, throw light on piping history as far back as 1890. The autobiography of John Wilson (1978) is very different. It aroused not so much criticism as embarrassment in piping circles, but however biased in view, or abrasive in tone, it carries conviction as a record of the thoughts and feelings of at least one 'Professional Piper in Peace and War'.

A considerable sensation was caused by the appearance in 1980 of Alistair Campsie's *The MacCrimmon Legend, the Madness of Angus MacKay*. The main theme of the book is that the contribution of the MacCrimmon family to piping has been grossly over-exaggerated, but the author attacks a number of other aspects of piping tradition, with less justification. He claims in particular that Angus MacKay's collections of pibrochs involved extensive plagiarism from the Campbell *canntaireachd* manuscript, and also that MacKay's reliability is undermined by his mental illness. There is no space here to enter into a detailed critique of Campsie's arguments (the two points just mentioned have been adequately dealt with in reviews by G.A. Dixon (1980) and A.G. Kenneth (1980)), but on the positive side it can be said that if Campsie's book inspires more pipers to study and defend the positions they hold, it will have done good rather than harm.

The literature in which the bagpipe is richest is of course the music itself. At the present time, new collections of tunes are multiplying faster than ever before, and there is no sign that the flow will cease. Useful indexes of tunes have been published — *The Piobaireachd Index* (1978), and two covering the small tunes (D. Varella, 1966; H. Bain, 1983). In my *Bibliography of Bagpipe Music* (1980) I have given an overview of the development of the written records of pipe music from the beginning, as well as locating and identifying copies of rare editions.

A great deal of valuable writing on pipers and pipe music has, however, appeared not in books but in articles in periodicals. Until the advent of efficient inter-library loan systems and photocopying these remained virtually inaccessible, and even now there is no simple way of locating an article on any particular topic. The last full bibliography of bagpipe writings was published by G.H. Askew in 1932, but it is hoped that the bibliography attached to this book, while not comprehensive, will help to fill the gap. Many of the articles have appeared in journals published by and for pipers themselves. The earliest of these was *Piping and Dancing*, which ran monthly for a number of years from 1935. After the war came the *Piping Times*, published by the College of Piping since 1948, and the *Pipe Band*, published by the Scottish (later Royal Scottish) Pipe Band Association from 1952. A number of other journals have appeared, some of them very short-lived, but notably also the *Piper and Dancer Bulletin* and the *Piping World*, both circulating mainly in Canada and the USA, and the *International Piper*, which started very well indeed, but sadly ceased publication after only a few years (1978–81). Probably the most keenly read sections in all of them were and are the reports of competition results, or better, detailed critiques of the playing; but there are also articles on piping matters, ranging from learned to topical, and regular series on such things as reed making, or the stories of tunes. Collected files of all these magazines are essential material for historians, as are the *Proceedings* of the Piobaireachd Society Conferences, published annually from 1973. Many piping societies produce news-sheets for their own members, and it is to be hoped that archives of these are being preserved as well, and may eventually become available.

Professional academic research into pipe music has effectively been pioneered by the School of Scottish Studies of Edinburgh University. To say this is not to deny that amateur research workers have also from time to time produced work of professional standard, as I have tried to make clear wherever possible in this book. But interest in piping has been slow to develop among the academic scholars who might have been expected to contribute most of our knowledge. Until the 1970s no musicologist had made any detailed study of pipe music, nor had any scholars begun the important task of evaluating the associated traditions. Studies of this kind are now appearing, however, particularly in the journal *Scottish Studies*. It is sad to report that so far few pipers admit the value of such work, and there have even been some expressions of hostility. But in the long run it is difficult to doubt that increased knowledge will be accepted as beneficial to piping tradition.

Oddly enough, until recently pipers frequently complained at the neglect of their art by academic scholars. Such complaints tend to overlook the fact that research can only be built on information, and the best kind of information is that provided by pipers themselves. Of all the items published in the piping journals, the most valuable in this respect are letters from experienced pipers, writing from their own knowledge. This has always been the hardest material to come by. Sixty years ago, the correspondence columns of the *Oban Times* were the main source of written information, but they are sadly disappointing, and one is forced to conclude that those who wrote most were the ones who knew least. There are understandable reasons for this. I have been told that serving members of the armed forces — a category that included most leading players — were actually prohibited from writing to the press; and as for other leading players, reading between the lines of the little they did write, one is forced to the conclusion that they dared not express themselves openly for fear of antagonising the judges. Do these considerations apply today? Some will say they do not, but I am not so sure. But in any case one thing that has certainly not changed is the simple reluctance of anyone not trained as a writer to put pen to paper on any subject whatever.

Recordings

As yet there is no published discography of pipe music, and it is only possible to make a few general remarks on this very important topic. Recordings of pipe bands have always been the most popular. Every sizeable record shop, in Britain at least, will have a few, mostly on well-known commercial labels. Solo piping records are less common. They are

H

often produced in short runs, but a large shop with a specific 'folk' or 'ethnic' division is likely to have at least one representative disc, possibly even of *ceòl mór*. Waverley Records, a division of EMI, have issued a number of good bagpipe records, as have most of the leading folk music specialists such as Topic and the Ethnic Folkways Library of the USA.

Tape recordings are also available commercially, including some particularly valuable archive recordings of past players, published by the School of Scottish Studies. But most tapes are made informally. The tape recorder has indeed revolutionised piping. Most players possess one, and tapes now circulate as freely as did manuscripts in the old days, and far more effectively. Tape recorders appear at all major competitions. Some pipers object to this, arguing that illicit copying inhibits the sale of authorised recordings and robs the players of royalties which they should receive, but it is difficult to see an end to the present practice. More constructive developments include tuition by tape, a service which several leading teachers now provide; examinations by tape, conducted by the College of Piping and the Institute of Piping; and even competitions by tape, pioneered by the Scottish Piping Society of South Africa, whose members are scattered hundreds of miles apart.

The reader of this book who wishes to listen to good piping now has plenty of opportunities, but still has to seek them out. In Scotland there are radio and television broadcasts, although the schedules vary from time to time. Until recently there was a weekly BBC programme which rotated between pipe-band and solo music, interspersed with a monthly magazine programme of piping affairs. At the time of writing this feature has disappeared as a result of the transfer of piping from the Gaelic Department to the Music Department of the BBC. In any case, these programmes cannot be heard in England, nor of course overseas, and efforts to have them more widely broadcast have not yet succeeded.

Competitions are still the best places to hear live playing. Full programmes of solo and band competitions are printed each year in the *Piping Times* and the *Pipe Band* respectively. Local tourist offices can often provide information about Highland Games to be held nearby, with at least some mention of the piping events, but national publicity is not good, and at the present time the Piobaireachd Society is looking for ways to remedy this. Although the most famous events are held indoors, there is no denying the attraction of the old-style open-air competitions held alongside all the other events of a traditional Highland Games. Arriving at the field, the visitor will have no difficulty in following the sound of pipes to its source — although this might turn out to be the 'tuning park' where the players are warming up their pipes. The actual competition is held on a raised square platform; seats for the audience may or may not be provided. The piobaireachd event will be in the remotest part of the field, with a small but completely dedicated audience. What is lacking at nearly all these events is any kind of useful information for interested non-piping spectators. Occasionally there will be a printed programme, listing the names of the competitors; but normally, only the name of each competitor, and his tune, will be announced before he plays. At the end of the competition the judges give out the names of the winners, and that is all. On the other hand, as already noted, the audience at these competitions consists largely of experts, and the visitor who has found his way there should not hesitate to ask questions. Pipers today realise that they have a cause to promote, and more than any previous generation they will welcome the interest that underlies any intelligent question.

NOTES

1. *PT*, *6*, No.2; *8*, No.11; N.A. Malcolm Smith [1984], 52.
2. For some press accounts, see *The Times* (London), 24th March, 1972; *PT*, *30*, No.3, editorial; *IP* editorials, Jan. 1979 and Feb. 1980; F. Blacklaws, letter in *IP*, March, 1980.
3. See, for example, *PT*, *30*, No.11; *32*, No.11.

Bibliography

'Amateur' (1818) *The Bagpipe Preceptor.* Edinburgh.

An Comunn Gaidhealach — see e.g. *Coisir a Mhòid.*

Aird, James (c.1790) *A selection of Scotch, English, Irish and foreign airs adapted for the fife, violin or German flute.* James Aird, Glasgow.

Anon. (1893) 'An interview with the Queen's bagpipemaker'. Reprinted from the *People's Journal* (Dundee) 4 Nov. 1893. A typed copy of the booklet is in the National Museum of Antiquities of Scotland, Edinburgh (MS Archive, 1976/8); also reprinted *PT* **16**, No.9.

Anon. (1950) 'Piping Timber', *PT* **3**, No.3.

Anon. (1953a) 'Edinburgh City Police Pipe Band, 1882–1953', *PT* **6**, No.3.

Anon. (1953b) 'Famous Pipe Bands: No.1. The City of Glasgow Police Pipe Band', *PT* **6**, No.2 [This series of articles was not continued; but see also *PT* **3**, Nos.7–8; **6**, No.11, and *The Pipe Band* Sept/Oct. 1978 and Nov/Dec 1978, for accounts of two other pipe bands].

Anon. (1961) 'The Army School of piping, Edinburgh Castle', *PT* **13**, No.9.

Anon. (1964) see Anon. (1893).

Anon. (1973) 'The Strathy Pipes', *PT* **25**, No.4.

Anon. (1978–9) 'The Army and its Pipers', *IP* **1**, Nos. 2, 4, 7, 10.

Anon. (1980) Editorial in *IP* **3**, No.6.

Anon. (1981a) 'An Introduction to pipe chanter reedmaking', by 'A traditional reedmaker', *IP* **3**, Nos.10, 11.

Anon. (1981b) 'The Highland Society of London', *PT* **33**, No.12.

Anon. (1984) 'A Letter from Boreraig', *PT* **36**, No.4.

Anon. (1985) 'The Scottish Pipe Band Association. The First Fifty Years', *The Pipe Band*, No.7 (Jan/Feb. 1985).

'A.M.' — probably Archibald Campbell, Yr of Kilberry (c.1903) — 'The passing of the piobaireachd'. A series of articles in the *Oban Times*, reprinted as a pamphlet. Quoted, J. Campbell (1977).

Allardyce, A. (1888) *Scotland and Scotsmen in the Eighteenth Century from the Ochtertyre MSS.* Edinburgh, 2 vols.

Army Manual of Bagpipe Tunes and Drum Beatings. Music for massed pipes and drums. Patersons Publications Ltd., London. Books 1–2, 1934, 1936.

Askew, Gilbert H. (1932) *A Bibliography of the Bag-pipe.* Newcastle upon Tyne.

Askew, Gilbert, H. (1934) 'The Lowland bagpipes: notes on the instruments in Wilton Lodge Museum, Hawick'. *Trans. Hawick Archaeological Soc., 1934,* 42–45.

Bain, H. (1983) *Bain's Directory of Bag-Pipe Tunes*. Edinburgh.

Baines, Anthony (1957) *Woodwind Instruments and their History*. 3rd edn., London, 1977.

Baines, Anthony (1960) *Bagpipes*. Revised edition, Oxford 1979.

Baines, Anthony (ed.) (1961) *Musical Instruments through the Ages*. Harmondsworth.

Baines, Anthony (1973) 'The Wooden Pipe from Weoley Castle', *Galpin Society Journal* 26, 144–145.

Baines, Anthony (1975) Review of F. Collinson, 'The Bagpipe' (1975), in *Early Music* 3, 269 (July, 1975).

Bartholomew, Sheriff John (unp.) *Account of the Campbells of Nether Lorn and their system of canntaireachd*. Unpublished typescript. National Library of Scotland (Edinburgh) MS 2260. The typescript is anonymous but the author's name is given in NLS MS 3716.

Beague (1556) *Histoire de la Guerre d'Ecosse*, Paris, quoted Dalyell (1849), p.20.

Blades, James (1961) 'Orchestral Instruments of Percussion', in A. Baines (1961), Ch. 14, pp. 327–349.

Blankenhorn, V.S. (1978) 'Traditional and Bogus elements in MacCrimmon's Lament', *Scottish Studies* 22, 45–67 (1978).

Boag, W.G.F. (n.d., a,b) 'Drums on Parade' and 'The Tenor Drum'. Two published articles, copies of which were supplied by the author. The original references have not been traced.

Boag, W.G.F. (1975) 'Pipers in the Scottish Regiments; in *The Bulletin: Military Historical Society*, Vol.XXVI, No.101, 26–30.

Boag, W.G.F. (1976) 'The Rise of the Scottish Style of Side Drumming', in *Talking Drums* (Premier Drum Company Ltd, Leicester) (volume and issue number not traced).

Boone, Hubert (1983) *La Cornemuse* (Bruxelles).

Boswell, James (1785) *The Journal of a Tour to the Hebrides with Samuel Johnson*.

Breathnach, Breandàn (1971) *Folk Music and Dances of Ireland*. Dublin (revised ed., 1977).

Bruford, A., and Munro, A. (1973) *The Fiddle in the Highlands*. Highland Information Series, An Comunn Gaidhealach, Inverness 1973; see also G.S. Emmerson (1971), 50–52.

Bryan, J.F. (1970–1) 'A note on the 'Glen 1409' pipes', *Proc.Soc.Antiquaries Scotland*, 103, 240–241 (1970–1).

Bunting, Edward (1796, 1809, 1840) *A general collection of the Ancient Irish Music; A general collection of the ancient music of Ireland; A collection of the ancient music of Ireland*. Reprinted in one volume, *The Ancient Music of Ireland*, Dublin, 1969.

Burnett, John (1968) *Plenty and Want*. Harmondsworth.

Burt, E. (1754) *Letters from a Gentleman in the North of Scotland* . . . 2 vols. 5th edition with appendix, 2 vols, 1818. See also A.J. Youngson (1974).

The Cabar Feidh Collection. Pipe Music of the Queen's Own Highlanders (Seaforth and Camerons). London, 1983.

Campbell, Alexander (1814) MS diary, quoted F. Collinson (1975), 195–6.

Campbell, Alexander [1815] A slight sketch of a journey made through parts of the Highlands and Hebrides ... Edinburgh University Library, MS. La.51.

Campbell, Archibald (unp.) *Notes on the Campbell canntaireachd MS and on Angus McKay's Specimens of Canntaireachd.* Typescript, National Library of Scotland, MS 3716.

Campbell, Archibald (1948) *The Kilberry book of ceol mor.* The Piobaireachd Society (Glasgow).

Campbell, Archibald (1949) 'The grace-noting of competition marches', *PT* 1, No.5.

Campbell, Archibald (1950a) 'The history and art of Angus MacKay', *PT* 2, Nos.5–7.

Campbell, Archibald (1950b) 'The MacGregor pipers of the Clann an Sgeulachie', *PT* 2, Nos.10–12; cf. J.G. Dalyell (1849), 8; 'Fionn' (1912).

Campbell, Archibald (1953) 'Piobaireachd', *PT* 5, Nos.6–7.

Campbell, Archibald (1955a) 'Piping Competitions 1844–1859', *PT* 7, No.4.

Campbell, Archibald (1955b) 'Ceol Mor and the London Competition of 2nd April, 1955', *PT* 7, No.7.

Campbell, Archibald (1955c) "Togail nam Bo' or 'The MacFarlane's Gathering", *PT* 7, No. 12. See also M. MacFarlane (1894); G. D. MacDonald, letter in *PT* 8, No.2; and J.E. Scott, letter in *PT* 8, No.3.

Campbell, Archibald (1958) Letter in *PT* 10, No.11; see also A. MacNeill, *PT* 11, No.4.

Campbell, Archibald (1961a) Introduction to *PS* 10, iii–iv.

Campbell, Archibald (1961b) 'The Campbell Canntaireachd MS', *PS* 10, v–vi.

Campbell, Archibald (1967) 'Argyll, or Western Fencible Regiment', *PT* 19, No.11.

Campbell, Archibald (1968–9) 'Some aspects of Highland pipe music', *PT* 21, Nos.3, 4.

Campbell, Sir George (1944) 'The Story of the Piobaireachd Society', *J. Edinburgh Chamber of Commerce*, August, 1944.

Campbell, G. (1962) *Highland Heritage.* London.

Campbell, James (1977) 'History of the Piobaireachd Society', *PSC* March 1977, 30–48.

Campbell, James (1983) 'Piobaireachd Technique' (extract from notebook of A. Campbell, Kilberry), *PT* 35, No.9.

Campbell, James (1984) *Sidelights on the Kilberry Book of Ceol Mor. Notes on instruction received by Archibald Campbell of Kilberry.* Glasgow, The Piobaireachd Society.

Campbell, John and Archibald [1909] *The Kilberry book of ceol meadhonach.* Peter Henderson Ltd, Glasgow.

Campbell, John F. (1880) *Canntaireachd: articulate music.* Archibald Sinclair, Glasgow.

Campbell, John Lorne (1975) *A Collection of Highland Rites and Customs copied by*

Edward Lhuyd from the MS of the Rev. James Kirkwood (1650–1709). The Folklore Society.

Campbell canntaireachd MS (c.1800). 2 vols., National Library of Scotland, Edinburgh, MSS 3714–15. A complete typescript copy is also in the National Library, MSS 2259–2260. For accounts of the MS, see J. Bartholomew, unp; A. Campbell, 1961b; A.G. Kenneth, 1965; J. McIver, 1966.

Campsie, Alistair K. (1980) *The MacCrimmon Legend*. Edinburgh.

Cannon, Angus, F. MS collection of pipe tunes, compiled mainly in 1916 (Author's collection; photocopies now in the National Library of Scotland).

Cannon, Roderick D. (1969) 'The Glen family', *PT* **21**, No.11.

Cannon, Roderick D. (1971) 'The bagpipe in Northern England', *Folk Music Journal*, **2**, No.2, 127–147.

Cannon, Roderick D. (1972) 'English bagpipe music', *Folk Music Journal* **2**, No.3, 176–219.

Cannon, Roderick D. (1974) "The Battle of Harlaw' — a lost piobaireachd?', *PT* **26**, No.12.

Cannon, Roderick D. (1976) 'A bibliography of bagpipe music' (paper read at conference) *PSC* March, 1976, 30–49.

Cannon, Roderick D. (1977) 'The Red Coat', *PT* **30**, No.3.

Cannon, Roderick D. (1978) 'Cha Till Mi Tuille', *PT* **30**, No.7.

Cannon, Roderick D. (1979) 'My Home', *PT* **31**, No.5.

Cannon, Roderick D. (1980) *A Bibliography of Bagpipe Music*. Edinburgh.

Cannon, Roderick D. (1981) 'War or Peace', *PT* **33**, No.7.

Cannon, Roderick D. (1982a) 'Tune of the Month' (i.e. 'The Old Woman's Lullaby'), *PT* **34**, No.5.

Cannon, Roderick D. (1982b). Letter in *PT* **34**, No.5.

Cannon, Roderick D. (1984) 'Arniston Castle', *PT* **36**, No.10.

Cannon, Roderick D. (1987) '70 years ago: a piper in the first world war'; *PT* **39**, No.10.

Cannon, Roderick D. (unp.) *The music of John MacCrimmon*. Unpublished MS.

Carolan, N. (1981) 'Shakespeare's Uilleann Pipes', *Ceòl* V, (1), 4–9.

Carruthers, Alex, R. (1977) 'Technical Aspects of the Highland bagpipe', *PT* **29**, No.9.

Celtic Melodies, being a collection of original slow Highland airs, pipe reels and canntaireachd. Robert Purdie, Edinburgh, 2 vols. [c.1823 and 1830].

Chambers, Christine K. (1980) Non-lexical vocables in Scottish traditional music. Ph.D. thesis, with tape recording, Edinburgh University.

Chappell, William (1855–9) *Popular Music of the Olden Time*, 2 vols., London.

Charlton, G.V.B. (1927) 'The Northumbrian bagpipes', *Archaeologia Aeliana*, 4th Ser., vii, 131–142.

Cheape, Hugh (1983a) *A check-list of bagpipes in the Edinburgh University Collection of Historic Musical Instruments*. Edinburgh.

Cheape, Hugh (1983b) 'The Making of Bagpipes in Scotland' in D.V. Clarke and

A. O'Connor (eds.), *From the Stone Age to the Forty Five: Studies Presented to R.B.K. Stevenson*, Edinburgh, 594–615.

Clan MacCrimmon Society — see G.C.B. Poulter and C.P. Fisher (1936).

Clark, A. (1845) 'Duirinish', in *The New Statistical Account of Scotland*, Vol.14. Edinburgh & London.

Cocks, William A. (1935) 'James Allen's Organ Pipes', *Proc.Soc.Antiquaries Newcastle upon Tyne*, 4th Ser. **6**, 213–216.

Cocks, William A. (1954) 'Bagpipe', in *Grove's Dictionary of Music and Musicians*, 5th ed., London.

Coisir a Mhòid. The Mòd collection of Gaelic Part Songs, 4 vols., 1896–1912, 1913–1925, 1925–1931, 1932–1937. Alex MacLaren & Sons, Glasgow.

Collinson, Francis (1966) *The Traditional and National Music of Scotland*. London.

Collinson, Francis (1970) 'Syrinx and bagpipe: a Romano-British representation', *Antiquity* **43**, No.142, 305–8 (1969); reprinted *PT* **23**, No.3.

Collinson, Francis (1975) *The Bagpipe. The history of a musical instrument*. London.

Common Stock. The Journal of the Lowland and Border Pipers' Society, Vol.1, No.1 (December, 1983).

Connell, William (1980) *Ceol Mor. A self tuition book written in authentic Cameron style of playing*. London, Ontario.

Cooke, Peter (1972) 'Problems of notating pibroch: a study of 'Maol Donn'', *Scottish Studies* **16**, 41–59.

Cooke, Peter (1976–7) 'The Pibroch Repertory: some research problems', *Proc.Royal Music Assoc.*, **102**, 93–102.

Cooke, Peter (1978) 'Changing styles in pibroch playing. Cadence E's and beats on A', *IP* **1**, Nos.2,3. See also M. MacInnes (1951).

Cooke, Peter (unp.) *The case of the "Redundant A"* (unpublished MS).

Cornish, Eric E. (1952) 'The Chanter Scale', *PT* **4**, No.9.

Currie, James (1800) *The Life of Robert Burns ... with ... Observations on the Scottish Peasantry*. Liverpool. Quoted J.F. & T.M. Flett (1964), 28.

Dalyell, Sir John G. (1849) *Musical Memoirs of Scotland*. T.G. Stevenson, Edinburgh.

de Maeyer, R. (1976) 'The Bagpipes in Europe', *Brussels Museum of Musical Instruments Bulletin*, Vol.VI, 1/2.

Dixon, George A. (1980) Letters [following A. Campsie (1980)], *The Scotsman* (Edinburgh), August 2, 1980; August 14, 1980. See also I. Grant, *Ibid.*, August 14, 1980.

Dixon, George A. (1981) 'The 1743 Lord Lovat/David Fraser Piping Indenture', *IP* **4**, No.5.

Dixon, George A. (1983). Private communication, 28 Sept. 1983, quoting the Stirling Kirk Session Register of 24 May, 1604. Central Regional Archives Dept., Stirling, CH2/1026/1.

Dixon, George A. (1984) 'From the Past', *PT* **36**, No.5.

Donnelly, Sean (1981) 'The Warpipes in Ireland', *Céol* V (1), 19–24.

Doran, Jackie (1971), 'Red Hackle Brian Boru Band', *PT* **24**, No.1.

Dow, Daniel (c.1771). *A collection of ancient Scots music for the violin, harpsichord or German flute.* D. Dow, Edinburgh, n.d.

Drill (all Arms) (1965) . Prepared under the direction of the Chief of the General Staff, Ministry of Defence, London.

Dwelly, Edward (1901–11) *The Illustrated Gaelic-English Dictionary.* Glasgow, 9th edition, 1977.

Emmerson, George S. (1971) *Rantin' Pipe and Tremblin' String. A history of Scottish dance music.* London.

Emmerson, George, S. (1972) *A Social History of Scottish Dance.* Montreal, London.

Farmer, Henry George (n.d.) *Handel's Kettledrums and other papers on Military Music.* Hinrichsen. Includes 'Scots Duty, the old drum and fife calls of Scottish Regiments'. 33–38; and 'The Scots March', 48–55.

Fergusson, William (1939) *Fergusson's bagpipe melodies.* London.

'Fionn' (1896) 'Gille-Calum — The Sword Dance', *Celtic Monthly* IV, 49 (January 1896); cf. Scott, J.E. (1969a).

'Fionn' (1904) *The Martial Music of the Clans.* John MacKay, Glasgow.

'Fionn' (1911) *Historic, Biographic and Legendary Notes on the Tunes,* appended to *Collection of Ancient Piobaireachd,* by David Glen, Edinburgh.

'Fionn' (1912) 'History of the Rankins, pipers to MacLean of Coll', *Celtic Monthly* **19**, 195–198.

'Fionn' (1912–13) 'The Clan MacGregor Pipers. 'Clann an Sgeulachie'', *Celtic Monthly,* **19**, 239–240 (1912); ''Clann an Sgeulachie'. A famous family of pipers', *Ib.,* **20**, 207–208.

Flett, J.F. and Flett, T.M. (1956) 'Some Early Highland Dancing Competitions', *Aberdeen University Review* **36** (115), 345–358.

Flett, J.F. and Flett, T.M. (1964) *Traditional Dancing in Scotland.* London.

Fraser, A. Duncan (1907) *Some Reminiscences and the Bagpipe.* Edinburgh.

Fraser, M. Kennedy and MacLeod, Kenneth (1909–21) *Songs of the Hebrides.* London, 3 vols.

Fraser, Simon (1816) *The Airs and melodies peculiar to the Highlands of Scotland and the Isles,* Edinburgh. New edition, revised by W. MacKay, Inverness 1874.

Geoghegan, John (c.1746) *The compleat tutor for the pastoral or new bagpipe.* London.

Gesto — see MacLeod, Niel.

Glen, David (1876–1901) *David Glen's collection of Highland bagpipe music.* David Glen (later David Glen & Sons), Edinburgh, 17 vols.

Glen, David (1881) *David Glen's Highland bagpipe tutor* ... David Glen, Edinburgh.

Glen, David (1900) *The music of the Clan MacLean.* David Glen, Edinburgh.

Glen, David [c.1903–8] *The Edinburgh Collection of Highland Bagpipe Music.* Edinburgh, Parts 1–11.

Glen, David, & Sons (1927) 'Bagpipe Making. Methods Employed in an Edinburgh Workshop'. Full-page article under headline 'Evolution of the Bagpipe', reprinted from *The Weekly Scotsman* (Edinburgh), Saturday, June 18, 1927.

Glen, John (MS) *Account book kept by John Glen 1848* [i.e. Day-book of the firm of Thomas Glen & Sons, Edinburgh]. Now published as *The Glen Account Book 1838–1853*. A. Myers (ed.)., Edinburgh, 1985.

Glen, John (1900) *Early Scottish Melodies*. J. & R. Glen, Edinburgh.

Glen, John and Robert (c.1870) *Glen's Collection for the great Highland bagpipe*. Edinburgh, 3 vols., n.d.

Glen, Robert (1880) 'Notes on the Ancient Musical Instruments of Scotland', *Proc.Soc.Antiquaries Scotland* Vol.XIV, 114–125.

Glen, Thomas (c.1840–3) *A new and complete tutor for the great Highland bagpipe*. T. Glen, Edinburgh.

Gordon, Seton L. (1923) *Hebridean Memories*. London. Chapter XIX, 'The Island Piper'. The piper is not named, but in private correspondence Mr. Gordon confirmed that he was John Johnston, and added other details regarding his playing.

Gordon Highlanders (1983) *The Gordon Highlanders, Pipe Music Collection*, Vol.1, Paterson's Publications Ltd, London.

Graham, G. Farquhar (1908) *The Popular Songs and Melodies of Scotland*. Balmoral Edition, revised by J. Muir Wood. London.

Grainger and Campbell [c.1961]. *The Care and maintenance of the Great Highland bagpipe*. Grainger & Campbell, Glasgow, n.d.

Grant, Isobel F. (1959) *The MacLeods, the history of a clan*. New edition, Edinburgh, 1981.

Gray, Pipe-Major W. See 'Shamateur'.

Gray, William and Seton, John [1922] *Bagpipe and drum tutor ... with various marches ... & long reveille with their accompanying drum settings*. Published by the authors, Glasgow.

Grimble, Ian (1979) *The World of Rob Donn*. Edinburgh.

Gunn, William (1848) *The Caledonian repository of music, adapted for the bagpipes*. Glasgow.

Haddow, Alexander J. (1974) 'The MacKay Tunes, the story of some Sutherland Piobaireachd', *PSC* March 1974, 42–61.

Haddow, Alexander J. (1982) *The history and structure of Cèol Mór* [ed. D.R. Hannay]. M.R.S. Haddow [Glasgow].

Haddow, Alexander J. and MacFadyen, John (1973) 'A preliminary note on the structure of 'uneven line' piobaireachd', *PT* 25, Nos. 7, 8. For a more extended account, see A.J. Haddow (1982), 155 ff.

Hale (c. 1690) *The Derbyshire Hornpipe*. The music appears, without title, on an engraving which includes a portrait of the composer, Hale, piper of Derbyshire. Published by S. Nicholls. British Museum Cat.No.1851-3-8-352. Reproduced J. Offord (1985), 125.

Hamilton, A.D. (1946–8) 'Music or Noise' (extracts from a series of lectures given to the Scottish Pipe Band Association, 1947–48). *The Pipe Band* Jan-Feb. and Mar-Apr. 1978.

Hannay-MacAuslan MS. MS collection considered to have been compiled by Donald MacDonald. National Library of Scotland, Edinburgh, Dep.201. Watermarked date 1811.

Harris, Cyril, M., Eisenstadt, Maurice, and Weiss, Mark R. (1963) 'Sounds of the Highland bagpipe', *Journal of the Acoustical Society of America* **35**, 1321–1327.

Hawkes and Sons (1922) *The great Highland, Irish War and Scottish System Brian Boru bagpipe*. London.

Henderson, Peter [1888] *Henderson's Collection of Marches, Strathspeys, Reels and Jigs*. P. Henderson, Glasgow (cf. R.D. Cannon (1980) No.**324**)

Henderson, Peter [1900] *Henderson's tutor for the bagpipe and collection of pipe music*. P. Henderson, Glasgow.

Hesketh, C. (1961) *Tartans*. New York.

Hillocks, David, MS. Collection of tunes compiled by David Hillocks, Fife Major, Centre Forfar Local Militia. Early 19th Century. Now in the County Library, Forfar.

HSL Notes. Transcripts of entries in the minute book of the Highland Society of London, copied by A. Campbell (typescript kindly loaned by Mr. G. Tregear).

IP *The International Piper*. Edited by C.M. MacLellan and J.A. MacLellan. Edinburgh. Monthly, Vol.1, No.1 (May 1978) — Vol.4, No.6 (October 1981).

J.D.B. (1969) 'The Drum in the Highland Band', *The Pipe Band* Jan/Feb, 1969, 31.

Johnson, David (1972) *Music and Society in Lowland Scotland in the Eighteenth Century*. London.

Johnson, David (1984) *Scottish Fiddle Music in the 18th Century*. Edinburgh.

Johnson, James (1787–1803) *The Scots Musical Museum*. Edinburgh, 6 vols. Reprinted as the *Scots Musical Museum ... with illustrations of the lyric poetry and music of Scotland by William Stenhouse ...* Foreword by Henry George Farmer, Folklore Associates, Hatboro, Pennsylvania, 2 vols., 1962.

Johnson, Samuel (1775) *A Journey to the Western Isles of Scotland*. London, 1924.

Johnston, John. MSS (Letters to Seton Gordon). National Library of Scotland, Edinburgh, Acc.7451, box.1.

Johnstone, Duncan (1979) *Collection of Jigs and Hornpipes*. Glasgow.

Keltie, Sir John Scott (1875) *A History of the Scottish Highlands ... with an account of the Gaelic language, literature and music by ... T. MacLauchlan*, 2 vols., Edinburgh and London.

Kennedy, David V. (1977) 'Chanter reeds', *PT* **29**, No.5.

Kennedy, David V. (1980) 'Reeds and Chanters', *PT* **32**, No.5.

Kenneth, A.G. (1965) 'The Campbell canntaireachd', *PT* **17**, No.8.

Kenneth, A.G., Murray, D.J.S. and MacFadyen, J. (1977) 'The Emendation of Piobaireachd', *PSC* March 1977, 49–67.

Kenneth, A.G. (1980) 'The Music Mistakes in 'The MacCrimmon Legend'', *PT* **33**, No.2.

Kenneth, A.G. (1984) 'Some mistakes in Angus MacKay's settings, and where they came from', *PT* **36**, No.6.

Kermack, W.R. (1957) *The Scottish Highlands, a short history*. Edinburgh.

Kilberry — see Campbell, Archibald.

Kirkwood, Rev. James — see J.L. Campbell (1975).

Langwill, Lyndesay G. (1950) 'The Stock and Horn', *Proc.Soc.Antiquaries Scotland*, lxxxiv, 173–180.

Langwill, Lyndesay G. (1980) *An Index of Musical Wind Instrument Makers*, 6th edn., Edinburgh.

Laughter, J.C. (1977) Letter in *PT* **29**, No.11; see also D.R. MacLennan (1976).

Lenihan, John M.A. and MacNeill, Seumas (1954) 'An Acoustical Study of the Highland bagpipe', *Acustica*, 4, 231–232.

Logan, James (1831) *The Scottish Gaël*. Edited with Memoirs and Notes by the Rev. Alex. Stewart, 2 vols., Inverness, 1876; reprinted Edinburgh, 1976.

Logan, James (1841) — see J. MacKenzie (1841).

Logan's collection of Highland bagpipe music ... Logan & Co., Inverness, 7 vols. [1899?–c.1909].

Logan's complete tutor for the Highland bagpipe ... Inverness [c.1901]. Many subsequent editions, e.g. 1910, 1923, 1963; entirely revised by Pipe Major John MacLellan, Paterson's Publications Ltd., London, 1963.

London Scottish R.V. Pipers Music, n.d., privately printed for the London Scottish Regiment. Copy supplied by Major R.J. Powell.

Lorimer, R.L.C. (1941) 'Piobaireachd: prolegomena to an unwritten study', *Scots Magazine*, December 1941, 206–14.

Lorimer, R.L.C. (1962) 'Studies in pibroch. 1. The '4:6:4:1 (or 2)' metre in pibroch reconsidered in terms of Joseph MacDonald's 'antient rule'', *Scottish Studies* 6, 1–30.

Lorimer, R.L.C. (1964) 'Studies in pibroch. 2. The metre of 'Bodaich Dhubha nan Sligean': a definitive account', *Scottish Studies* 8, 45–79.

MacArthur, A. MS. Collection of piobaireachd. National Library of Scotland, Edinburgh, MS 1679. On the history of this MS, see R.H. MacLeod (1982).

MacAulay, Alexander (1964) 'The art and history of the MacDougalls of Aberfeldy', *PT* **16**, Nos. 4, 5. See also Anon. (1893).

MacBain, Alexander (1899) 'The history of the Highland bagpipe. A lesson in anachronism'. *The Highland News* (Inverness), February 4, p.9.

MacBain, Alexander 'The Highland Bagpipe — a lesson in anachronism', *Celtic Monthly* 15, 191. Continuation — by K.N. MacDonald, 15, 171.

MacColl-Botly, F.C. (1980) Letter in *PT* **32**, No.10.

MacDonald, Alexander (1914) *Story and Song from Loch Ness-Side*. Inverness; reprinted, Inverness, 1982.

MacDonald, Archibald (1934) *Am Port Mor a bha air Chall agus Sgeulachdan eile na h-Airidh* (translation of N. Munro, *The Lost Pibroch and other Shieling Stories*). Stirling.

MacDonald, Donald [1822] *A collection of ancient martial music of Caledonia called piobaireachd*. Edinburgh. (As regards the date, see R.D. Cannon, 1980.) Reprinted with a new foreword by S. MacNeill, Wakefield, 1974.

MacDonald, Donald (1828) *A collection of quicksteps, strathspeys, reels and jigs. Arranged for the Highland bagpipe*. Donald MacDonald & Son, Edinburgh; 2nd edition, 1831.

MacDonald, Donald (1831) See previous entry.

MacDonald, Donald. MS (1826) *A select collection of the Ancient Music of Caledonia called Piobaireachd*. National Library of Scotland, Edinburgh, MS 1680.

MacDonald, Donald — see also Hannay-MacAuslan MS.

MacDonald, John (1942) 'Pipe Major John MacDonald's Memoirs', *Oban Times*, 4 April, 1942; reprinted in A. MacPherson (1955), 66–68.

MacDonald, Joseph [1760] *A compleat theory of the Scots Highland bagpipe*. Edinburgh University Library, MS La.III 804.

MacDonald, Joseph [1760] *A compleat theory of the Scots Highland bagpipe* [compiled 1760]. P. MacDonald, Edinburgh 1803; reprinted Inverness, 1927; republished Wakefield, 1971.

MacDonald, K.N. (1901) *Puirt-a-beul, Mouth-Tunes*. Oban.

MacDonald, Patrick (1784) *A collection of Highland Vocal Airs ... and some specimens of bagpipe music*. Edinburgh. (On the dating of the book, see R.D. Cannon, 1980.)

MacDonald, Patrick (1803) See above, J. MacDonald [1760]. In the present book the reference 'P. MacDonald (1803)' denotes only passages in the printed edition of J. MacDonald's 'Compleat Theory' which are not in the MS of 1760.

MacFadyen, Ian (1975) 'Teaching Piping in the Highlands', *PSC* March 1975, 43–46; with discussion, 46–60.

MacFadyen, John (1966) *Bagpipe Music*. London.

MacFadyen, John (1975) 'Aspects of Piobaireachd Playing', *PSC* March, 29–42.

MacFadyen, John and MacLeod, Donald (1977) *The Piobaireachd Tutor*, Part 1, Glasgow.

MacFarlane, Malcolm (1894) 'Piobaireachd Chloinn Pharlain — Clan Farlane's Pibroch', *Celtic Monthly* **3**, 39 (1894) (article signed C.M.P., i.e. Calum Mac Pharlain).

MacGregor, Alexander (1878) 'John MacDonald — an adherent of Prince Charles', *Celtic Magazine*, Vol.III, 462.

MacGregor, John (1801) *Orain Ghàelach* (ed. R. MacGregor). Edinburgh. See also *Celtic Monthly*, XIV, 191–2 (July, 1906); and A. MacKintosh (1918).

MacInnes, Malcolm (1951) 'Reminiscences of Pipe-Major Robert Meldrum', *PT* **3**, Nos.4–8.

MacIver, J. (1966) 'Remarks on titles of ceol mor tunes from the Campbell canntaireachd collection', *PT* **19**, Nos.2, 3.

MacKay, Angus (1838) *A Collection of Ancient Piobaireachd or Highland pipe music.* Edinburgh. Reprinted with a new foreword by Seumas MacNeill, Wakefield, 1978.

MacKay, Angus (1843) *The piper's assistant, a collection of marches, quicksteps, strathspeys, reels and jigs.* Alexander Glen, Edinburgh; and Angus MacKay, London.

MacKay, Angus. MSS. Collection of piobaireachd, two volumes. National Library of Scotland MSS 3753–4.

MacKay, I.L. (1954) 'The MacKays of Gairloch', *PT* 6, No.10.

MacKay, William (1840) *The complete tutor for the great Highland bagpipe.* Alexander Glen, Edinburgh.

MacKenzie, Lt.Col. B.D. (1984) 'Major-General Charles Simeon Thomason', in N.A. Malcolm Smith [1984], 57–66; see also 'The Life and Work of General Thomason', *PSC* March 1983, 1–15.

MacKenzie, John (1841) *Sar-Obair nam Bard Gaelach. The Beauties of Gaelic Poetry*, with introduction by James Logan. John MacKenzie, Glasgow. Reprinted Edinburgh, 1907.

MacKenzie, John M. (1970) 'The Crimean Long Reveille', *PT* 22, No.4.

MacKenzie, R. (1901) *Duty Calls and Favourite Tunes of the Seaforth Highlanders*, Elgin. (Privately printed as 'Pipers Equipment' for the Seaforth Highlanders, see R.D. Cannon (1980), No.**331**.)

MacKinnon, R. (c.1905) *Robert MacKinnon's Collection of Highland Bagpipe Music ... including a new tutor.* P. Henderson, Glasgow.

MacKintosh, A. (1918) 'English and Gaelic words to strathspeys and reels', *Trans. Gaelic Soc.Inverness* **28**, 287–326.

MacKintosh, A. (1922) 'Gaelic and English words for old Highland marches, strathspeys and reels', *Ibid.* **29**, 81–94.

MacLauchlan, T. (1875) 'Gaelic Literature, Language and Music', in J.S. Keltie (1875), vol.ii, 66–115.

MacLellan, John (c.1905) *The Cowal Collection of modern Highland bagpipe music.* J. Quigley, Dunoon.

MacLellan, John A. (1964a) *The piper's handbook; a complete non-musical guide for the piper to all aspects of the great Highland bagpipe.* Paterson's Publications Limited, London.

MacLellan, John A. (1964b) 'The Sovereign's pipers', *PT* 16, No.11.

MacLellan, John A. (1966a) 'Angus MacKay of Raasay', *PT* 18, No.6.

MacLellan, John A. (1966b) *Bagpipe Music for Dancing.* Paterson's Publications Limited, London.

MacLellan, John A. (1979) 'The Tree of Piping', published under the heading 'The History of Piping', *IP* 1, Nos.9–11.

MacLellan, John A. (1980a) 'The Sovereign's Pipers', *IP* 3, No.1.

MacLellan, John A. (1980b) 'The MacKays of Gairloch', *IP* 3, No.7.

MacLellan, John A. (1982) *The Notation and Tuning of the Highland Bagpipe.* J.A. MacLellan, Edinburgh.

MacLellan, John A. and Campbell, James (1980) 'The set tunes for 1980', *PSC*, March 1980, Session III.

MacLennan, D.R. (1976) 'Reminiscences of Pipers and Piping', *PSC* March, 1–14.

MacLennan, George S. (1929) *Highland bagpipe music*. G.S. MacLennan, Aberdeen. Reprinted R.G. Hardie and George McLennan, n.d.

McLennan, Iain (i.e. Lt. John MacLennan) (1925) *The Piobaireachd as performed in the Highlands for ages, until about the year 1808.* Edinburgh.

McLennan, John (Lieutenant) (1907) *The Piobaireachd as MacCrimmon played it.* Edinburgh. See also previous entry.

MacLeod, Angus (1952) *Orain Dhonnchaidh Bhàin, The Songs of Duncan Ban MacIntyre.* The Scottish Gaelic Texts Society, Edinburgh. Reprinted Edinburgh, 1978.

MacLeod, D. (1954 — n.d. [1974?]) *Pipe Major Donald MacLeod's Collection of Music for the Highland Bagpipe.* 6 vols., Glasgow.

MacLeod, D. (n.d.) *Donald MacLeod's collection of piobaireachd.* Book 1, Glasgow.

MacLeod, Mary (17th century Gaelic poet). See J.C. Watson, 1934.

MacLeod, Morag (1974) 'Canntaireachd', *PSC* March 1974, 20–41.

MacLeod, Niel (1828) *A collection of piobaireachd or pipe tunes.* Edinburgh.

MacLeod, Norman (1841), article in *Cuairtear nan Gleann*, quoted as "Trial or Competition of Pipers" by W. Gray, *PT* **2**, No.6 (March, 1950).

MacLeod, Ruairidh H. (1973) 'Sir Rory Nor MacLeod's influence on piping', *PT* **26**, No.3, 10–15.

MacLeod, Ruairidh (1977a,b,c) 'Early MacCrimmon records', 'The Mac-Crimmons and the '45', 'The end of the MacCrimmon college', *PT* **29**, Nos.5,6,8.

MacLeod, Ruairidh H. (1981) The greatest piper of his time. Unpublished MS, loaned by the author. See also *PSC* 1981 (to be published).

MacLeod, Ruairidh H. (1982) 'The Highland Society of London and the Publication of Piobaireachd', *PT* **34**, Nos.9,11.

MacLeod, Torquil W. (1949) 'A Reader Comments', *PT* **1**, No.8.

MacNeill, Archie (1956) 'More about Chanters', *PT* **8**, No.10.

MacNeill, Archie (1958) 'Bagpipes and other Instruments', *PT* **10**, No.4.

MacNeill, Seumas (1951) 'The music of James Mauchline', *PT* **3**, No.81. See also *NP* **25**, No.11 and J. & R. Glen (1870), ii, iii. On the authorship of 'The Barren Rocks of Aden', see also D. Glen (1881), *NP* **24**, No.9 and J.E. Scott (1969b).

MacNeill, Seumas (1960) *The Seumas MacNeill Collection of Bagpipe Music.* Book 1, Glasgow.

MacNeill, Seumas (1965) 'Piobaireachd — the Celtic Symphony', *PT* **17**, No.7.

MacNeill, Seumas (1968) *Piobaireachd. Classical music of the Highland bagpipe.* British Broadcasting Corporation, Edinburgh.

MacNeill, Seumas and Richardson, Frank (1987) *Piobaireachd and its Inter-pretation.* Edinburgh.

MacNeill, Seumas (1972) Untitled editorial comment (signed S.M.) on letter of R. Smith, *PT* **24**, No.5.

MacNeill Seumas (1976) 'Views on the Structure of Piobaireachd', *PSC* March, 25–29.

MacNeill, Seumas (1978) Introduction to A. MacKay (1838), reprint edition.

MacNeill, Seumas (1980) 'Some Pipers of the 19th Century', *PSC* March, 1–19.

MacNeill, Seumas and Lenihan, John M.A. (1960–1) 'The Scale of the Highland bagpipe', *PT* **13**, Nos. 2–6.

MacNeill, Seumas and Pearston, Thomas (1953, 1968, 1969) *The College of Piping Tutor for the Highland bagpipe*. Parts 1–3, Glasgow.

MacPhee, Donald [1876] *A Selection of Music for the Highland Bagpipe*. Glasgow.

MacPherson, Angus (1955). *A Highlander looks back. The Oban Times*, Oban, Argyll.

MacRae, Alex. (1932) 'The MacKays of Gairloch', *PSC*, 1–16.

Malcolm, Charles A. (1927) *The Piper in Peace and War*. London.

Malcolm Smith, N.A. (ed.) (1984) *The First One Hundred Years. A History of the Royal Scottish Pipers Society*. (Edinburgh).

Manson, W.L. (1901) *The Highland Bagpipe: its History, Literature and Music*. Paisley.

Marr, Robert A. (1887) *Music and Musicians at the Edinburgh International Exhibition 1886*. Edinburgh.

Matheson, W. (1970) *An Clarsair Dall, The Blind Harper. The Songs of Roderick Morison and his Music*. Scottish Gaelic Texts Society, Edinburgh.

Menzies, D.P. (1894–5) 'Notes on the 'Bannockburn' bagpipes of Menzies', *Proc.Soc.Antiquaries Scotland*, **29**, 231–4.

Mooney, Gordon J. (1982, 1983) *A collection of the choicest Scots Tunes for the Lowland and Border bagpipe*. Parts 1, 2, Linlithgow. Published for the Lowland Pipers' Society.

Morier (1679) *Account of Scotland*; quoted J.G. Dalyell, 1849, 35.

Morrison, Alick (1967) 'The Contullich Papers, 1706–1720', *Trans.Gaelic Soc. Inverness*, XLIV, 310–348.

Morrison, H. (1899) *Songs and Poems in the Gaelic Language, by Rob Donn*. Edinburgh.

Moss, George (1969) (*Deòrsa Moss*) 'Ainmean Gaidhlig sa' Phiobaireachd' (Gaelic names in Piping), *Gairm* (Glasgow), No.69, 41–46.

Moss, George (1956) 'Ceol Mor playing — old and new styles', *PT* **8**, No.11.

Moss, George (1957) 'Piobaireachd playing', *PT* **9**, No.8.

Moss, George (1959) 'Canntaireachd', *PT* **12**, No.1.

Moss, George (1979–81) Correspondence in *IP* **1**, No.12; **2**, Nos.3,4,6; **3**, Nos.3,4,5,12; **4**, Nos.3,6.

Moss, George (1983) *Pibroch* (Scottish Tradition, Cassette Series, No.6), ed. P. Cooke, School of Scottish Studies, Edinburgh.

Mumby, Keith (1976) 'Poor Boreraig', *PT* **28**, No.6.

Munro, Niel (1906) 'The Looker-on, Twa Hundred Pipers and a' and a'', *Glasgow News*, 20 August, 1906; reprinted in *IP* **1**, No.11.

Murray, Lieut.Col. D.J.S. (1975) 'Piping in the Army', *PSC* March, 1–28.

NP Notices of Pipers — i.e. MacLennan, John; Scobie, I.H.M., and Campbell, Archibald, 'A Dictionary of pipers and piping', *Piping Times* 19, No.7 (1967); continued as "Notices of Pipers", in various issues of the same journal, 19, No.11 to 27, No.12 (1967-1975). References to individual 'notices' are given by citing the volume and issue of the *Piping Times* in which they occur, i.e. *NP* 19, No.7 etc. For the dates of issue, note that issue 1 of the *Piping Times* is dated October of each year, issue 2 November, etc.

Offord, J. (1985) *John of the Greeny Cheshire Way. The famous 'double' hornpipes of Lancashire & Cheshire*. Published by Friends of Folk Music, 55 Kingsway, London.

Orme, Barrie J. (1979) *The Piobaireachd of Simon Fraser with Canntaireachd*. Published by the Editor.

Oswald, James (c.1745-1770) *The Caledonian Pocket Companion ... containing all the favourite Scotch tunes ... for the German flute or violin*. London, 15 books.

Peacock, John (c.1805) *A favorite collection of tunes with variations adapted for the Northumbrian small pipes ...* Newcastle. W. Wright. Reprinted as *Peacock's Tunes*, ed. Colin Ross, The Northumbrian Pipers' Society, Newcastle, 1980.

Pearston, Thomas, (1950) 'A little about the bagpipe chanter', *PT* 2, No.7.

Pearston, Thomas (1951-2) 'Bagpipe Cane', *PT* 3, Nos.10-12; 4, Nos.1-5. See also *Ibid.*, 'Cane selection' (with illustrations), *PT* 8, No.11.

Pearston, Thomas (1973) 'Bagpipe Tuning', *PT* 25, No.4.

Pennant, T. (1774) *A Tour of Scotland and Voyage to the Hebrides*. Chester.

Perdue, Robert E., Jr., (1958) *'Arundo Donax* — Source of Musical Reeds and Industrial Cellulose', *Economic Botany*, 12, No.4, 368-404 (Oct.-Dec. 1958).

The Piobaireachd Index (1978), published by the Piobaireachd Index, 333, Franklin Avenue, N.J. 07604, USA.

Piobaireachd Society (1st series, 1905-13) *A collection of piobaireachd, selected and edited by the Piobaireachd Society*. Part 1, Inverness [1905]; parts 2-4, Glasgow [1906, 1907, 1910]; part 5, no imprint [1913]. According to J. Campbell (1977), the first book appeared early in 1905, not 1904 as stated by R.D. Cannon (1980).

Piobaireachd Society (1980) *The Piobaireachd Society ... collection of Ceòl Mór composed during the twentieth century* (no imprint).

The Pipe Band. Official organ of the Scottish Pipe Band Association. (incorporating 'Piping, Drumming and Highland Dancing Journal'). Published by the Scottish Pipe Band Association, No.1 (1952-).

Piping World. Edited by John Allen. Published by Donald Varella, James Coldren, 57, Clark Street, Glen Ridge, New Jersey, 07028, USA. Vol.1, No.1 (September 1968) — ?

Poulter, G.C.B. and Fisher, C.P. (1936) *The MacCrimmon Family*. Camberley, Surrey.

Powell, Richard J. (1980) 'Piping in Pakistan', *IP* 3, No.3.

Powell, Richard J. (1985) *The Drums - finally beaten*. A radio programme, presented in the British Forces Broadcasting Service, January.

PS (The Piobaireachd Society, New Series). *Piobaireachd ... edited by Comunn na*

Piobaireachd (The Piobaireachd Society) ... Books 1–13, 1925–[1980]. The original files from which Books 1–10 of this series were compiled are now in the National Library of Scotland, Edinburgh, as 'The Campbell of Kilberry Papers', Acc.8373.

PSC. Proceedings of the Piobaireachd Society Conference. Published annually, from 1973 (except for the 1981 volume which has not yet appeared).

PT. Piping Times. Edited by S. MacNeill. Published by The College of Piping, 20, Otago Street, Glasgow G12 8JH. Monthly (October 1948 — continuing). For the dates of issue, note that issue 1 is dated October of each year, issue 2 November etc.

Ramsay, Pipe Major Donald S. [1953, 1958] The Edcath collection of Highland bagpipe music. Books 1,2.

Ramsay, John, of Ochtertyre (1784) 'Of the influence of Poetry and Music upon the Highlanders', unsigned article included in P. MacDonald (1784) [8], 9–15. The attribution to Ramsay is given by A. Allardyce (1888) and accepted by W. Matheson (1970), xxxi.

Reid, Peter (The Reid manuscript of Pipe Music, c.1820). Privately owned — see PS 13 (1980), preface. A photocopy is in the National Library of Scotland, Edinburgh. MS, Acc. 5585.

Reid, Robert (c.1933) The Piper's Delight. Paterson's Publications Ltd., London.

Richardson, Major-Gen. Frank M. (1968) Foreword to S. MacNeill (1968).

Roberts, P. (1983) 'Francis Markis, 'Cold Wind' Piper', Common Stock, 1, No.1, 4–5.

Robertson, J. and Ramsay, D.S. (1953) Master Method for the Highland Bagpipe. London.

Ross, David (1974) 'Some of the old pipers I have met', PT 26, No.4.

Ross, G.F. (1926) Some Piobaireachd Studies. Glasgow.

Ross, G.F. (1929) A collection of MacCrimmon and other Piobaireachd. Glasgow.

Ross, James (1957) 'A classification of Gaelic Folk-Song', Scottish Studies 1, 95–151.

Ross, Roderick [1959–1967] Binneas is Boreraig. Edinburgh, 5 vols.

Ross, William Ross's collection pipe music (London) 1869; new edition [London, 1876]; revised edition, Inverness [1885]; reprint with foreword by S. MacNeill, Wakefield, 1976.

Ross, William (1925–1950) Pipe-Major W. Ross's collection of Highland Bagpipe Music. London, 5 vols., 1925–1950. (Vols.1–4 were revised at various times between 1943 and 1950. For details see R.D. Cannon, 1980.)

Royal Scottish Pipe Band Association (1962, 1971) The Scottish Pipe Band Association Tutor and Text Book. Glasgow, 2 vols.

RSCDS. The Royal Scottish Country Dance Society.

RSPBA — see Royal Scottish Pipe Band Association.

Sanger, Keith (1983) 'The MacArthurs. Evidence from the MacDonald papers', PT 35, No.8.

Scots Guards (1954) *Standard Settings of Pipe Music*. Paterson's Publications Ltd., London.

Scott, James E, (1960) 'The Cock o' the North', *PT* **13**, No.1.

Scott, James E. (1969a) 'Gille-Calum', *PT* **21**, No.5.

Scott, James E. (1969b) 'The Barren Rocks of Aden', *PT* **21**, No.11.

Seton, Brevet-Col. Sir Bruce, and Grant, Pipe Major John (1920) *The Pipes of War, a record of the achievements of pipers ... during the War 1914*-18. Glasgow. Reprinted Wakefield, 1975.

'Shamateur' (i.e. W. Gray) (1940) 'Ceol Mor. Cumha Mhic an Toisich (Mackintosh's Lament)', *Piping and Dancing*, **5**, No.9.

Smith, N.A. Malcolm — see Malcolm Smith, N.A.

SOBHD. Highland Dancing. The official textbook of the Scottish Official Board of Highland Dancing. London, 1955.

Starck, H. (1908) *The complete tutor for the 'Brien Boru' war pipes*. London.

Stewart, D. (1822) *Sketches of the Character, Manners and present state of the Highlanders of Scotland, with details of the military service of the Highland Regiments*. Edinburgh, 2 vols. Reprinted Edinburgh, 1977.

Sutherland, Ronald (1967) 'The bagpipe in old English Literature', *PT* **19**, No.4.

Thomason Charles S. (1893) *Ceol Mor Notation, a new and abbreviated system of musical notation for the piobaireachd ... with examples*. Dehra Dun. The text is included (perhaps with revisions?) in Thomason, 1900, i–xi, 1–13, plates I–VI.

Thomason, Charles S. (1900) *A collection of piobaireachd, as played on the great Highland bagpipes. Ceol Mor. Compiled edited and rendered in a new and easily acquired notation*. London, 1900. Revised edition (also dated 1900) c.1905? The texts of both editions are included in the reprint of 1975.

Thomason, Charles S. (1975) *Ceol Mor Notation, a new and abbreviated system*. Republished Wakefield, 1975. (In spite of the title, this edition contains the complete text and music of both editions of the complete collection.)

Thomason, Charles S. *Ceol Mor Legends*. National Library of Scotland, Edinburgh, MS 3749.

Thomson, Derick S. (1963) 'The MacMhuirich Bardic Family', *Trans. Gaelic Soc. Inverness* **43**, 276.

Thomson, Derick S. (1968) 'Gaelic Learned Orders and Literati in Mediaeval Scotland', *Scottish Studies* **12**, 57.

Thomson, Derick S. (1974) *An Introduction to Gaelic Poetry*. London.

Thomson, Derick S., ed. (1983) *The Companion to Gaelic Scotland*. Oxford.

Thomson, Robert (1955) 'Country of Origin?', *PT* **8**, No.1.

Van der Meer, J.H. (1964) 'Typologie der Sackpfeife', *Anzeigen der Germanischen Nationalmuseums*, 123–146.

Van der Meer J.H. (1969) 'Beitrag zur Typologie der westeuropäischen Sackpfeifen', in *Studia instrumentorum musicae popularis* I (E. Stockman, ed.), Musikhistoriska Museet, Stockholm, 98–111.

Varella, Donald [1966] *Bagpipe Music Index*, published by Bagpipe Music Index, 57, Clark Street, Glen Ridge, N.J. 07028, USA.

Varella, Donald [1976] *The United States Bicentennial Collection of Bagpipe Music, Volume II, 'The Peter MacLeod Memorial Collection'*. Piping Press, Michigan, USA.

Walker, Rory (1967) Letter on the tune 'Loch Duich', *PT* **20**, No.3.

Wardlaw MS. Chronicles of the Frasers, ed. William MacKay, Scottish History Society, 1st series, Vol.47, Edinburgh 1905.

Watson, J. Carmichael (1934) *Gaelic songs of Mary MacLeod*. Edinburgh. (Reprinted, 1965).

Weatherall, G.A. (Deputy Adjutant-General) 'Circular Memorandum issued to the Infantry at Home and Abroad', Horse Guards, 11th February 1854.

Whyte, Henry — see 'Fionn'.

Wilson, J. (1937, 1957, 1967) *John Wilson's Collection of Highland Bagpipe Music*, Books 1–3, Ontario, Canada.

Wilson, John (1973) Letter on jig playing, *PT* **25**, No.4.

Wilson, John (1977) Letter quoted in D. Varella [1976].

Wilson, John (1978) *A Professional Piper in Peace and War*. J. Wilson, Willowdale, Ontario, Canada.

Winstock, Lewis (1970) *Songs and music of the Redcoats. A history of the War Music of the British Army, 1642–1902*. London.

Youngson, A.J. (1974) *Beyond the Highland Line, Three Journals of Travel in Eighteenth Century Scotland: Burt, Pennant, Thornton*. London.

Index